A SMILE MAKES A LOUSY UMBRELLA

Peanuts Parade Paperbacks

A SMILE MAKES A LOUSY UMBRELLA

Cartoons from *You're Something Else, Charlie Brown*
and *You're You, Charlie Brown*

by Charles M. Schulz

Holt, Rinehart and Winston / New York

Published simultaneously in Canada by Holt, Rinehart
and Winston of Canada, Limited.

First published in this form in 1977.

Library of Congress Catalog Card Number: 77-71352

ISBN: 0-03-021406-8

Printed in the United States of America

10 9 8 7 6 5 4 3 2 1

Copr. © 1951, 1952 United Feature Syndicate, Inc.

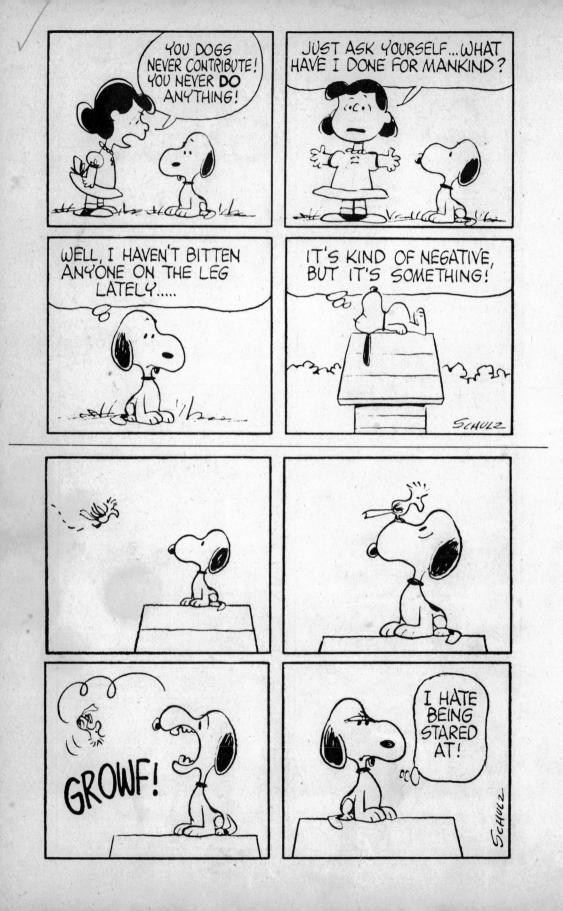

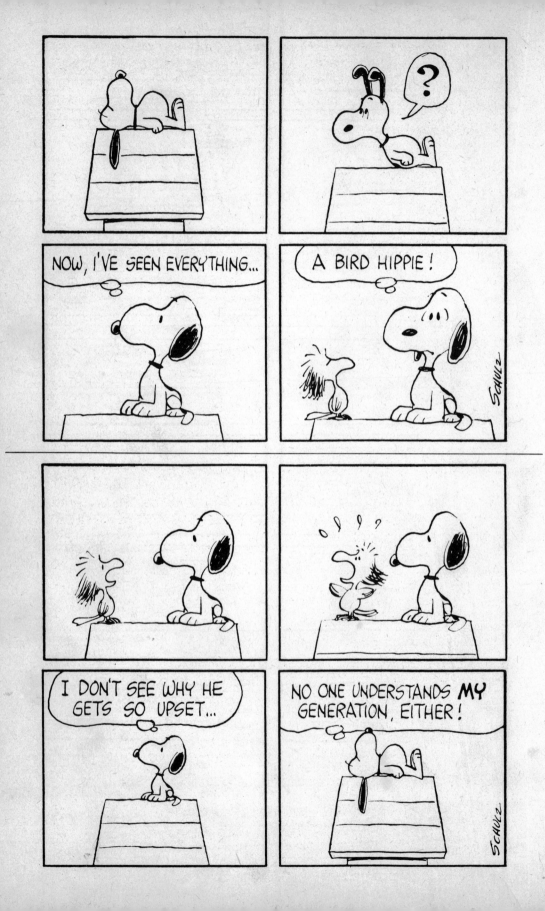

THAT'S HIS "HA-HA, YOU HAVE TO SHOVEL IT, AND I DON'T" DANCE!

SCHULZ

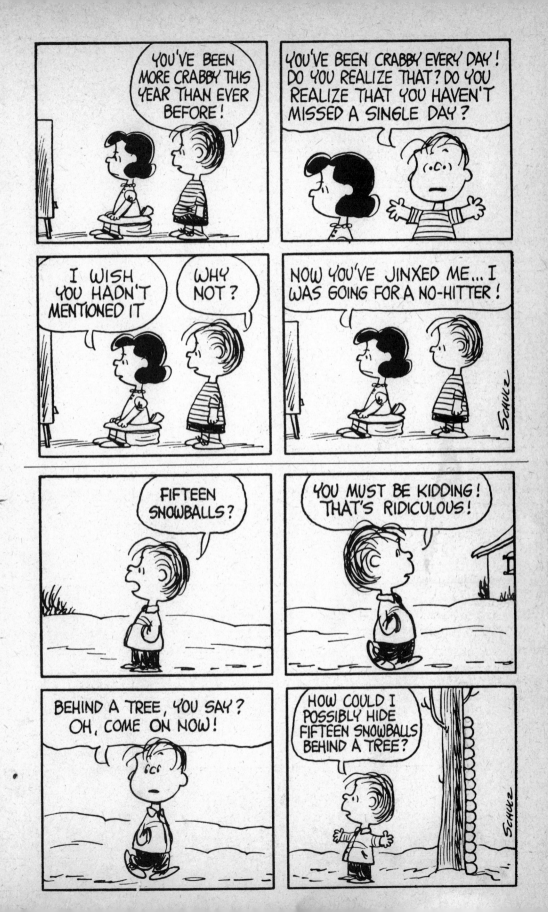

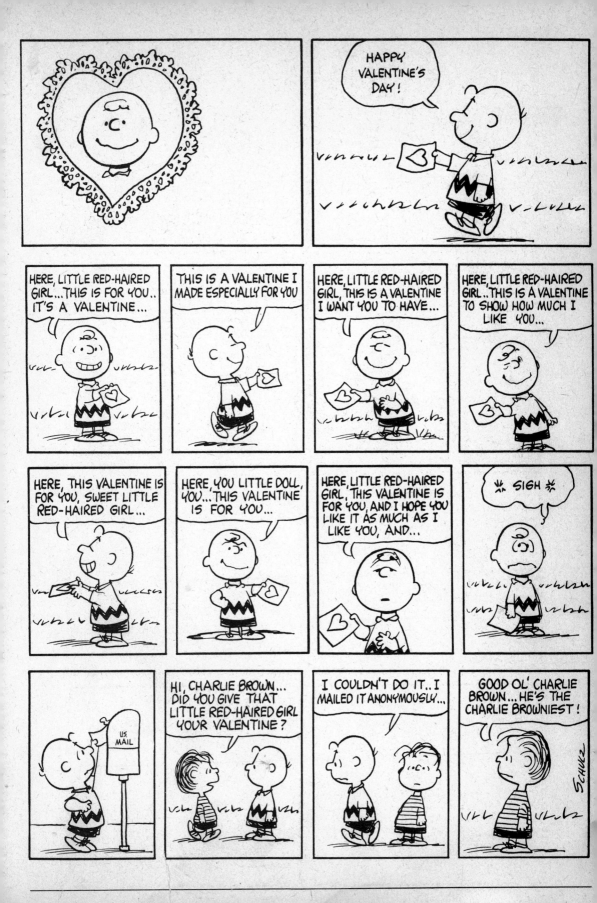

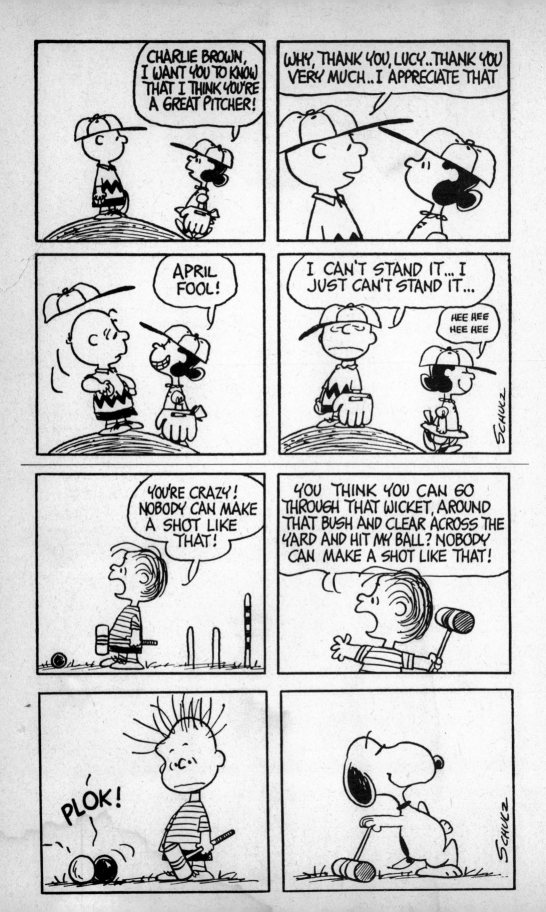

The Book of the Grail
by Josephus

The Book of the Grail
by Josephus

The Forgotten Early Account
of the Arthurian Legend

Transcribed and Edited by
E. C. Coleman

AMBERLEY

First published 2016

Amberley Publishing
The Hill, Stroud
Gloucestershire, GL5 4EP

www.amberley-books.com

British Library Cataloguing in Publication Data.
A catalogue record for this book is available from the British Library.

ISBN 978 1 4456 5658 8 (print)
ISBN 978 1 4456 5659 5 (ebook)

Map design by Thomas Bohm, User design.
Typesetting and Origination by Amberley Publishing.
Printed in the UK.

Contents

For the Lord of Neele made the Lord of Cambrein this book to be written, that never tofore was treated in Romance but one single time beside this; and the book that was made tofore this is so ancient that only with great pains may one make out the letter. And let Messire Johan de Neele well understand that he ought to hold this story dear, nor ought he tell nought thereof to ill-understanding folk, for a good thing that is squandered upon bad folk is never remembered by them for good.

Josephus c. 1205

Introduction to this Edition

It is not known when *The Book of the Graal* (known also as *Perlesvaus*) was first written, or by whom. There may have been a 'good clerk' named Josephus who was told to write it down upon the instructions of an angel, but more detail would be a greater incentive to acceptance of his authorship.

Nor can the date of its writing be pinned down with any great accuracy. If the 'Lord of Cambrein', who also ordered the book to be written, is the Bishop of Cambrai, subsequent datings suggest that he had to be one of two succeeding bishops who held the position between 1200 and 1237. The 'Lord of Neele' or 'Johan de Neele', for whom the Lord of Cambrein had the book written, is probably John de Nesle who is mentioned as living in 1214 and 1225. Written in medieval French, *The Book of the Grail* was translated into Welsh prior to 1368, and records in its translated title that it was originally written about the year 1200.

The Welsh translation, a sixteenth-century French version and a few surviving pages of a thirteenth-century copy were used in 1866 to transcribe the book into medieval French once again. This, in turn, was translated into Middle English under the title of *The High History of the Holy Grail* by Sebastian Evans in 1898. Since that time, apart from one modern language version, it has remained available only in the form presented by Evans, an academic curiosity ignored by much of the Arthurian world who preferred the later works of Mallory and Tennyson. It is the Evans edition that has been used as the basis of this edition.

No claim is made for the accuracy of the language used for this transcription. The main purpose has been to give a feel of antiquity and yet remain readable. Words such as 'aby' (to redeem by penalty), 'brachet' (a spoilt child), 'sithence' (subsequently, or since), 'guige' (a strap attached to a shield enabling the wearer to carry the shield on his back), 'Confiteor' (a prayer of general confession), 'gramercy' (an expression of surprise, or 'thank you'), and 'wot' (knowledge) have been replaced by more understandable equivalents. A few unresolved matters have been tidied up for the sake of narrative fluency, but no changes have been made to the order of events. Consequently, the following from Sebastian Evans' Introduction to his 1898 translation still applies:

> I commend the 'Book of the Graal' to all who love to read of King Arthur and his knights of the Table Round. They will find here .... what I take to be in all good faith the original story of Perceval and the Holy Graal, whole and incorrupt as it left the hands of its first author.

Percival and his quest for the Holy Grail first appear in Chrétien de Troyes' poem *Perceval, le Conte du Graal*, written somewhere around 1185. The poem breaks off after some 9,000 lines, possibly on the death of Chrétien. The work was then completed in a series of four 'continuations', each by a different writer. *The Book of the Graal*, however, is presumed to be by a single author who, nevertheless, also takes up the story where Chrétien breaks off. Consequently, the reader is assumed to know that Percival had already seen the Holy Grail, but had failed to achieve it by not asking the required question:

Whom doth the Grail serve?

Chrétien's Grail is, however, different to the one in *The Book of the Graal*. To Chrétien, it was simply a dish or paten which held a wafer for consumption at the Mass. It was the wafer which would help cure the Fisher King – the wounded king whose realm turns to wasteland around him. In his *Joseph d'Arimathie*, written at the end of the twelfth century, Robert de Boron first tells the story of the cup, or chalice, which was used to collect the blood of Christ as he hung on the Cross. Brought to England by Joseph of Arimathea, the chalice had now become the Holy Grail – the same object for which the Grail Knights of *The Book of the Graal* set out in quest. De Boron also introduced the 'sword in the stone' to the Arthurian myth, but *The Book of the Graal* had both a sword and an arrow which had to be drawn from stone columns. The annual beheading, which became the basis for *Gawain and the Green Knight*, makes its first appearance, and Camelot is the castle of the Widow Lady, the mother of Percival, although a comment, which has all the appearance of a later insertion, points out that this Camelot is not the same one as that belonging to King Arthur, Kay is not the good knight of other versions, Excalibur does not exist, Merlin is but briefly mentioned, and Queen Guinevere suffers a tragedy rather than the exposure of her love for Lancelot.

It may be of interest to note that no claim of historical accuracy can be made for King Arthur passing laws which demanded that, from the time the Holy Grail was achieved, all communion services in England should use a chalice styled after the Holy Grail – or that bells should be hung in churches. Nevertheless, the earliest communion chalices in England of the Grail type are from the thirteenth century – shortly after the publication of *The Book of the Graal*.

Clearly, although no date is indicated in *The Book of the Graal*, the story was set firmly in early thirteenth-century England. King John was on the throne and the aristocracy spent much of their time in jousting, hunting, and making courtly love. Their main theme in life was chivalry. The weak and the innocent – which was bound to include women – were to be protected. Honour and reputation is everything. There were strict rules of courtesy and loyalty, mercy had to be shown where possible and the truth always told. On the other hand, Jerusalem was in the hands of Islam and the Fourth Crusade has just been completed with the sack of Constantinople – guilty of being in the hands of the wrong sort of Christians. Already there was talk of a Fifth Crusade; therefore, there could be no compromise on the question of religion. *The Book of the Graal* was quite content that those heroes within its pages were undeviatingly Christian; to be otherwise was to place your head at very great risk. In this, *The Book of the Graal* did not shirk its responsibilities and, consequently, could be described as a handbook for the twelfth and thirteenth-century Military Orders such as the Knights Templar, the Knights of St John and the Teutonic Knights.

Here, then, is the frequently dark tale of a time that was already legendary by the beginning of the thirteenth century; a time when good, fearless men went out in search of adventures in which they could defend the weak, defeat wickedness and right wrongs. But only the very best of them can seek the Holy Grail and restore order where there is chaos, light where there is darkness, and good where there is evil. However, this is no place for weak, simpering damsels in distress. Time and again, the women encountered by the knights show courage, initiative and enterprise. Where they are treated badly by men, either with physical cruelty or mere disdain, they lose no time in appealing to the knights for help. Together they form a society where there is little moral shading, where the individual is either good or wicked, and glories in or suffers the consequences accordingly.

E. C. Coleman, 2016

The Original Introduction

This is the history of that most sacred vessel that is named by men the Holy Grail, wherein the precious blood of Our Saviour was received on the day that He was crucified that He might redeem His followers from the pains of Hell. This history was written by the good clerk Josephus by command of the Lord God who spoke to him through an angel. Thus may the truth be made known to good knights, worthy men, and all those willing to suffer pain and to work for the spread of the rule of Jesus Christ made new by His death upon the Cross.

This High Book of the Grail beginneth in the name of the Father, and of the Son, and of the Holy Ghost. All three being of one substance, which is God. And it was God's command to write this High Book. All those that read it should dwell upon its meaning, and forget the wickedness they bear in their hearts, for great goodness shall it bring them that hear it in their heart.

This Holy history was written for the sake of those worthy men and good knights whose deeds shall be remembered, and for the great and good knight whose family came of the soldier Joseph. Good knight he was without fail, for he was chaste in mind and body, hardy of heart, and of great strength. Boasting was unknown to him, and he hid his great courage beneath a mantle of kindliness. All these virtues were his for his lack of wickedness. But it needs be told, that Greater Britain fell beneath great misfortune, and sorrow covered the lands and islands when the good knight failed to utter but small words. Nonetheless, by his deeds of knighthood, he alone brought back gladness throughout the lands.

The good knight was of the family of Joseph of Arimathea, the uncle of his mother. This same Joseph had been a soldier in the service of the Governor Pilate for seven years. Such was the service done by this Joseph that when Pilate offered him wealth and land or any other reward of his choosing, Joseph requested only the body of Our Saviour when he was taken down from the Cross. For Pilate, such a reward was as of naught. He granted Joseph's wish under the belief that the soldier would treat the body of Christ in the manner of the meanest thief. But Joseph treated our Lord's body with all due reverence and laid Him in the Holy Sepulchre and placed alongside Him the spear that had pierced His side, and the most Holy vessel that had gathered the Holy blood from the wound.

The mother of the good knight was named Yglais. She was the sister of the grievously maimed Fisher King, of King Pelles, and of the King of Castle Mortal whose evil was matched only by the twin goodness of his brothers. Yglais was a good and loyal mother to the good knight, and to his sister, Dindrane. His father, whose family descended from Nichodemus, was Alain le Gros, son of Gais le Gros who dwelt by the Hermit's Cross. This Alain had eleven brothers, each of whom died young in the service of our Lord bearing their arms in defence of the Saviour's cause. Alain was the eldest; Gorgalians was next; Bruns Brandalis was the third; Bertholez le Chauz the fourth; Brandalus of Wales was the fifth; Elinant of Escavalon was the sixth; Calobrutus was the seventh; Meralais of the Palace Meadow was the eighth; Fortunus of the Red Land was ninth; Melaamaus of Abanie was the tenth, Galians of the White Tower the eleventh; Alibans of the Waste City was the twelfth. All smote the enemies of the Lord with the uttermost of their power, all died in the defence of His name. Of such family was the good knight whose history is written by Josephus the good clerk, and who shall tell you of his name and manner presently.

Part the Ist

The authority of the scriptures tells us that since the death of our Lord upon the Cross, no earthly King has taken up the cause of Jesus Christ more boldly than King Arthur of Britain. To him alone, and in company with the good knights that attended his court, fell many great adventures thanks to his high belief in God. Many true knights, the best the world hath seen, attended to the King and sat at his Round Table. Such was the noble manner of his Kingship that all the princes and barons strove to follow his example, yet none was praised as much as he.

But after some years had passed, a weariness fell upon King Arthur and the pleasures of charity and gallant deeds left him. Christmas, Easter and Pentecost passed without remembrance and many of his knights departed in sorrow at the change. His Queen, Guinevere, a lady of great beauty, became downcast and knew not what to do of her husband's malady. Even the Lord God did not send her comfort. It is from this time that this history beginneth.

On one Ascension Day, when the King was at his Castle Cardoil, he walked through the Great Hall and saw his Queen seated at a window. Sitting beside her, the King saw that her eyes shone with tears.

'What ails you, my Lady?' said the King, 'Why do you weep?'

'I weep, Sire,' the Queen replied, 'for neither you nor I have any cause to be joyous.'

'It is true, Madam, that I have little of which to feel joy.'

'Right, indeed you are,' said the Queen. 'On a high day such as this, the court would be thronged with knights, more than could be numbered. Now I am ashamed that so few are your knights, and adventures are but memories. I fear that God has truly made you forget your honour.'

The King replied with great sadness, 'Again it is true, my Lady. I have no will to work charity, nor can I face anything that may turn to honour. I have a great feebleness of heart that loses me my knights and the love of my friends.'

With great tenderness, the Queen said unto the King, 'My Lord, I know of a way to restore the courage of your heart. In the White Forest is the chapel of Saint Augustine which can be reached only by the bravest of knights. Should you repair to the chapel and ask God for His counsel He will listen unto you for He will know you have a good heart. Upon your return, with the Lord's assistance, you will again find your desire to do good.'

'Madam,' replied the King, 'your words have pierced my soul and I can no longer gaze upon your downcast form. I have oft heard of this chapel, and I believe it to be a worthy site to restore my spirit.'

'But remember, Sire, that the chapel is girdled with perils and adventure. Once it is gained, however, you will find a most wonderful hermit who lives by the building. He lives now only to glory God, and will aid you in your prayers.'

'Then,' sayeth the King, 'I shall proceed thither, armed and alone.'

'No, my Lord,' sayeth the Queen. 'Pray take with you a knight and a squire for the perils are great.'

'I will not, my Lady, for the adventures faced alone are greater than those faced in company. If it is the Lord's will that I succeed, then succeed I shall whether alone, or with others.'

'Please God, my Master, take at least a squire to aid you,' cried the Queen.

Knowing that her heart would be injured by refusal, the King replied, 'To please you, my Lady, I shall take a squire, but I cannot deny the notion that evil will come of it.'

As the King spoke these words, a tall, strongly-made young man entered the Great Hall. He was Chaus, the son of Yvain le Aoutres.

The King turned to his Queen and sayeth, 'Think you that I should take this one?'

'Indeed, I do, Sire, for I have heard much of his valour.'

At this, the King called out to the squire who came and knelt before him. Raising him up, the King said, 'Chaus, tonight you shall sleep in the Great Hall and, on the morn, you shall prepare my horse and my arms. We both shall leave at break of day without other company.'

That night, as the King and Queen left the Great Hall, the squire remained behind. Fearful of his duties, Chaus removed not his clothing nor his shoes with the intent of remaining awake throughout the night. But sleep enveloped him and he dreamed that the King had left the castle, alone and unarmed. Waking in fright, the squire put on his spurs and his sword, mounted his horse and rode with great fury after the King he imagined to be already near the White Forest.

And before long, the squire came upon a great forest. Entering the darkness, he found a track which, to his mind, had been made by the King. Then a clearing in the trees appeared before him and, upon casting around, he saw a chapel surrounded by a burial-ground in which were many graves. Alighting from his horse, Chaus entered the chapel which was empty save for the body of a knight which lay before the altar covered in a rich silken cloth. Around the knight were four gold candlesticks with candles lit. The wonder of the sight struck the squire for he knew not how the knight had been so arrayed, nor by whom the candles were lit. He knew not either where the King was, nor where to search for him. At this, Chaus removed one of the candles and hid the gold candlestick about his clothing and left the chapel to regain his horse and continue in his search for the King.

The squire had not continued long before he came across a fearful sight. In his path, lit only by a low moon, stood a foul-featured man dressed in black. So tall was the stranger that his head was above the squire even though the young man was on his horse. The light of the moon showed that the man held a two-edged knife in his hand. Pushing aside his fear, the squire demanded of the stranger, 'Have you met King Arthur in this forest?'

'I have not,' returned the man. 'But I am pleased to have met you, for you have left the chapel as a thief. You have carried off a candlestick of gold that was placed in honour of the knight that lay dead in that chapel. I demand that you yield it up to me that I may return it. Should you choose not so to do, I shall obtain it at a cost most dear to you.'

'By my faith,' replied the squire, 'I shall never yield it to you for I intend to present it to King Arthur.'

At this, Chaus gave spur to his horse but, as he rode past the stranger, the man thrust the knife deep into the squire's left side and he gave a loud cry of 'Dear God! I am a dead man!' So loud was his shout that it woke him from the dream he was suffering. The cry also brought the King and the Queen to his side as he lay in the Great Hall.

'What ails you,' sayeth the King.

As he lay on the floor of the Great Hall, the squire recounted his dream to the King and Queen.

'Then it was just a dream,' sayeth the Queen.

'Aye, my Lady,' replied the squire. 'But a dream like none other.'

Having spoken thus, Chaus lifted up his left arm and the King and Queen saw the handle of a great knife, its two-edged blade deep inside the squire's body. The squire then withdrew a gold candlestick from his clothing and gave it to the King with the words 'For this candlestick that I present to you, am I wounded to death!' He then continued by saying, 'Draw not forth the knife of my body, Sire, until I have made my confession.'

A priest was sent for and did take the squire's confession. Then the King withdrew the knife and the squire's spirit departed forthwith. In concord with the squire's father, the King sent the gold candlestick to the newly founded church of Saint Paul's in London with the command that the squire's adventure should be everywhere known and that prayers should be made for the soul of the squire who was slain on account of the gold candlestick.

That morning, King Arthur armed himself to go to the chapel of Saint Augustine. On his preparing to leave, the Queen said unto him, 'Whom will you take with you?'

'Madam,' replied the King, 'I seek no other company than God, for He has shown that I must travel alone.'

'Then so be it, Sire,' answered the Queen. 'May God guard you and grant your safe return. I know you have the will to do well and to see your praise raised up once again.'

Sayeth the King, 'May God remember it.'

The King took to his horse on the mounting-stage and received the shield and spear of Yvain Le Aoutres in honour of that man's noble son. At his side hung his sword and the King appeared in every aspect a brave warrior. His spurs caused his horse to leap forward as he rode toward his destiny in the White Forest. At this, the Queen asked of the assembled knights, 'Is he not a good man?'

'Yea,' they replied as one, 'yet the loss to the world of his charity, courtesy and noble character is felt beyond all horizons. May he return to his good beginnings with God's early blessing.'

King Arthur rode fearlessly into the forest and continued on until the time of evensong. At that time he came across a clearing wherein lay a chapel and a small house that seemed to be a hermitage. Alighting before the house, he opened the door and entered, taking his horse with him for fear of what may remain outside. Within its walls, the King laid down his spear and shield, unbuckled his sword and raised his helmet visor. Before him he saw food such as for horses and so removed his horse's bridle and allowed him to eat thereof.

A noise then assaulted his ears as if of strife in the chapel. It was as if the voices of angels were met by the sound of the fiends of Hell. Marvelling at this, the King went to the chapel and opened the door. At this the sounds ceased and nought could be seen inside but the images of our Lord and his Lady mother and the crucifixes. Entering further, the King saw an open coffin before the altar wherein lay the hermit who was named Calixtus, his long beard down to the girdle of his vestments. And he was on the point of death. But though night had fully come, the light as if of many candles remained around the hermit. The King, knowing him to be in the presence of a good man, decide to remain at his side until the spirit departed but, as he did so, a loud and fearful voice fell upon his ear telling him to leave forthwith, for the spirit could not be departed whilst he remained.

19

Much saddened by this, the King returned to the house and heard the chapel strife continuing. And his sadness deepened when he heard the angel voices weakening as the fiends grew louder and more clamorous. Then the angel voices were stilled and the King looked to the ground in despair. But then he heard the sweetest voice of a Lady. So sweet and clear did she speak that the sound of her voice would have lightened the heaviest grieving. The Lady spoke to the devils and sayeth, 'Begone from this place, for you have no right over the soul of this good man. Whatever he has done, he has made ample amends in the service of my Son and in mine own. The penance he hath done in this hermitage has washed away his sins.'

But the devils replied, 'True, my Lady. But longer hath he served us than he hath served you and your Son. For forty years or more he hath been a murderer and robber in this forest, and he hath but served you for five years. And now you wish to steal him from us.'

'I do not. No wish have I to take him by theft, for had his life ended in your service as it ended in mine, yours he would have been by right.'

At this the devils groaned with a terrifying sound as the sweet Mother of our Lord God took the departing spirit into her arms and gave it to the angels to deliver to Her dear Son in Paradise. And the angels sang the praises of the Lord God as the Holy Lady led them to the Realms of Light.

The next morn broke clear and fair and the King returned to the chapel expecting to find the hermit remaining within his coffin. But there was neither coffin nor hermit, but a new and gloriously carved tomb-stone in the floor marked by a red cross. And incense lay upon the air as the King made his prayer before departing.

Armed again, the King rode through the forest until he came across an open land most fair. At its entrance a spear barred the way whereby stood a damsel of great beauty. The King turned to her and saluted her by raising his helmet visor. 'Damsel,' he said, 'May God give you joy and good fortune.'

'Sire,' sayeth the woman, 'So may he unto you.'

'Damsel,' returned the King, 'Where is there hospitality in this land?'

'Sire,' replied the damsel, 'there is none save a holy chapel with a hermit beside.'

Astonished, the King asked, 'Is this then Saint Augustine's chapel?' For, but a night before he had believed himself to be at that chapel.

'It is, Sire, but the lands about and the forest are so perilous that no worthy knight hath yet returned but he be dead or deeply wounded. Yet the place of the chapel is of such worthiness that none go there without finding refreshment of the spirit. May God guard you for you appear a most noble knight and I pray you are not harmed. Indeed, Sire, I shall remain here until I see you again.'

'May it please God then, that I shall return to greet you.'

'May it please God indeed, for I then may ask you of tidings of him that I seek.'

At this, the King advanced to the spear that barred his path, and it fell away to let him pass.

Ere long, the King found himself in a fair wooded valley where he chanced upon the chapel of Saint Augustine and a hermit's house close by. Reining his horse to the bough of a nearby tree, the King sought to enter the chapel but found he could not so do though the door be open and no one barred his way. Again he tried to enter, and again he could not as if he was held back invisibly. Falling to his knees he implored Our Saviour to admit him. As he did so, the King heard the opening prayers of the Mass and saw the hermit approach the altar with his right hand holding that of the fairest child he had ever seen. The boy was dressed in a white linen robe and wore upon his head a golden crown in which jewels shone with great brightness. From the other side of the chapel there then appeared a Lady of great beauty and serenity. As the hermit sayeth his prayers, the Lady crossed to the altar, took up the child, and sat upon a rich throne, and kissed the child on her lap saying, 'Sire, you are my Father and my Son and my Lord, and guardian of me and of all the world.'

At this, the King marvelled and his wonderment grew as a flame of light came through a window behind the altar. A light brighter than any from sun, from moon or from star and brighter than any light from all the world. Then there were the voices of angels as they responded to the hermit's prayers. The Lady then offered the child to the hermit who took him and placed him on the altar as he began his sacrament. At this the King bowed his head. Upon looking up, and to his great astonishment and consternation, he saw that the child had vanished and been replaced by the body of a man bleeding from his side, from his hands, and from his feet. The man's brow was crowned with thorns. The sight moved the King's heart to tears and he felt wretched that he could do nothing to aid the wounded figure. But, as he wiped tears from his eyes, he saw that the dying man was gone and the child had returned to his mother.

At the final singing of the Mass, the voice of an angel sayeth, 'It is finished.' And the Lady took the child into her arms and the great flame of light flared to dazzle the eyes only to vanish leaving none within the chapel save the hermit knelt before the altar. Rising, the hermit turned from the altar and spoke to the King. 'Sire, now you might enter herein for you have known the presence of our Lord and His Holy Mother.'

The King entered the chapel as the hermit sayeth unto him, 'Sire, I know you well, as I also knew your father, Uther Pendragon. Your sins prevented you from entering the chapel whilst the Mass was being sung. Nor will you ever enter again until you shall have first made amends for your misdeeds towards God and towards the Saint of this chapel. Though you be the richest King in the World and your adventures, charity, and honour be set as examples to all men, of late your example is one of idle indolence. Nothing short of the greatest misfortune can become you if you do not return to that high point which once you obtained. Your court was the sovereign court of all the world, but now it is the least worthy. Sorry is the man who goes from honour to shame, but never shall a man be reproached who comes from shame to honour, for the honour wherein he is found rescues him to God. But never shall be rescued the man who hath renounced honour for shame, for the shame and wickedness wherein he is found shall declare him guilty.'

'Sire,' sayeth King Arthur, 'I have come here to make amends and to be better instructed than I have been. Well do I see that this place is most holy and I pray that you ask God that he show me how to amend my endeavours hereafter.'

Sayeth the hermit, 'God grant that you may amend your ways that you may help to fight evil by means of the grace given by our Lord on his crucifixion. For we have great sorrow in the land through a young knight that abideth in the castle of the Fisher King. God caused the Holy Grail and the Spear of the point which runneth with the Holy Blood to appear unto him, but he did not ask whom the Grail served or from whence it came. Accordingly, foul war is abroad in the land, famine and disease are everywhere, and the people starve. When knight meets knight they meet not in fellowship, but in combat. Of this you shall see when you return to your castle.'

'Sire,' sayeth King Arthur, 'May God defend me from wickedness and an evil death. From henceforth my ways shall be amended, thus may He bring me safely home.'

'Amen sayeth I. May God hear your plea.'

At this the hermit departed, commending the King to God.

King Arthur took again to his horse and began his return with great pace. As he met with the forest he was surprised upon by a tall knight on a black horse and carrying a black shield. The black knight also bore a lance that burned with bright flame from its point to the knight's gauntlet. Already at great pace, the knight closed fiercely with the King and would have struck him from his horse had not the King swerved before contact.

'What, Knight,' cried the King, 'have I done that you should so act towards me?'

'I have good reason not to have love for you,' replied the knight.

'But why, Sire, why?'

'For you have my brother's gold candlestick that was foully stolen from him.'

'You know then, who I am?'

'Yea,' sayeth the black knight. 'You are King Arthur that once was good and true, but are now evil. I shall do nought but defy you as my mortal enemy.'

This said, the knight ran again at the King as the King gave his horse spur and pointed his lance at the knight. They clashed most fiercely that both moved in their saddles and lost their stirrups. The shock of combat caused blood to flow from the King's mouth and nose and he marvelled that the burning lance of his enemy had not shattered to ashes. Again they rushed at each other with mighty pace. The King aimed his lance and hit the black knight on the shield with such force that the knight bent backwards in his saddle, but such was the knight's resolution that he reached forward and struck the King's shield such a blow that his lance pieced the shield and the King's armour and the King felt the iron of the lance in his arm. To the King's marvelling and the knight's consternation, the flame of the knight's lance was thereupon extinguished.

With the flame went the knight's courage, and he pleaded with the King to let him live. But King Arthur knew the world to be a better place without the black knight and charged at him, thrusting his lance through the knight's body and bringing him to the ground. There he left the knight's body as he turned his horse towards the forest entrance.

The King had not travelled far when he heard the noise of a great company of knights reach the place of his combat and saw them cast their eyes upon the dead knight. Sore afraid that the knights numbered many beyond challenge from him, the King applied his spurs to his horse when he saw the damsel he had left by the barrier spear come near.

'Sire,' sayeth she, 'for pity's sake, return and fetch me the head of the knight that lieth there dead.'

The King looked back and saw the multitude of armed knights and the great peril thereof. 'What, damsel,' sayeth he, 'would you have them slay me?'

'No, Sire, I would not. But I must have the head of that knight. No knight has yet refused me any request. Please, Sire, do not be the first so to do.'

'But, damsel, I am sore wounded in the arm and cannot bear my shield.'

'I know that well, Sire,' she replied, 'but I know further that your arm will never heal until you bring me the head.'

King Arthur turned his horse again and stiffened his body. 'So shall it be, damsel, whatever may befall me.'

The King rode towards the massed knights and was astonished to see that they had cut the dead knight's body asunder and each was carrying off an arm or leg or other part. He then saw a knight who had the black knight's head at the point of his lance. Riding up to the knight, the King cried out, 'Abide, Knight and speak with me.'

The knight stopped his horse and sayeth, 'What, Sire, is your pleasure?'

'Knight, I beseech you to give me the head that you carry at your lance point.'

'Indeed, I will, Sire, on but one condition.'

'What is your condition?' sayeth the King.

'That you tell me who slew the knight whose head I carry.'

'Otherwise I may not have it?'

'No, Sire, you may not.'

'Then I will tell you,' sayeth the King. 'In truth before God, it was King Arthur who slew him.'

'And where is King Arthur?' sayeth the knight.

'Sire,' replied the King, 'I have attended to your condition. You must seek King Arthur yourself. Render me the head as by our agreement.'

'Willingly,' sayeth the knight and lowered his lance for the King to take the head which he did.

As the King rode away, the knight took from around his neck a great horn which he blew. The loud blast caused all the other knights to return and close with the knight. On their return, the knights asked him why he had blown his horn.

'For this,' he replied. 'The knight you see riding away told me that King Arthur slew the black knight. I summoned you that you may know and wish to follow him.'

'We will not so follow,' the knights sayeth, 'for it is King Arthur himself that carries off the head and we have no power to do him evil since he has passed the spear barrier. But you shall suffer the penalty of letting him escape.'

With that, the knights killed the knight and cut his body asunder as they had done with the black knight.

Beyond the spear barrier, the King found the damsel and presented her with the black knight's head.

'Sire,' sayeth she, 'I thank you for your gift and the courage that brought it.'

'Tis of nought,' replied the King, 'for with gladness I was able to meet your request.'

'Sire,' sayeth the damsel, 'you may alight from your horse, for there is no danger to you this side of the spear barrier.' And the King obliged.

'Sire,' she continued, 'take off your coat of mail that I might bind up your wound, for none save me can make you whole again.'

The King took off his coat of mail and the damsel took the blood, which ran still warm from the head and washed the King's wound. After which the King put on his coat of mail.

'Sire,' sayeth the damsel, 'under God's dominion you would never have healed the wound save by the blood of the black knight. It was for this that the knights carried off the body in pieces, for they knew that you would have need to return to be healed by the blood. For myself, I had to have the head. By it, shall a castle be yielded up to me that was taken from me by knavery. I now needs must seek for the knight through whom it shall be rendered to me.'

'Damsel,' sayeth the King, 'and who is the knight?'

'Sire,' sayeth she, 'he is the son of Alain le Gros of the Valley of Camelot, and is named Perceval.'

'Why Perceval?'

'When he was born, Sire, his father was asked what name he should have for the baptism. He replied that the boy would have the name Perceval which would remind him throughout his life that the Lord of the Moors had stolen from his family much of the Valley of Camelot. With God's aid, Perceval might one day become a knight. Indeed, the boy was fair of image and gentle and, ere long, went to the forest to learn how to hunt deer with a spear. One day his parents, who much loved him, took him to a small chapel close by their house. Mounted on four pillars of marble and roofed with timber, the chapel had therein a small altar with, before it, a costly coffin engraved with the figure of a man. The boy asked his father and mother who lay within the coffin. His father told him that he knew not and knew little else though the coffin had been there since the time of his father's fathers. All that may be said is that letters carved upon the coffin told the reader that, when the best knight in the world shall come to that place, the coffin will open and the joints fall asunder. Then will be seen he that lieth therein.'

Sayeth the King, 'Damsel, have many knights passed thereby since the coffin was set there?'

'Knights beyond number, Sire, yet none have caused the coffin to open. When the boy was told the story he asked his father and mother how was a knight made? His mother made reply by saying that he had eleven uncles who had been made knights, yet none had survived beyond twelve years of their knighthoods. The boy replied that his question still remained. His father then replied that knights were good and worthy men of great valour who were clad in coats of mail to protect their bodies and with helmets upon their heads, and with shields, and lances, and swords to defend their bodies. On the morrow, the boy Perceval took one of his father's horses and, with his spear, entered the forest to hunt deer. Ere long, he came into a clearing and saw two knights engaged in combat. One knight had a red shield, the other a blue. In time he saw that the Knight of the Red Shield was about to vanquish the Knight of the Blue Shield. At this he threw his spear at the Knight of the Red Shield piercing the knight's heart, whereupon the knight fell dead. He had not known that a spear might pierce a knight's armour. As the Knight of the Blue Shield left the field in great joy, the boy took the dead knight's horse home to his father and told him the story and his parents did grieve that their son had taken the life of a knight. Sometime after, the boy left his home to attend the court of King Arthur as a squire. So well did he impress the King with his prowess and courage that the King made him a knight. Perceval then departed the court in search of adventure becoming of a knight and travelled throughout many kingdoms bringing help to the weak and sustenance to the poor. Now he is the best knight in the world and I must seek him. If you see him, Sire, you shall know him by his shield which is of green and beareth a white hart. Pray tell him that his father is dead and that his mother is at war with the Lord of the Moors who is strengthened by the brother of the Knight of the Red Shield whom he slew.'

'May God grant me such a meeting,' sayeth the King, 'for well will I send forth your message.'

'Now, Sire,' sayeth the damsel, 'I have told you of him that I seek but I have yet to discover your name. Pray tell me, Sire, what is it?'

The King replied, 'I am known as Arthur.'

The damsel stepped back as if in dread and sayeth, 'Arthur? Have you indeed such a name?'

'In truth I have.'

'So help me God, for I am indeed sorry for you. You have the name of the worst King in the world. Never again will he move from his Castle Cardoil, such dread hath the Queen lest anyone should take him from her. So it is said, for I have never seen either or any of them. I had hoped to go to his court but many knights I met who told me that the court of King Arthur is the most vile in all the world, and that all the knights of the Round Table have denounced it for the evil therein.'

'Damsel,' sayeth the King, 'I heard that at his beginning he did well beyond measure.'

'Well begun may be half ended. But what care anyone for his beginning when the end is bad?' sayeth the damsel. 'I am sorry beyond measure that such a seemly knight and worshipful man as you are should bear the name of so evil a King.'

'Damsel,' sayeth the King, 'a man is not good by his name, but by his heart.'

'It is true, Sire, but your name marks you in my heart with the same image of evil as the King. Whence go you now, Sire?'

'I go to Castle Cardoil where I shall find King Arthur.'

'Go then, and quickly. For I have no better hope of you since you go hence.'

'Damsel,' sayeth the King, 'you must say as you please, but it is to Castle Cardoil I go. God be with you.'

'And may God never guide you to such a place, the court of King Arthur.'

With that the King departed and entered into the deep forest where he heard a loud and terrifying voice saying, 'King Arthur of Greater Britain. You should be right glad at heart that God hath sent me hither unto you. He bids you to hold court at the earliest that you may, for the world that is made worse by you shall be greatly amended by your coming honour.'

In the silence left by the great voice, the King's heart grew large with joy for God had forgiven his many failings and now suffered him to restore the glory and honour as before.

At his arrival at the mounting stage at Castle Cardoil the Queen and the loyal knights made great joy of his coming. And he repaired to his chamber and dressed in a great robe of crimson silk with ermine. And the Queen sayeth unto him, 'Sire, such pain and suffering have you had.'

'Lady,' the King replied, 'good men must suffer to find honour, for none shall be found without suffering.' He then told the queen of his adventures and the manner of the wound in his arm, and of the damsel that had taken against him because of his name.

'Sire, sayeth the Queen, 'well you now know how right it is that a man of great wealth and power should have great shame of himself when he becometh sinful.'

'Indeed, it is so. Much did the damsel do for me by her speech, but nought can compare to the great voice in the forest telling me that God commanded that I hold court presently, and that I shall see an adventure that can right the world of the wrongs I have done. It shall be the fairest adventure that ever hath been known.'

'Sire,' sayeth she, 'your joy should be unbounded that your Saviour hath remembered you. Therefore, fulfil His commandment.'

'That I shall do, Madam, no one has more desire to do good, find honour, and give charity than I at this time.'

'Then, Sire, God be praised.'

Part the IInd

From Castle Cardoil, King Arthur sent forth messages under his seal for the barons and knights to assemble at Castle Pannenoisance on the feast of Saint John. Carried throughout all the lands and islands, his words caused wonder to those that read the King's summons. Whereas before, the well-doing of the King had waxed so feeble that none believed it could ever be restored, now a new desire was abroad. The King, under God's command, was well intent to make amends for his evil idleness.

With great joy the Knights of the Round Table that were scattered well abroad learned of this new desire and returned to the court with great celebration. Only Lancelot and Gawain came not thither on Saint John's day. By number there were one hundred and five knights in the great hall when the King and his Queen sat at the table. Kay and Yvain, the son of King Urien stood as stewards and saw that all had meat and drink. The Butler, Lucan, served the King with the great golden cup that was his alone by reason of his past glories. The sun shone through the windows upon the flowers and herbs that lay upon the floor and gave the great hall the scent of balm.

Upon the first meat having been eaten, the King and the knights looked in wonder as three damsels entered the hall. The first was riding a white horse which beareth a golden bridle and a saddle of ivory over a silken cloth of crimson and gold. This damsel was fine and seemly of body but not so fair of face. The damsel was richly clothed in a robe of green silk laced with gold. Her right arm was rested on the richest pillow decorated with tassels of gold and her hand bore a silver box bearing a golden crown wherein lay the head of a King. Her arm, the pillow, the box all held close to her by a cloth of gold around her neck. On her head, the damsel wore a close hat that covered all but her face. The hat flamed with the brightest of jewels as if it burned.

The second damsel rode a much broken down horse less white and appeared as a squire. On her back she bore a bag in which was carried a hound. She bore also a white shield bearing a red cross. In her left hand she carried a box made of lead bearing a copper crown. In the box was the head of a Queen. This damsel was of fairer face than the first.

The third damsel had no horse and appeared on foot with her gown tucked up for ease of running. This damsel bore a whip with which she prompted the animals forward. Of all the damsels she was the most fair.

As the first damsel approached the King at his table she sayeth, 'Sire, may our Lord grant you honour, and joy, and good adventure, and may the Queen and all the knights in this hall love you as their wise sovereign. Pray, Sire, do not hold it to be churlish of me not to alight from my animal, for I may not alight where knights are present until such time as the Grail shall be achieved.'

'Damsel,' replied the King, 'gladly I do not take it as churlish and would easily have you remain for your comfort.'

'Thank you, Sire. May I now tell you of the errand that I am about?'

'Pray do so, damsel, tell us at your pleasure.'

'Sire,' she sayeth, 'the shield born by this damsel belonged to Joseph, the good soldier who took down the body of our Lord from the Cross. This shield shall you take from me and hang on the great column of this hall. None shall touch it until it be a knight come hither for the shield. You shall know him to be the Knight of the Shield for he shall put in its place a shield that will be of red bearing a white hart. With the shield he shall bear away shall he achieve the Grail. Furthermore, Sire, you will tend the hound which, although now of sad countenance, will be alive with joy when the good knight comes.'

'Damsel,' sayeth the King, 'we shall full and properly keep the shield and the hound safely, and we thank you for bringing them to this place.'

'Sire, I have more to tell you. The best King that lives in the world, the most loyal and the most righteous, sendeth you greeting. But he is saddened to the depths of his soul that he has fallen into great troubles.'

'Damsel,' sayeth the King, 'full saddened am I to hear of such a thing. Pray, tell me, who is this King?'

'He is, Sire, the Fisher King upon whom great grief has fallen upon. Know you why, my Lord?'

'I do not, but would know for I might come to his aid.'

'His grief, Sire, came upon him from the want of a deed of a guest knight at his castle. To this knight appeared the most Holy Grail, but he failed to ask whom the Grail served, and the lands were turned to strife and pestilence thereof. Thereafter, knights fought with knights, men fought with men, and the land suffered. You, Sire, know well of this, for your goodwill did ebb away likewise and you have received much blame. For you, Sire, were the example to the world in well-doing but now you are the mirror of all that is calamitous. Even I, though at first bearing a good heart, have suffered and I will show you thus.'

At this, the damsel took off her hat where under grew not a single hair. 'Sire,' sayeth she, 'before the knight came to the Fisher King's castle, I had tresses of golden hair. But he did not ask the question of the Holy Grail. Nor will my hair return until such time as a knight goes thither to the castle of the Fisher King and asks the question. When that happens, the land will turn to plenty, knights and men will live in fellowship, and I will know my golden hair again. But, good Sire, and good knights, the adventure will be difficult as may be seen at the door of this hall. There you will find a great carriage drawn by three white harts. The traces are of silk, the axles of gold, and the carriage is made of ebony. All is covered with black silk in which is woven a golden cross. Beneath this cover are the heads of a hundred and fifty knights, some in boxes of gold, some of silver, and some of lead. The damsel bearing the shield holds the head of a Queen who betrayed the King whose head I hold, and the knights within the carriage. I pray you, Sire, send to see the costliness and manner of the carriage.'

King Arthur sent Kay to see the carriage. The knight looked and saw that it was indeed a remarkable carriage but thought himself to bring a jest to the King saying, 'Never beheld I a carriage so rich, nor have I seen three such white harts that draw it. They, my Lord, would serve us well for our table for they are full fat and tall.'

But the King grew hot with wrath at the words of Kay. 'No, Sire, I will not have such notions, not even for another kingdom.'

The damsel then sayeth, 'Sire, I know that Kay speaks in jest. Let him speak so, for I know well that you will pay him no heed. Sire, we must leave you now for we have stayed too long. Pray have the shield and hound secured as by our request.'

At the King's command, Yvain took the shield and hung it on the great column, and the Queen's maids took the hound to her apartments where it lay quiet and sad.

As the damsels departed, the King and Queen and the knights looked out of the castle windows and all said that they had never seen a damsel without hair, and felt full sorrow for the damsel with no horse who followed the others on foot.

As they came close by a great forest, the damsels saw a knight on a tall and bony horse. The armour of the knight was full rusty and his shield had been pierced in so many places that the colours thereon could not be seen, and he carried a strong and thick lance. Raising his helmet visor, the knight sayeth, 'Fair welcome, damsel, to you and to your companions.'

'Sire,' sayeth she, 'may God grant you both joy and good adventure.'

'Damsel. Whence come you?'

'From the court of King Arthur who is at Castle Pannenoisance. Is that where you are bound?'

'No,' sayeth the knight, 'I have oft seen the King, but glad I am that he has amended his taking up of good works.'

'Where then do you go, Sire?'

'To the land of the Fisher King, God willing.'

'What, Sire, is your name?'

'I am called Gawain, the nephew of King Arthur.'

'That name, Sire, is such as my heart would have chosen for you. Pray, Gawain, abide with us as our protector for we must soon pass a castle whereof there is some peril.'

'That I shall do willingly,' sayeth the knight.

As they passed through the empty forest, the damsel told Gawain the story of the shield and hound she had left at King Arthur's court and of the knight who had not asked the question.

Though eager to hear, Gawain could not stir his mind from the damsel on foot. 'Pray tell me, why may the damsel on foot not ride upon the carriage?'

'She may not, Sire, for as I have no hair upon my head, she may not go otherwise than on foot. This has come about for the lack of the knight who did not ask the question. Thus are the lands and islands in sorrow and strife. Only when the question is asked by a valorous knight may she ride.'

'Then let us pray that God will grant me the courage and the will to carry out your wish, whereof I may win the notice of God and the praise of the world.'

And thus they went through the green forest until all around began to change. The trees had no leaves and the wood was blackened as though by fire and no birds sang. The ground was also black and split asunder with great cracks from which came forth a stench truly great. And Gawain looked upon the damsels that were distressed by their fortune and grew angered that he could not amend their ills.

They then chanced upon a great valley wherein lay a great black castle surrounded by a tall and black wall. The place seemed to Gawain to be an abode of evil. Upon closing with the castle it was seen to be misshapen and suffered a black stream that issued from a mountain to pass through it with a noise of thunder. From the gateway he heard cries of lamentation from within saying, 'Oh God! What hath become of the good knight, and when will he come?'

'Damsel,' sayeth Gawain, 'what is this foul and hideous castle wherein so many suffer and cry for the coming of the good knight?'

'Sire,' she replied, 'it is the Castle of the Black Hermit. I beseech you not to intrude here for they cannot help me and your death will be at hand. Against them you have no might or power.'

When within a bow-shot of the castle gate they beheld the terrible sight of a hundred and fifty knights pour forth. The knights came to the carriage, lifted up the cover and took the heads thereunder and those of the King and Queen for the heads were their own and the rest their sovereign's. Then, as if in great joy, the knights returned to the castle.

Gawain had remained still to see this and felt great shame that he had allowed such a thing in sight of the damsels but they said unto him, 'Now knoweth you the strength of them and how little your might would have availed you.'

'Damsel,' sayeth Gawain, 'this is an evil castle from where people are robbed in such a manner.'

'Sire,' sayeth she, 'this evil will never be amended, nor this outrage be done away, nor the evil-doer therein be stricken down, nor shall the prisoners therein be set free until such time as the good knight shall come.'

And Gawain replied, 'And glad that knight shall be when by his valour and his boldness he shall destroy so much evil.'

'Therefore, Sire, shall he be the best knight in the world,' sayeth the damsel. 'I despair though that I know him not for I have better reason to see him than anyone alive.'

Gawain sayeth, 'I also wish to see him, for I wish also to turn and continue my journey to the castle of the Fisher King.'

'Then,' sayeth she, 'stay with me until we are beyond the black castle. Then shall I show you the way.'

At this they reached the end of the castle wall and saw a knight issue forth on a great horse. The knight held a strong lance and bore a shield of red whereon was a golden eagle. He spoke to Gawain with the words, 'Knight, I pray you bide a while.'

'What do you want of me?' sayeth Gawain.

'You must fight with me and take from me this shield, or I shall conquer you. This shield is greatly precious and you should try to take it from me for it belonged to the best knight in the world in his time, faithful, wise, and powerful.'

'Who was this knight?'

'Judas Machabeus, he who drove the Syrians from the Temple at Jerusalem and restored and purified it thereafter.'

'You speak truly,' sayeth Gawain, 'for he was a great and good knight.'

'Then you must try and take the shield, for your own is the poorest and most battered that any knight bore. Hardly may a man know the colour thereon.'

Then spoke the damsel. 'Thereby you may well see that his own shield hath not been idle, nor has his horse been as well stabled as yours.'

But the knight replied, 'I will have no long pleading. He must fight with me for I intend to defy him.'

At this the horses drew back and came together at a great pace. The knight smote Gawain on his shield and his lance passed through but breaking against Gawain's armour. Gawain's lance entered the knight's breastplate and drove through his body till he lay on the ground. Pulling his lance free he saw the knight leap to his feet and return to his horse to place his foot in the stirrup and thereby remount.

The damsel then cried out, 'Gawain! Do not permit him to mount his horse again for if he does his strength will increase mightily and you will not conquer him!'

The knight stayed his foot and sayeth, 'Is this then the good Gawain, the nephew of King Arthur?'

'It is,' sayeth the damsel. 'He it is without fail.'

'Sire, sayeth the knight, 'are you he?'

'I am Gawain.'

'Then, Sire,' sayeth the knight, 'I hold myself conquered. Had I known, I would not have been so bold to have challenged so noble a knight.'

The knight took then the red shield bearing an image of a golden eagle and gave it to Gawain. 'Take this shield that once belonged to the best and most faithful knight in the world in his time, for by none I know shall it be better employed than by you. Now, Sire, will you give me your shield as you have no use for it?'

Readily acceding to the knight's request, Gawain made to hand his shield to the knight when, to the surprise of all, the damsel on foot spoke for the first time to them. 'Hold, Gawain! If you deliver him your shield it will be born into the black castle such as only the shields of the defeated are born. The many knights inside will take it that you have been conquered and will come to claim you for the foul prison therein.'

Gawain then sayeth to the knight, 'Is it as the damsel sayeth?'

'It is, Sire,' replied the knight, 'and truly glad am I that I have been conquered for a second time. This second victory of yours has freed me from my sore troubles.'

'Of what troubles do you speak?'

'For I have for many a long time been engaged in jousts with many passing knights. Some have been cowardly, many have been brave, and much is the wounding I have suffered but none bore me to the ground with such force as did you. Since you now carry away the shield, never again shall knights dread to pass this castle, and never again shall I have to contend with them.'

'Then I am truly glad of my conquering of you, and I wish you well.'

'Sire,' sayeth the knight, 'I now must leave and return to the Castle of the Black Hermit, there to display my shame at my defeat.'

'God grant you do well,' sayeth Gawain.

Then spoke the damsel of the lost golden hair. 'Gawain, give me the shield that the knight would have carried off.'

'Willingly, damsel,' sayeth he and gave the shield to the damsel on foot who put it in the carriage. As she did so, a great alarming noise issued from the black castle that resoundeth through the blackened forest.

'It is the fate of the defeated knight. So great is his shame that he has been cast into the foul prison.'

With the black castle left behind them, Gawain sayeth, 'When it shall please you, I must return to my journey.'

And the damsel made reply, 'Truly it is so. May God guard you on your passage.'

Sayeth Gawain, 'Forget not, damsel, I am yours to command.'

'Thank you, Sire, and thank you for your company. Ahead thou shalt see a great Cross beyond which the forest returns well fair and you shall bid farewell to this foul blackness.'

Gawain turned to go, but the damsel on foot cried out to him, 'Sire! I had supposed you to be more heedful.'

'On what account, damsel?' sayeth Gawain in surprise.

'For this,' sayeth she, 'that you have never asked of my damsel why she carries her arm from a cloth of gold around her neck, nor of the precious pillow whereon her arm lieth. I believe that no greater heed will you take at the court of the Fisher King, nor will you ask the question needed.'

'My sweet friend,' sayeth the damsel on the white horse, 'blame not Gawain alone, but also King Arthur before him and all the knights that were at the court. For none of them was so heedful to ask me. Go on your way, Gawain, for it is now too late to ask for I will tell you not, nor shall you ever know it save only by the most cowardly knight in the world. That is mine own knight who goeth out to seek me but knoweth not where to find me.'

'Damsel,' sayeth Gawain, 'nor shall I ask you.'

With that the damsels departed and Gawain set himself forward again towards the great Cross and the fair forest beyond.

Part the IIIrd

Upon entering the green forest Gawain's mind was all turbulent, for the damsel on foot had sayeth he had failed to ask a question of the damsel that had lost her golden hair. Thereby, how might he ask the question of the Holy Grail? Thus troubled, he rode until evensong when he chanced across a small chapel and the house of a hermit in the forest. Before the chapel ran a clear stream beside which sat a damsel holding the reins of a mule. At the saddle-bow of the animal was hung the head of a knight.

'Damsel,' sayeth Gawain, 'may God be with you this evening.'

'Sire,' sayeth she, 'and with you also.'

'Dost thou wait for someone?'

'I do, Sire, I await the return of the hermit of this holy chapel for I would ask him if he knows of a certain knight.'

'Do you think he knows of such people?'

'I have been told so.'

At this the hermit came from the forest and gave greeting to the damsel and Gawain. He invited them into his house and gave their animals feed. He then made to take off the saddles when Gawain sayeth, 'Hold Sire! That is not work for you.'

The hermit replied, 'Though I be a hermit, I know well how to do such matters for I was a squire and a knight for forty years at the court of King Uther Pendragon before coming here twenty years since.'

'But,' sayeth Gawain, 'your features give you the appearance of a man of not yet forty years in this world.'

The hermit bowed his head.

After the saddles had been taken off, the hermit took the damsel and Gawain into the chapel, telling the knight to keep his sword by his side as the forest was perilous. And most fair was the chapel inside.

On return to the house the hermit gave them meat to eat and water from the stream. Then the damsel sayeth to the hermit, 'I am seeking a knight and am come to ask if you know of him.'

'Who is this knight?' sayeth the hermit.

'Sire, he is the pure knight of most holy lineage. He hath a heart of gold and steel, the courage of a lion, the body of a battle-horse, and is without wickedness in everything.'

'Damsel,' sayeth the hermit, 'of little can I tell you of him but that he stayed with me twice within the last twelvemonth.'

'Do you know of another who may know of him?'

'I do not, damsel.'

'And you, Sire,' sayeth she to Gawain, 'do you know of him?'

'I would tell you willingly damsel,' sayeth Gawain, 'but nothing I know of him nor of others that might.'

'And do you know the damsel without hair?'

'Yes, it is ere long since I left her.'

'Does she still carry her arm on a pillow from a cloth of gold round her neck?'

'She does.'

'Sire,' sayeth the hermit, 'what is your name?'

'I am called Gawain, King Arthur's nephew.'

'Then you have my highest esteem.'

'But, Sire,' cried the damsel, 'you are kindred to the worst King that is. Through King Arthur all the world is made worse. For hatred of him I hated a knight that found me nigh to Saint Augustine's chapel, and yet he was the finest knight I ever saw. He slew a knight within the barrier spear most bravely and put himself at much peril to gain for me the head that now hangs from my saddle-bow. But when he told me his name was Arthur the joy fell away for he had the name of that evil King.'

Sayeth Gawain, 'You must speak as you find, but I tell you that King Arthur hath just held the richest court that ever was held, and he has put away all evil and now seeks to bring more good and charity than was ever known before for as long as he shall live. And, damsel, I know of no other knight that beareth the name Arthur.'

'It is right that you come to his rescue for he is your uncle, but your words will mean nothing until he has proved his good intent.'

'Sire,' sayeth the hermit, 'the damsel must say as her heart commands. I say God defend King Arthur for his father made me a knight. Now am I a priest serving the Fisher King by the will of Our Lord and His commandments. All that do serve the Fisher King partake of His reward, for to serve a year seemeth like unto but a month. Such is the holiness of the place and of his castle where I have oftentimes done service in the chapel where the Holy Grail appeareth. Thus it seemeth that all who so serve remain youthful.'

Gawain then asked, 'Sire, by what path may a knight go to his castle?'

'None may show you the way, Sire. Only the will of God may lead you. Do you desire to go thither?'

'It is the greatest wish that I have.'

'If God wills it, may God give you the grace and courage to ask the question when the Grail appears. Be not like the others who failed to ask thereof and caused much evil to befall many people.'

On the morrow, Gawain rose to find his horse and the damsel's mule with saddle and bridle. Going to the chapel he found therein the hermit clothed for the Mass and the damsel praying before an image of Our Lady. There she prayed that God and the sweet Lady would help and guide her. And the tears washed down her face. On her rising, Gawain asked her, 'Why, damsel, are you so downcast?'

She sayeth, 'I am cloaked in desolation for I have been unable to find the pure knight. Now I must go to the castle of the black hermit and bear with me the head of the knight that hangs at my saddle-bow. That head shall be my payment for my safe passage beyond the castle lest otherwise I should be cast into the castle prison or be shamed. Then will I seek the damsel who lost her golden hair and go through the forest in her company.'

When Mass had been sung, Gawain parted company with the hermit and the damsel wishing them God's protection and they him also.

The next day, in search for the lands of the Fisher King, Gawain chanced upon a young squire standing by a horse. Cordially they exchanged salutes and Gawain sayeth, 'Wither go you, my friend?'

'I go, Sire, to seek the Lord of this forest.'

'To whom does the forest belong?'

'It belongeth, Sire, to the best knight in the world.'

'What,' sayeth Gawain, 'can you tell me of him?'

'He ought to bear a shield of white with a red cross upon it. I say that he is a good knight but little call have I to praise him for before he was a squire he slew my father in this forest with a spear. I shall never be at ease until such time as I have avenged my father who was the best of knights.'

'My friend,' sayeth Gawain, 'take heed of what I say. Since your enemy is such a good knight, so much more will be the evil of your actions.'

'Perhaps,' sayeth the squire, 'but on his encounter I shall run upon him as my mortal enemy.'

'As your heart commands, my friend. Meantime, where in this forest may I rest for the night?'

'I know not, Sire, for there are no lodgings for many leagues in all directions. Already it is noon and thou shouldst not tarry if you seek a safe house for tonight.'

Gawain bid the squire God's guidance and went at a great pace through the forest until the sun was like to set. At this, he saw beyond fair meadows a castle on a mountain. Great was the castle and enclosed in high walls with, in its midst, a great tower. When within a bow-shot a squire came from the castle gate and saluted Gawain with a welcome.

'God be with you this evening,' sayeth Gawain. 'What is this castle?'

'It is, Sire, the castle of the Widow Lady.'

'And the name thereof?'

'It is Camelot, Sire. The castle belonged to Alain Le Gros, a loyal and worshipful knight who has been dead for many years. His Lady remains but without comfort or guidance and thus the castle is attacked by those who would remove her by force. Chief amongst these are the Lord of the Moors and another knight. Already they have robbed her of seven castles. Her greatest desire is to see the return of her son for she has none but her daughter and five old knights to help her guard the castle. The gates are barricaded and the draw-bridge raised, Sire, but if you will tell me of your name I will return and tell my Lady of your coming that you may enter and lodge therein tonight.'

'I thank you, Sire,' sayeth Gawain, 'but my name shall already be known therein to your Lady.'

At this, the squire rode off at great pace to the castle and Gawain attended at a chapel near the castle mounted on four columns of marble and was a fair sepulchre. Inside he saw a coffin wherein it was not known who lieth there. And the coffin remained still and whole.

Meanwhile, the squire entered the great hall of the castle and sayeth to the Widow Lady and her daughter, 'Lady, beyond the walls cometh the finest knight I have ever seen. He is well armed and alone and requests to be lodged herein this night.'

An excitement beating within her breast, the Lady asked, 'What name hath he?'

'He told me, Lady, that you should well know his name.'

The Lady then wept with great joy as did her daughter. 'Dear Lord God,' sayeth she, 'it is my son returned. This is the greatest day of my life for now I shall not be robbed of mine honour, nor shall I lose my castle now I have a champion for my cause.'

Straightway the Lady and her daughter left the castle saying 'Haste! At the coffin shall we see whether it be he!' But they found Gawain at the chapel and the coffin not opened. At this, the Widow Lady fell down in a faint and returned only with great weeping.

The daughter of the Widow Lady sayeth to Gawain, 'You are welcome, Sire, but my mother took you to be her son arrived back and made great joy. Now, alas, it is plain that you are not her son for the coffin remains closed and whole, and still we know not who lies therein.'

Gawain raised the Widow Lady and sayeth she, 'Sire, what is your name?'

'Lady,' sayeth he, 'I am called Gawain, the nephew of King Arthur.'

'Then, Sire, you shall be welcome both for your own and for sake of my son.' The Widow Lady then biddeth a squire to take the horse and shield and lance of Gawain to the castle. She took the knight into the great hall and fetched him water to wash for his rusty armour had begrimed him mightily. She apparelled him in a robe of silk and gold and ermine and sat next to him with the question, 'Sire, can you tell me aught of my son whom I hath not seen for many a year and of whom I am in sore need?'

'Lady,' sayeth he, 'I can tell you nought of your son and mighty is my wish that I could for I also would wish to meet him. Pray tell me, how is he named?'

'His name is Percival which meaneth 'lost valleys' and he was the boldest of squires when he departed from this castle. Now I heareth that he is the best knight alive and the most strong and without taint of wickedness. But it is for his slaying of the knight with the red shield that I now much need his courage. For seven years he hath been gone from this castle and from his mother and his sister, Dindrane. Now the brother of the knight he slew and the Lord of the Moors do war upon me and would rob me of my castle. Of my brothers, King Pelles hath given up his land and become a hermit, and the evil King of Castle Mortal lays war against the Fisher King that he might have the most Holy Grail and the Spear of the eternally bleeding point. Pray God that they should never fall to him.'

'Lady,' sayeth Gawain, 'there was a knight at the court of the Fisher King before whom the Holy Grail appeared three times yet he failed to ask whereof it served nor whom it honoured.'

The daughter of the Widow Lady replied, 'Sire, it is truly as you speak and he was the best knight in the world, but though I love my brother and all brave knights it was by the failing of that knight that mine uncle the Fisher King hath fallen upon evil times.'

Sayeth the Widow Lady, 'Sire, it is the duty of all good knights to call upon the Fisher King. Will you therefore go?'

'Lady, I have no greater wish for long has that been my intent.'

'Then you are sure to see my son. Tell him of my evil plight and that of my brother the Fisher King. Moreover, Gawain, remember your duty should you be blessed with the sight of the most Holy Grail.'

'I shall do, Lady, as my God commands.'

As they spoke, five knights of the castle entered the great hall from the hunt and brought much good food. They knelt before the Widow Lady and sayeth, 'Lady, there is to be a great tournament in the valleys that aforetime belonged to you. Great tents are already put up and the brother of the Knight of the Red Shield and the Lord of the Moors are in attendance with many knights. It has been ordained at the tournament that the victor shall have garrison of your castle.'

And the Widow Lady weepeth, saying to Gawain, 'Sire, now you may see how I am to be treated. These knights say already that my home is theirs.'

'They may say as they wish,' sayeth Gawain, 'but it remaineth a great dishonour and sin among them.'

At this, the daughter of the Widow Lady fell at the feet of Gawain but he raiseth her up and sayeth, 'Damsel, be of brave heart.'

'For the sake of God, Sire, take pity on my mother and on me!'

'I have great pity for you both.'

'And therefore, Sire,' sayeth the daughter, 'these straits shall reveal you to be a good knight for by their goodness are great knights known unto God.'

That night Gawain slept with the other knights in the great hall but he slept most poorly for his mind troubled him greatly. On the morn he arose, took food and put on his armour and heard Mass in the castle chapel. Then asked he of the other knights whether they would go to the tournament. All sayeth, 'Yes, Sire, do you so go?'

'In faith, I do,' he replied.

Gawain and the knights took to their horses and bid farewell to the Widow Lady and her daughter who made great joy at Gawain attending to their cause.

After a great gallop, Gawain and the five knights came upon the fairest of lands with green forests and high rocks wherein sported many deer. 'Sire,' said the knights to Gawain, 'we are in the valleys of Camelot of which the Widow Lady and her daughter have been robbed by those that took also her seven castles.'

'That, brother knights, is a wrong and a sin to be avenged.' sayeth Gawain.

Soon they saw the pennants and the shields and the tents of the tournament where many knights were seen to be riding in gallop. The tents stretched from one hand to the other for many were the knights that rode there. One of the companions of Gawain showed him amongst the knights on the field of the tournament the Lord of the Moors and the brother of the Knight of the Red Shield who was named the Knight of the Red Chaos.

At this Gawain galloped into the affray laying low a knight who gave him challenge. The five knights followed and, though none had experience of battle, such was the example of Gawain that they sent their challengers from their horses. The Knight of the Red Chaos who knoweth not Gawain ran at him full tilt but was put aground with broken bones. Knight after knight fell to the lances of Gawain and his five companions. Upon seeing this, the Lord of the Moors rode up with a great band of knights. Gawain ran at him and they met with such ferocity that both their lances broke apart in splinters. The Lord of the Moors lost his stirrups and fell with such mighty force that his helmet gave a great dent to the ground. Gawain took the horse of the Lord of the Moors and gave it to one of the knights of the Widow Lady. Many a knight fell to Gawain and the five knights until the Lord of the Moors returned to the affray and ran at Gawain with the broken shaft of his lance. Again they met with great shock so that the lance-shafts were broken on shield and breast-plate. Crying to his knights not to enter the contest, the Lord of the Moors drew his sword, likewise Gawain. Many and heavy were the blows upon helmet and armour and the Lord of the Moors did bleed with much blood from the mouth and nose until his armour was all bloody. No more could he endure the assault of Gawain and he yielded himself up and his knights to Gawain and his five knights. Gawain took the horse of the Lord of the Moors and sayeth to one of his knights, 'Guard this horse for me.'

The many knights repaired to their tents and took counsel one of the other, all agreeing that the knight with the red shield bearing a golden eagle had done better than all of them. And they asked of the Lord of the Moors if he accorded with them. At this, he answered, 'Aye, it is so.'

To Gawain the Lord of the Moors sayeth, 'You, Sire, are the warden of the Castle Camelot.'

'Thank you, my Lord,' sayeth Gawain. And to the five knights he sayeth, 'Brothers, it is my will that the safe keeping of the Castle Camelot and the Widow Lady and her daughter be in your hands as witnessed by all the knights here present.' This they agreed right gladly.

To the Lord of the Moors, Gawain sayeth, 'You, my Lord, will go to Castle Camelot where you shall be the prisoner of the Widow Lady.'

But the Lord of the Moors sayeth, 'No, Sire. You defeated me in tournament, not in war, and you are not right to make me prisoner. Instead, ransom will I pay. What, Sire, is your name?'

'It is Gawain. I am the nephew of King Arthur.'

'Sire, although I have never met you, your name is oft spoken abroad. As the Castle Camelot is now in your keeping you have my promise that for a year and a day neither the castle nor the Lady need fear me or any other that I may prevent from molesting her or her daughter. This I pledge in the presence of these knights here present and I shall give you gold and silver in ransom.'

'Thank you, my Lord,' sayeth Gawain. 'I agree to those terms which you have said.'

At this, Gawain and the five knights returneth to Castle Camelot where Gawain gave the daughter of the Widow Lady the horse of the Lord of the Moors. Great was the joyous feast that night at which Gawain told the Widow Lady that she and her daughter were in the safe keeping of the five knights for a year and a day.

On the morn Gawain took leave after attending Mass, for such was his custom. He departed with commendation unto God from the Widow Lady and her daughter for he had left them in better keeping than when he found it.

It should be known by all that the Castle Camelot of the Widow Lady lies in the west whereas the Castle Camelot of King Arthur guardeth the entrance to England.

Part the IVth

Guided by God and adventure, Gawain went in search of the
castle of the Fisher King praying that he might succeed in his holy
errand. At evensong he came across a mighty house surrounded by
large waters. Thinking this house to be the home of a worthy man,
Gawain went to the gate of the house. As he drew nigh to a bridge
leading to the gate he saw a dwarf who sayeth to him, 'Gawain.
You are indeed welcome.'

'Dear friend,' sayeth Gawain, 'may God bless you for your
kindness. Do you know me?'

'I know you well, Sire,' sayeth the dwarf, 'for I saw you at the
tournament. You could not have chosen a better moment to have
come hither, for my Lord is absent. But you will find my lady, the
most fair and gentle and courteous in all the realm and she is not
yet of twenty years.'

'My friend,' sayeth Gawain, 'what is the name of the lord of the
house.'

'Sire, he is called Marin, lord of the Castle Gomeret.' Then
sayeth the dwarf, 'I will go and tell my lady that the good knight
Gawain is come and bid her to make great joy.'

On entering the chamber of the lady, the dwarf sayeth, 'Haste,
Lady! Make great joy for Gawain is come to stay with you.'

Sayeth the Lady, 'Your news makes me both glad and sorry. Glad
I am that the good knight will abide here tonight, yet sorry that

he is the knight that my lord hateth most in the world. He has oft warned me against this knight saying that Gawain keeps not faith with any lady or damsel but would have his will of them, for what is bred in the bone will never be out of the flesh.'

'My Lady,' sayeth the dwarf, 'so I have heard it said, but it is not true.'

When Gawain entered the courtyard and dismounted he was greeted by the lady who took his hand and led him to the hall and made him to sit down upon a cushion. A squire led his horse to the stable and other squires helped him to remove his armour and brought him water to wash. And the dwarf brought him a scarlet and ermine robe to sit at the table with the lady. Many a time as they ate meat Gawain looked at the lady and thought her to be of great beauty. Had he been minded to trust his eyes and his heart he would have changed his purpose, but so strong was his heart that he quenched his desires so that he fell not in to wickedness and deceit for the sake of the high pilgrimage that he was on.

After meat, Gawain went to his bed chamber saying to the lady, 'May God be with you this night.' And the lady answereth the same.'

The dwarf sayeth to Gawain, 'Sire, I shall stay by the door of your bed chamber until you be asleep.'

Gawain replieth, 'Thank you, you shall be rewarded for your kindness.'

Seeing that Gawain had fallen in to sleep, the dwarf left the house and took a boat upstream of the river to a small island whereon was a small house. There slept Marin the Jealous, the master of his lady. The dwarf waketh him roughly, saying, 'Sire, how do you sleep so well when you cannot be sleeping with as much ease as does Gawain.'

The knight sayeth, 'How can you know such a thing?'

'I know, Sire, for I left your lady and Gawain abed together in warm embrace.'

'But,' sayeth Marin the Jealous, 'I forbade that she should ever allow Gawain to enter the house.'

'In truth, Sire,' sayeth the dwarf, 'he has brought her greater pleasure than I have ever heard or known of any man that ever brought pleasure to any lady. Pray haste yourself, Sire, for there is great danger that he may take her away from you.'

'No, I will not go,' sayeth the knight. 'But be assured that she shall pay dearly for this treachery even though she depart with him.'

Knowing nought of this, Gawain rose the next morn. There he met the lady who wept with distress for she knew the dwarf had gone to her master. 'Sire, for the sake of God have pity on me, for the dwarf hath betrayed me. You will depart for the forest and leave me to my lord who will cause me great hurt for that which I have not done. This will be a great sin for you to do.'

'Truly do you speak,' sayeth Gawain. At this he armed himself and left the house to watch from the forest. On his departing, Marin the Jealous returneth. 'Sire,' sayeth the lady. 'Welcome my lord.'

'You, lady,' he replieth, 'may you have nought but shame and evil fall upon you as the most disloyal woman that ever lived. I know that this night you took into my bed the very knight I have warned you against.'

'Sire, I gave him room in the house, but your bed hath never been shamed by me, nor never shall be.'

'You, lady, are a false woman and you lie.' At this he tore her clothing until nought but rags remained although she pleaded with him for mercy. Taking her long tresses he gave them to the hand of the dwarf and told him to drag her to the forest as he rode behind armed on his horse. At the forest they came across a pond of cold water and the knight threw her in as he cut rods from the nearby trees. Thus armed, he beat her until the water took the colour of her blood and her cries resounded through the trees.

On hearing the cries, Gawain galloped at great pace and arrived by the pond saying, 'Hold your hand, Sire! Why do you so treat the best and most loyal lady that I have ever known? Never have I found a lady that did me so much honour in her goodness, in her speech and in her bearing. You should have nought but praise for her. Pull her from the water, Sire, and I will swear on any holy relic that I never sought evil of her nor had I desire so to do.'

'Sire,' replieth Marin the Jealous, 'I will pull her from the pond on one condition. That you will joust at me and I at you. Should you defeat me then she shall be free of all blame, but if I conquer you she shall be held guilty. This shall be the judgement of the matter.'

'I ask for no more,' sayeth Gawain.

Bidding the dwarf to take the lady out of the pond, Marin the Jealous walked back his horse that he might fall upon Gawain in full strength. Both knights came at each other in a might rush, but as they were about to meet shield to shield, Marin the Jealous pulled his horse and rode at his weeping lady piercing her though with his lance. He then rode at great pace to his house with the dwarf running behind. Seeing the foul deed, Gawain raced thereafter and trampled the dwarf beneath his horse until he was slain, but the bridge was raised and the gate of the house was barred.

From the roof of the house, Marin the Jealous cried out, 'This, Sire, is your entire fault. It is you that hath brought shame and misadventure upon me. But you shall pay for it.'

At this, Gawain turned his horse and returned to the place where lay the lady that was slain. Taking her bleeding body upon his horse he found a chapel and lay her modestly inside praying that someone should care for her in death. He then departed with a heavy heart.

Deep in the green forest, still sore of heart, Gawain chanced across a sight he had not thought possible. Coming towards him was a knight of the strangest appearance. The knight was riding his horse whilst sat with his face towards the tail, his armour was hung loose around his neck and his shield and lance were borne with both with their tops at the bottom. As the knight came closer, Gawain heard him cry out, 'Gentle knight, for the sake of God do me no harm for I am the Knight Coward!'

'No, Sire,' returned Gawain, 'I shall not harm you. Indeed I know of no one who would.' Had it not been for his downcast thoughts, Gawain would have laughed to have seen such a sight. 'No, Knight, you shall have nothing to fear from me.'

On their drawing abreast, Gawain asked of the knight, 'Whose knight are you?'

'I am the knight of the lady who hath lost her golden tresses.'

'Then, Knight, you are most welcome, and be well assured that I mean you no harm.'

'May God be praised,' sayeth the knight, 'for I see from your shield of red with the golden eagle that you must be Gawain. In your presence I shall adjust my armour to its proper station and ride my horse as do other knights.' At this, Gawain helped the Knight Coward to arm himself properly.

Thereupon came another knight at a great gallop. He had a shield of black and white equal. 'Wait, Gawain,' he cried, 'I am here on behalf of Marin the Jealous whose wife you caused him to slay. I shall defy you ere you leave this ground.'

Replieth Gawain, 'I am heavy of heart for her death was undeserved.'

'That will avail you not for I hold you to answer for her death. If I conquer you the blame shall be yours, but if you defeat me my lord will still hold your life forfeit.'

'To this I will not agree for God knoweth well that no blame do I have.'

At this spoke the Knight Coward to Gawain, 'Fight him not, Gawain, for you may not depend upon me for help.'

'It is of nought,' replieth Gawain. 'I have long fought and had adventures without you, and with the help of God, I shall continue so to do.'

Seeing that the black and white knight was determined to bring him to combat, Gawain backed his horse before they met at a great gallop. Both their lances were shattered on the shields but Gawain overturned the knight and his horse. He then drew his sword and set to fall upon the other knight but the knight cried out, 'Hold, Gawain! Do you think to slay me? I am defeated and have no wish to die for another's folly. Pray, Sire, have mercy.'

Thereupon Gawain did think that the knight had done no more than follow his lord's bidding. Taking the hand of the knight in his, Gawain bid him fare well and the knight departed.

'Sire,' sayeth the Knight Coward, 'I cannot be as brave as you. As God may witness, had the knight defied me in such a manner I should have run away or fallen to my knees to beg his mercy.'

Gawain replieth, 'You wish for nought but peace, and a full noble wish that is. May God grant you as you desire.'

'In the name of God I thank you for your wish, for of war and battle comes nothing but evil. Nor have I the seams and scars that mark you in many places. Instead I ask God to defend me. And to God I commend you, Sire, for I am now to depart to find my lady without her tresses.'

'Before you depart, Sire, I have a question I must ask. Why does you lady have her arm slung from her neck resting upon a pillow?'

'She holds her arm so, Sire, for that was the arm with which she held the Holy Grail up to the knight who would not ask of whom the Grail served. Since that day she will not use the arm again until she can return to the Fisher King's castle and a knight be found who hath the courage to ask the question. Sire, may I now go hither to find my lady?'

'Indeed you may, Knight, and may God go with you.'

'I thank you, Sire. But before I depart I wish to give you my lance. I have no use for it and yours is broken short.'

With that, the Knight Coward gave Gawain his lance and departed.

Gawain continued through the forest until the sun came close to set when he heard the sound of a great gallop. From the trees there came a wounded knight who cried out, 'What is your name, Knight?'

'My name is Gawain.'

'Then, Gawain, it was in your service that I was wounded thus!'

'How so?'

'This morn I went in to a chapel to pray and found the body of a lady you had borne there. I was minded to give her a burial and took her outside and beginneth to dig with my sword when the knight Marin the Jealous fell upon me and wounded me in many places. He seized the body of the lady and abandoned it to the wild beasts of the forest. Now I go to a chapel where I must confess to God, for well I know that I do not have long of this life. But I shall meet God more easily now that I have found you and told you of this story.'

'Sire,' sayeth Gawain, 'I grieve to find you thus and commend you most fully to God's care.'

They parted company and Gawain rode in to the night.

On the next day, Gawain came upon a castle that was both rich and fair. From the castle gates came an ancient knight with a hawk upon his hand. They both gave salute and Gawain asked the knight of whom belongeth the castle. And the knight replied that it was the Castle Orguelleux. The castle of the Proud Maiden that never asked a knight of his name.

The knight continued. 'And those of us who are her knights dare not ask the name of a knight on her behalf. But you will be well lodged within for she is both fair and courteous otherwise. She hath never had any lord nor will she so do until he be proved to be the best knight in the world. Come, Sire, let me escort you therein.'

From the mounting-stage before the hall the knight took Gawain within where squires removed his armour and he was given a robe of scarlet and fur. Then entered the damsel of the castle.

Gawain rose and sayeth, 'Damsel. I greet you well.'

'And, Sire, you also. Welcome indeed you are. Will you see my chapel?'

'At your pleasure, Damsel.'

The maiden took Gawain by the hand and led him to the chapel which was the finest and richest he had ever beheld. Inside were four tombs carved richly. On the right hand were three openings in the wall that were lined with gold and precious stones. Within each, lighted by a circlet of candles, lay a small chest of the finest work. The smell was of the sweetest balm.

'Sire,' sayeth she, 'see you these tombs?'

'I do, Damsel.'

'Three are made for the best knights in the world and the fourth for me. One tomb hath upon it the name Gawain, and the second hath the name Lancelot of the Lake. Each of them do I love for love's sake. The third hath the name Percival. Him do I love above the others. Within the three openings are hallowed chests wherein their heads may lie.'

At this, the maiden put her hand to the wall and took out a pin whereupon a broad blade of the sharpest steel fell and closed up the three openings.

'Thus shall I cut off their heads and place them in the chests therein. Afterwards their bodies shall be set in the three tombs which shall be shrouded both grand and rich. Thus I may never enjoy these knights in their life but they shall be mine until God calls me when I shall join them in company in the fourth tomb.'

Of his name, Gawain stayed silent and though given great honour by the maiden and her knights he wished well that the night may be over and he could leave the place. He heard also that the maiden sent knights in to the forest where they might meet the knights she sought and promised them great riches if one was brought in.

The next morn, after Mass and armed, Gawain said his fare well to the maiden and departed with no desire to remain longer within Castle Orguelleux.

As he rode at great pace through the forest he came upon two knights who mounted their horses at his coming and came to him with their shields up and their lances beneath their arms. 'Hold, Knight!' they cried, 'Tell us your name without falsehood.'

'I have no need of falsehood. I am called Gawain, the nephew of King Arthur.'

'Then, Sire, you are truly welcome. We have one request of you. Will you come with us to see the lady who most in the world wishes to see you and will make much joy at Castle Orguelleux where she waits.'

Gawain replieth, 'I have no leisure for such matters for I am bound elsewhere.'

'Sire,' they sayeth, 'we are commanded by the lady to take you thither whether by your will or not.'

'I have said plainly that I will not go with you.'

With that, the knights took his bridle and began to lead him towards the castle. But Gawain drew his sword and wounded one knight at which they both rode for the castle.

On receiving the knights, the maiden asked, 'Who hath done this to you?'

'It was, Damsel, Gawain. We found him in the forest but he would not come with us. We offered him force but he wounded my fellow knight.'

At this the maiden demanded a great horn be sounded which brought the knights of the castle to her full armed. She commanded them to follow Gawain and promised great riches to the knight that brought him in. Just as they were to depart at her command, two forest keepers came in to the castle. Both were wounded about the body.

'Who hath done this?' Sayeth the knights and the maiden.

'Gawain,' they replieth, 'He would not come to the castle with us and did cause us much hurt.'

'Is he nearby?'

'No, Damsel,' the keepers sayeth. 'He is far distant for he goes at great pace.'

At this, the knights sayeth to the maiden, 'Damsel, it will avail us nothing but shame and hurt to go after him. It was you, Damsel, that lost him for we knew him to be Gawain by his red shield that bears a golden eagle. But you forbade us giving you his name.'

'Then, but by the grace of God, my life is finished for I did not ask his name,' sayeth the maiden. 'Never again shall brave knights abide in my castle. I have lost the first of the great knights and thus I have lost the other two. Myself have I condemned by my pride.' The maiden then bowed her head and wept.

At that time, Gawain was riding through the forest when he heard a hound howling. The dog came to him keeping its nose to the ground whereupon it found a trail of blood that led off the trail. Gawain followed the hound until it led him to a decayed manor within a marsh. Passing over a near ruined bridge he came to the Waste Manor which was much cracked and crumbled. The hound stayed at his heel as Gawain entered. Therein he found the body of a knight which had been stricken through the breast unto the heart. Thereupon, a weeping damsel entered the room with a shroud with which to wrap the dead knight.

'You are welcome, Sire,' sayeth she to Gawain, 'but little cheer have I to offer you for I am in the midst of despair.'

Sayeth Gawain, 'May God grant you comfort and ease from your suffering.'

The damsel spoke to the hound saying, 'This knight is not the one I sent you to bring. I must have the knight that brought death to this knight.'

'Doest thou know who hath slain him?' sayeth Gawain.

'I do, Sire. It was Lancelot of the Lake that slew him in the forest. May God grant me vengeance upon him and all at the court of King Arthur who have brought nothing but evil upon us. This knight shall be avenged for he has a bold son whom is my brother and many good friends besides.'

With that, Gawain left the damsel after commending her to God. He departed the Waste Manor praying to God that he might meet Lancelot.

Part the Vth

Gawain travelled until the sun began to set when he came upon a fair manor and chapel. An orchard surrounded by a high wooden fence lay in front of the chapel. Thereby stood a hermit who looked in to the orchard and gave great shouts as of encouragement. Upon seeing Gawain, the hermit sayeth, 'Welcome, Sire.'

'May God be upon you,' replieth Gawain. At this the hermit had Gawain's horse taken to the stable. Taking the knight by the hand, the hermit led Gawain to the orchard and bid him look inside the fence.

Gawain looked therewithin and saw two damsels and a squire and a child that was riding a lion.

'Sire,' sayeth the hermit, 'this was the cause of my joyous cries. Saw you ever a child so fair?'

'No, Sire, I have not.'

They entered the orchard and the damsel brought Gawain a robe of scarlet and ermine.

'Sire,' sayeth the hermit, 'none may command the lion or ride him save for the child alone and yet the boy is of no more than six years. He is of noble family although his father is the most cruel man known. His father is Marin the Jealous that slew his wife on account of Gawain. The boy will not bide with his father for he knoweth him to be wrong. I am the uncle of the boy and see that he is tended by the damsels and the squire. But much the boy desireth to meet Gawain which is good, for on the death of his father he ought to be that knight's man. If you know anything of Gawain such news would be greatly welcome.'

'By my faith, Sire, I can give you tidings on that account. See you the shield I bore? That is the shield of Gawain.'

'Are you he?' sayeth the hermit.

'Truly, Sire, I am Gawain. And the death of the lady caused me much anger but her slayer retreated to his castle.'

The hermit sayeth to the boy, 'Fair nephew. That which you most desire is come. Come and greet him.'

The boy alighteth from the lion and put it in its den and closed the door thereon. To Gawain he sayeth, 'Welcome, Sire.'

'May you grow in honour before God,' sayeth Gawain. And he picked the boy from the ground and held him dear.

'Sire,' sayeth the hermit, 'through you his mother came to her death. He will be your man but he needeth your guidance and help.'

At this, the child fell to his knees in front of the knight and raised his hands as if in prayer.

'Look, Sire,' sayeth the hermit, 'he offers you his homage. Does not your heart move?'

Gawain took the child's hands in his own and sayeth, 'It is with gladness that I receive your homage and the honour therewith. Always shall you have my help and guidance when you needeth it. What, pray, is your name?'

'I am called, Sire, Meliot of England.'

'Truly he speaks,' sayeth the hermit, 'for his mother was the daughter of a rich lord of the kingdom of England.'

That night Gawain was treated well fair by the hermit and the damsels and the squire. After Mass, the hermit enquired of him, 'Wither go you, Gawain?'

'To the land of the Fisher King, God willing.'

'May God guide and protect you better than the knight that was here before you. Through him the lands are all fallen in to sorrow and the good Fisher King doth languish thereof.'

'May God have me do as His will directs. And you, Sire, may God stand beside you in the care of the boy Meliot.'

Thereupon the knight taketh his leave and came upon meadows and a forest most fair. At this, Gawain met a squire with a most sorrowful countenance.

'Where have you come from, my friend?' sayeth Gawain.

'I come from the forest, Sire.'

'Whose man are you?'

'I belong to the worshipful man that owns the forest.'

'You seem much downcast,' sayeth Gawain.

'I cannot be otherwise, for there is no joy in losing a good lord.'

'Who is your knight?'

'The best in the world,' sayeth the squire.

'Is he slain?'

'No, Sire, but he has been sore troubled this long time past.'

'And what is his name?'

'Those with him know him as Parluifer.'

'Will you tell me where he is?'

'I cannot, Sire, beyond that he abides in the forest. To tell you more would be against my knight's will.'

Gawain then saw that tears brightened the eyes of the squire and sayeth, 'What ails thee?'

'Sire, may I never know peace until I have entered a hermitage to save my soul for I have wrought the greatest sin any man can. I have slain my mother, the Queen, for she telleth me that I shall not be King after my father's death. Instead, she sendeth me to be a monk or a clerk and putteth my young brother in sight of the kingdom. Upon my father learning I had slain my mother he withdrew to this forest to make a hermitage and renounce his kingdom. Nor have I now any will to be King from the great disloyalty that I have wrought. I am, therefore, resolved that it is better that I should be banished than my father.'

'And what is your name?'

'My name, Sire, is Joseus. I am of the lineage of Joseph of Arimathea and my father is King Pelles and mine uncles are the Fisher King and the King of Castle Mortal. The Widow Lady of Camelot is mine aunt. The good knight Parluifer also is of this kin.'

With that the squire Joseus departed and Gawain entered the forest. There he found a spring from which flowed a fair stream by which there led a path much used. Journeying along the trail he came across a fair house and chapel. Outside the chapel sat a man of most pleasing appearance dressed as a hermit. He had white hair and no beard upon his face. At his side a squire held a strong and tall war horse on which was buckled a shield bearing a golden sun. In front of the hermit lay mail armour.

On seeing Gawain the hermit appealed to him saying, 'Ride gently, Sire, and make no noise, for we have no need of worse than we have at present.'

Gawain reined his horse and the hermit continued, 'Do not take it as a discourtesy, Sire, for willingly would I have asked you to lodge with us but within the chapel lieth a knight that is said to be the best in the world. Though he be sorely sick should another knight approach I could not prevent him from rising and challenging the coming knight. And if the sick knight was slain it would be a great loss to the world.'

'What is the name of this knight?' sayeth Gawain.

'I have named him Parluifer, meaning dearness and love.'

'May I see him?'

'Not, Sire, until he be whole again and of good cheer.'

'Is there nothing that I can say that will allow me to see him?'

To the sorrow of Gawain, the hermit replieth, 'No, Sire, nothing can you say.'

'May I then ask the lineage of the knight?'

'He is of the lineage of Joseph of Arimathea, the good soldier.'

Then came a damsel to the door of the chapel and calleth very low to the hermit who rose up and took his leave of Gawain. The damsel and the hermit entered the chapel and closed the door and the squire led the horse to the house taking the armour. Gawain turned his horse and entered the forest with inner hurt for the shame he felt for not knowing if the knight within the chapel was the son of the Widow Lady.

For many a long time Gawain journeyed through lands and kingdoms before he found the fairest of lands with a rich castle therein. Going thither he saw the castle with walls of great height. At the gate of the castle lay a lion chained. On either side of the gate were two engines that shot forth quarrels from their cross-bows with great force that none dare approach. On the walls walked men dressed in white robes as if of priestly manner and knights dressed in a manner ancient. On the same walls were many crosses and holders of relics. Three tall crosses rising from a chapel could be seen within the castle, one taller than the others. At the top of each of the crosses was a golden eagle. The priests and knights all knelt towards this chapel and made joy as if they could see God in Heaven with His Holy Mother.

Gawain was mightily confused. He could not approach the castle for fear of the great cross-bows, nor was there any way to the right or to the left and he was loath to return. At this a priest came forth from the castle. 'Sire,' sayeth Gawain, 'you are most welcome.'

'Good fortune to you, Knight,' sayeth the priest, 'what is you pleasure?'

'May I ask, Sire, what is the name of this castle?'

'It is the entrance to the land of the Fisher King wherein they are beginning the service of the Most Holy Grail.'

'Then, Sire, I seek your permission to advance further for I have journey long and hard to reach the land of the Fisher King.'

'Such a thing I cannot do, Knight, for to enter and approach the Holy Grail you must bring with you the sword with which Saint John the Baptist was beheaded.'

'Then must I be poorly treated for that I do not have the sword?'

'You should understand, Knight, that should you obtain the sword great joy will be made of you within these walls and wherever the Fisher King ruleth. But mark well, Knight, the sword is held by the most foul and unbelieving King that lives.'

'Therefore I must return,' sayeth Gawain, 'though most sorrowful I feel.'

'Thou needest not feel sorrowful, Knight, for should you capture the sword then it will be well known that you are worthy to behold the Holy Grail. But you should take great heed to remember the knight who did not ask whom the Holy Grail served.'

At this, Gawain departed in great sorrow that he had come close to the Holy Grail yet could not approach it. And he remembered not to ask of the priest where the sword that was used to behead Saint John the Baptist lay. But he remindeth himself that if God intended that he should be successful He would guide him to the place.

One day, Gawain came upon a small hill whereon was built a chapel. By the chapel was a townsman that sitteth upon a mighty battle-horse. They saluted each the other.

'Sire,' sayeth the townsman, 'I am of sorrow that your ride upon a horse that is lean and spare of flesh. It seemeth to me that you should be better horsed.'

'Nothing can be done, Sire,' sayeth Gawain, 'only when it please God shall I have a better horse.'

'Wither go you, Sire?' sayeth the townsman.

'I go to seek the sword wherewith the head of Saint John the Baptist was cut off.'

'Then, Sire, you run a sore peril for the King that hath it believeth not in God and is most foul and cruel. His name is Gurgalain and many are the knights who have gone thither but have not returned. Nonetheless, if God grant you the victory and you win the sword will you give me your word to bring it to me so that I may see it, for which I will give you my horse for your own?'

'Sire, you are most courteous but you know me not.'

'I do not doubt that you are an honourable and sincere man and that you will hold to your covenant.'

'And to this do I pledge you my word,' sayeth Gawain, 'that if God allows me to win the sword, I will show it to you on my return.'

And they departed that place on each other's horse.

Gawain rode at great pace until the night cometh but could find no castle nor house therein to lodge. With the rising moon he came across a broad meadow wherein a fair stream flowed. There he found a large tent white of sides and with a covering of red silk. The cords of the tent were of red silk and the pegs that pierced the ground were of ivory. The tops of the poles were golden and each bore at its top a golden eagle. At the door of the tent Gawain alighteth and took off his horse's bridle letting him feed upon the grass. Against the side of the tent he placed his lance and shield. Gawain then entered the tent and wondered at what he saw. In the centre lay a broad couch of red silk on which was placed a bed of feathers. A coverlet of ermine lay atop and at the head of the bed lay two pillows such as the fairest ever seen. All around lay a sweet scent as if of balm. On the ground were spread silken cloths. A seat of ivory was placed at each side of the couch each bearing a rich cushion. At the foot of the couch were two golden candlesticks with tall wax tapers therein. In the tent also was a table of ivory banded with gold and set with precious jewels. On the table was a cloth spread and a silver bowl and a knife with an ivory handle and golden vessels.

Gawain laid himself down on the couch and wondered at the tent and that not a soul was to be seen. At this he thought to take off his armour.

Thereupon a dwarf entered the tent and saluted the knight. The dwarf then came to the couch and began to take of Gawain's armour. The knight remembereth the lady who was slain though a dwarf and sayeth, 'Stand back from me, my friend, for I am not minded to disarm myself.'

'Sire,' sayeth the dwarf, 'you may disarm without misgiving for until the morrow you shall have no cause for alarm. Never were you lodged more richly or more honourably than tonight.'

With that Gawain began to disarm with the help of the dwarf but he brought in his lance and shield and sword by the couch. The dwarf brought him a silver bowl of water that he may wash, after which the dwarf brought him a robe of cloth of gold with ermine trimmed.

'Sire,' sayeth the dwarf, 'be not troubled over your horse for I shall see that he is at ease and fed and return him to you.'

Thereupon, two squires entered the tent with meat and wines and set them upon the table. They bid Gawain to eat and placed great torches in a tall stand of gold. They then departed.

As Gawain ate, two damsels of great beauty entered the tent and saluted him most courteously which he returned in kind.

'Sire,' sayeth the damsels, 'may God tomorrow grant you the strength to destroy the evil custom of this tent.'

'Of which evil custom do you speak, damsel?'

'Of a right foul practice, which causes me much grief, but it seemeth to me that you are the knight who, by the help of God, will cause the defeat of it.' In truth, though they would not give the evil custom a name, it was an eternal struggle against the armoured purity of chastity and honour.

Thus, the two damsels took him by the hand and led him to the stream in the meadow. 'Sire,' sayeth the elder damsel, 'what is your name?'

'My name is Gawain.'

'Then, Sire, we love you all the more for well we know that the evil custom of the tent shall be defeated. But only on the condition that you choose tonight the one of we two that most pleaseth you.'

But Gawain was most minded to sleep for he was weary and made his way to the tent. There the damsels helped him lay down and sat upon the bed and lighted the candles and awaited his requests. But Gawain said only, 'Thank you, damsels,' and closed his eyes.

'By God's wounds,' sayeth one damsel to the other, 'if this were truly Gawain, the nephew of King Arthur, he would not speak thus, nor would he deny such sport. This must be a false Gawain and we have done him honour for no purpose. Tomorrow he shall truly pay his reckoning.'

Then in to the tent came the dwarf and the damsels sayeth unto him, 'Keep a good watch over this knight that he might not flee for he is a false knight that gains lodging by the pretence that he is Gawain. We know this for if he had been the true Gawain and had spent a night in our company he would have wished for many another.'

'He will not go, damsels,' sayeth the dwarf, 'for his horse is in my safe keeping.'

But Gawain sleepeth not and heard all that had been said.

On the morn, Gawain awoke to find his armour and arms ready for wear. Outside the tent he found his horse with saddle and bridle and the dwarf waiting to help him depart. Sayeth the dwarf, 'Sire, you have not served the damsels as they would have wished and they make sore complaint of you.'

'If I deserve their complaint,' sayeth Gawain, 'then I am truly sorry. But I am not aware of any ill that I have done them.'

'They say, Sire, that you are most churlish, which a pity is for so gallant a knight as you appear to be.'

'They must say as they see. For myself I do not know who to render thanks for the good lodging I had last night save God. It would be right and proper to thank them.'

At this, two knights well armed rode up to the tent and thinking that Gawain was want to leave without a fair departing sayeth, 'Sire, last night we left the tent for you and all that was therein, and now you depart without payment. Pay for your lodging, Sire!'

'What would you have me do?' sayeth Gawain.

'You should pay for your victuals and the use of the tent.'

Then appeared the two damsels who addressed Gawain, 'Knight, now shall we see whether you are the nephew of King Arthur.'

And the dwarf sayeth, 'By my faith, I doubt much that we shall lose the evil custom that keeps good knights from coming by this knight.'

So Gawain felt him great shame so to be mocked and knew that he might not depart without a contest.

One of the knights descendeth from his horse as the other backed his horse for a charge. Then he came on at Gawain who met him full on with great blow. Gawain's lance pierced the knight's shield and the lance entered the body of the knight and threw him and his horse to the ground.

'By my faith!' sayeth the elder damsel, 'Look at Gawain the False. He doth do better than he did last night!'

Gawain pulled his lance from the knight's body and did dismount taking his sword from its scabbard. At this, the wounded knight cried out for mercy and holdeth himself vanquished. Gawain delayed his action for thought of what to do. Then the elder of the damsels sayeth unto him, 'Knight, the evil practice that keeps good knights away cannot be done away with until you slay this knight.'

The wounded knight turned to her and sayeth, 'Hear the great disloyalty of this woman. She who pretendeth to love me more than any in the world, now pleads my death.'

'I tell you plain, Sire,' replieth the damsel, 'the evil custom will not leave until you be slain.'

Thereupon, Gawain thrust his sword through the knight's body and killed him.

Now the other knight mounted his horse and backed away to charge in full measure. So doth Gawain and the two met with such hurtle that their lances break short, their shields pierce, saddle-bows splinter and girths burst asunder sending both knights to the ground whereon blood came from the mouths of both knights.

Then the dwarf cried out, 'Damsel, your Gawain the False doth most well!'

'Truly you speak,' sayeth the damsel. 'He must remain with us.'

Gawain was minded to let the knight live and did not further attack him when he cried out for mercy. But the damsels cried to Gawain, 'If you slay him not, the evil custom will not be overthrown. You must smite him at his foot for he is of the lineage of Achilles and cannot die otherwise.'

'Damsel,' sayeth the knight, 'you shame me with your love that hath turned against me. May there never be more such as you.'

Gawain still had pity on the knight and took the saddle from the horse of the dead knight and put it on his own. At this, the dwarf helped the knight to mount his horse, whereon the knight fled towards the forest at great pace. And the damsels cried out, 'Knight, your pity will be our death this day! For the Knight without Pity has gone for help, and if he escape, we shall be dead and you also.'

Thereon, Gawain mounted his horse and took a lance that was by the tent and followed the knight and smote him to the ground saying, 'No further may you go!'

'Much grief that causes me,' sayeth the knight, 'for I should have avenged me on you and the damsels before fall of night.'

And Gawain drew his sword and thrust it in to the knight's foot and the knight stretched himself forth and died.

The damsels make great joy of Gawain and tell him that he hath saved them from the evil custom. They made to tend to his wounds but he telleth them to take no heed.

'Sire,' they sayeth, 'again we offer you our services, for well we know you to be a good knight. Take as your lady-love which of us as you please.'

'Thank you, damsels,' sayeth Gawain, 'your kindness I am want to honour, but I can do no more than commend you to God.'

'But why will you leave us? Far better would it be for you to stay with us in this tent and be at comfort.'

'No, damsels, I have not the leisure to bide here and must return to the trail.'

At this, the younger damsel sayeth, 'Let him go, for he cannot be a true knight.'

But the elder sayeth with downcast eyes, 'It sore greiveth me that he goes, for had he stayed it would have pleased me right well.'

And thus Gawain departed and entered the forest.

Part the VIth

Gawain rode through the forest until he came across a high wall that went beyond sight wither it led. There was but one gate in the wall. On entering, Gawain beheld a land most fair with many orchards and well-garnished gardens. In the centre of the land was a great high rock on which a sat a great long-necked heron that kept watch over the land. On seeing Gawain, the bird cried out so loud that the lord of the land who was the King of Wales heard it and sent two knights to enquire who had arrived.

As the knights came to Gawain they cried out, 'Hold, Knight, for the King of this land would speak with you. No knight passeth through this land without the King speak to him.'

'Willingly,' sayeth Gawain, 'for I knew not the custom.'

The knights led him thither to the great hall wherein was the King and Gawain alighteth from his horse and set his lance and shield against the mounting stage. The King made great joy of him and asked him wither he goeth?

'I go, Sire,' sayeth Gawain, 'into a country where before I have never set foot.'

'Well I know this,' sayeth the King, 'for you are passing through my land to reach the country of King Gurgalain to capture the sword whereby Saint John the Baptist was beheaded.'

'It is true what you say, Sire. May God grant that I take the sword.'

'That may indeed be the will of God, but it is my will that you shall remain in my land for a year before you may depart.'

'God's mercy!' crieth Gawain. 'Why should I be so constrained?'

'For well I know that you will take the sword but not return by my land.'

'Sire, I pledge you my word that with the help of God, should I obtain the sword, I will return by you.'

At this, the King relenteth and sayeth, 'Then I will allow you to depart from me as you will for there is nought that I more wish to see than the sword.'

Gawain departed the next morn and entered a dark and gloomy forest. At noon he came by a marble fountain. Rich pillars surrounded the fountain and all were banded in gold and set with precious jewels. On the main pillar was a golden dish held by a silver chain. In the midst of the fountain was an image carved so finely that it seemed to live. As Gawain approached the image went down below the water and was hidden. Thinking to take a drink with the golden dish, Gawain reached towards it when a voice cried out, 'You are not the good knight who is served herein and who thereby is made whole.'

Gawain looked and saw a young clerk clad in white come to the fountain. On his arm the clerk bore a white napkin and he carried a small square vessel of gold. Then three most fair damsels came dressed in white robes with white cloths upon their heads. One carried bread in a small gold vessel, another carried wine in an ivory vessel and the other carried meat in a vessel of silver. They came to the dish on the chain and put therein the vessels that they carried and made the sign of the cross. They then went back as before but to the marvelling of Gawain there seemed to be but one damsel returning. The clerk took the golden dish from the chain and replaced it with the one he carried and walked in to the forest.

Gawain went after the clerk and sayeth, 'Young, will you speak with me?'

'What is your pleasure?' sayeth the clerk.

'Whither carry you the golden dish and that which is therein?'

'To the hermits that live in the forest and to the good knight that lies sick in the house of his uncle King Hermit.'

'Is it far from hence?' sayeth Gawain.

'To you, Sire, but I shall be there much sooner than thou shall.'

'By God,' sayeth Gawain, 'I wish I were there now that I might see him and speak with him.'

'So may you wish, Sire, but you are not there now and he is not here.'

At this, Gawain departed and rode through the forest until he chanced upon a hermitage. 'Sire,' sayeth the hermit, 'whither goest thou?'

'To the land of King Gurgalain, Sire. Is this the way?'

It is, Sire, but many good knights have passed hereby that have never returned.'

'Is it far?' sayeth Gawain.

'The King and his land are close by, but the castle wherein is the sword is far off.'

Gawain bided at the hermitage and after Mass rode to the land of King Gurgalain. There he encountered many folk expressing great sorrow. On the trail he met a knight riding at great pace to a castle. 'Sire,' sayeth Gawain, 'why do the folk of this castle, the land about and the country express such sorrow? For on every side I hear them weep and hold their heads in their hands.'

'I will tell you, Sire,' sayeth the knight. 'King Gurgalain hath but one son and he hath been taken by a giant who hath done much other mischief and wasted much of the land. Now hath the King sent word abroad that whosoever shall kill the giant and bring back his son he will give the fairest sword in the world and as much treasure as can be carried. But the King hath not found a knight with the courage so to do and blames his own faith and thus invites Christian knights to bring their aid.'

Joyous of these tidings, Gawain rode on to the castle of King Gurgalain where the King greeted him greatly and asked his name and whereof he came.'

'Sire,' sayeth Gawain, 'my name is Gawain and I am of the land of King Arthur.'

'And a goodly land that truly is,' sayeth the King, 'but mine own hath no one with the courage to rescue my son. Should, howsoever, you have the necessary valour to act on my behalf and place yourself in danger for the sake of my son, I will give you the richest sword that ever was forged and which was used to cut off the head of Saint John the Baptist. Every day at noon the blade flows full bloody for at that hour the good man hath his head cut off.'

The King sent for the sword and showeth Gawain the scabbard that was heavy with precious stones and had mountings of silk and fastenings of gold. The hilt of the sword was of gold also and the pommel was set with a most holy sacred stone that Enax, a high Emperor of Rome, hath had set therein. The King then drew the blade from the scabbard and it came full bloody for it was noon. And the King held it before Gawain until the time had passed and the blade came as clear and as green as an emerald. It seemed as long as a full sword but when put in the scabbard it seemed but two hand spans in length. Gawain's desire for the sword grew at the sight he had seen.

'Knight,' sayeth the King, 'this sword will I give you, and I shall do another thing whereof you shall have joy.'

'And I, Sire, with the help of God and His Holy Mother will do as you need.'

And the King showeth Gawain the way to the lair of the giant and the good knight left with the prayers of the people after their own faith. He rode until he came to a land much wasted by the giant wherein was a great high mountain. Thereon lived the giant most cruel and horrible who feared no man in the world and no knight had the courage to seek him. The path to the giant's castle proved to be a pass so narrow that Gawain could not take his horse, nor his shield, nor his lance and had to press himself through the rocks armed with sword alone. Such the giant could with ease step over but not an earthly divide man.

As he cleared the pass, Gawain came to a level land wherein sat the giant with the son of the King before his castle. When the giant seeth Gawain he gave a fearful shout and took up a great axe and ran to the knight. The giant, thinking to strike Gawain on the head, swung the axe but Gawain stepped aside and with a leap cut off the giant's arm, axe and all. At this the giant went back to the King's son and took him in his good hand and crushed him to death. Then the giant returneth to Gawain and picked him up in his good hand to crush him also but falleth down from his great wound. As he fell Gawain thrust his sword into the giant's heart and slew him.

Gawain cut off the giant's head and with much sorrow took up the body of the King's son and returneth to his horse. He then rode to the castle of King Gurgalain and delivered up the body of the King's son which brought much sorrow throughout the land. But the King was an honourable man and heaped much praise upon Gawain for slaying the giant and gave him the sword for which the deed had been done. And the head of the giant was hanged at the gate of the castle.

The King did then cause a great fire to be lit and had the body of his son set in a great brass bowl wherein it was soon on boil and cooked and fed to the high men of the land.

The King sayeth to Gawain, 'There is yet more I would do for you.' And he sent for all his knight and people to attend upon him at the castle.

The King told his knights and people that from the example of Gawain it was his wish that he baptised a Christian. And a hermit was sent for and did baptise the King with the name Archis. The King did then tell the knights and people that if any were not willing to believe in God, he would command Gawain to cut off their heads.

Thus by the miracle of God and by Gawain was the King of Albanie baptised.

At this, Gawain departed and rode to fulfil his vow to the King of Wales to whom he showed the sword as he had given his word. The King ordered the sword to be placed in his treasury and Gawain cried 'This, Sire, is betrayal!'

And the King sayeth, 'I am of the lineage of the man who cut of Saint John the Baptist's head, therefore it is mine of better right than yours.'

But the knights of the King joined with Gawain and sayeth, 'Sire, Gawain hath been a true and loyal knight. You should yield to him that which he won fairly else the world think evil of you for your deed.'

The King wondereth at this and was loathe to give up the sword but sayeth, 'I will yield the sword only on the condition that the request of the first damsel Gawain meets and sayeth my name shall not be denied her request in full whatsoever that request might be.'

At this, Gawain readily agreed for he was much anxious to be gone from the place. With the sword he departed and went to the place whereat he had vowed to show the sword to the townsman who had exchanged his horse for his own. When the townsman arrived he took the sword and looked at it closely before smiting his horse with his spurs and galloping towards the nearby town.

Gawain set after him at great pace but the townsman had entered the town before he could catch him. There the knight seeth a great procession of priests and clerks and many crosses and relics and he saw the townsman entered the church before the procession. On entering the church Gawain sayeth loudly, 'My lords, yield up to me the sword the townsman hath plundered from me by treachery!'

But sayeth the priests, 'Sire, we know well that the sword is that which was used to cut off the head of Saint John the Baptist and the townsman hath brought it to this place to consecrate as a holy relic and to provide a holy sanctuary. He sayeth that it was given to him freely.'

'Not so, my lords,' sayeth Gawain. 'I showed it to him to fulfil my pledge and he hath taken it by treachery.'

Seeing him to be a good knight, the priests ordained the return of the sword and Gawain departed most joyfully.

Gawain had gone scarce far when he encountered a well armed knight that appeareth ready for combat. 'Sire,' he sayeth to Gawain, 'I have come to help you for it is known that you were treated evilly in the town, I am from the castle that gives help to all stranger knights that pass by whenever they have need thereof.'

'May God bless such a castle,' sayeth Gawain. 'But I complain not for right was done me by the town. What, Sire, is the name of the castle?'

'It is the Castle of the Ball. Since you have been delivered as of your right, will you come hither with me and lodge the night at the castle? My lord is a good man and will welcome you rightly.'

Thither they went to the castle which was fair and welcoming and were met at the mounting stage by the lord and his two fair daughters who played with a ball of gold. The lord greeted Gawain right well and bid his daughters take him in to the great hall. There he disarmed himself and was given a red robe. After dining on meat the two maidens sat with him and provided great cheer.

At this, a dwarf came rushing from a side door and began to beat the maidens about the face and head with a whip. 'You fools!' he cried. 'Know you not that you make cheer with him whom you should hate! For this is Gawain, King Arthur's nephew, who hath slain your uncle!'

The maidens left the hall in great shame and Gawain was greatly chastened. When the dwarf had left the hall the father of the maidens sayeth unto Gawain, 'Be not troubled by what he sayeth, for the dwarf is our master, he teacheth my daughters and he is with great anger that you have slain his brother the day that Marin the Jealous slew his wife on your account. Since that time there has been much sorrow in this castle.'

'I also am sorry,' sayeth Gawain, 'for blame of her death is neither mine nor hers as God knoweth.'

On the morn, Gawain rode many a day until he came again to the castle at the entrance to the land of the Fisher King. There he saw that the lion had gone from the gate and the cross-bow engines were not there. He saw a grand procession of priests and rulers from the castle coming to meet him. A squire, fully clothed in his rank, took the horse and armour of Gawain and the good knight went forward to meet the procession. There he displayed to them the sword at noon and the blade came all bloody and they bow down and sang hymns to the Lord. Great joy was made of Gawain and all prayed that God should lead him to the castle of the Fisher King and that the Holy Grail should appear unto him and he should ask the question. To which he answereth that he would do as God commanded.

The chief priest sayeth unto Gawain, 'You, Sire, have great need for rest for you have travelled long and hard.'

'It is true and I have seen many things of which I am ashamed. Tell me, Sire, what is this castle called?'

'It is the Castle of Inquest where there is nought that you may ask that may not be answered. This has been ordained by the Holy Ghost.'

'Then, Sire,' sayeth Gawain, 'pray tell me of the three damsels that were at the court of King Arthur. One held the head of a King, the other of a Queen. And they hath a carriage wherein was the heads of a hundred and fifty knights some in gold, some cased in silver and some in lead.'

'It was, Sire, a Queen that betrayed and hath slain the King and the knights and the heads were carried in remembrance of our first King Adam who was betrayed by his Queen Eve. And the people that were after him and the people yet to come remain in much sorrow for her treason. The heads of the knights sealed in gold signify God's new law, those sealed in silver, God's old law, and those sealed in lead signify the false law of the unbelievers. Of such is the world made.'

'Tell me also, Sire, of the Castle of the Black Hermit whereof the heads were all taken from the Damsel of the Carriage. That damsel sayeth to me that the Good Knight should cast them all out when he comes to the relief of the folk that are therein.'

'As you know well, Sire, when Eve gave Adam to eat of the apple, all mankind went to Hell, alike both the good and the evil. Thus God became man to save these good souls with His Grace and Might. Thus also the Castle of the Black Hermit doth signify Hell and that the Black Hermit doth signify the Devil and the Good Knight shall cast them out those within. By such allusion and example doth unlearned hermits come to know God's will.'

'What of the marvel of the damsel without tresses who sayeth that she should never again have hair until the Good Knight achieveth the Holy Grail?'

'The damsel is without hair from the time that the knight did fail to ask the question of the Holy Grail. This doth signify the good soldier Joseph who was without hair on his head until Our Lord redeemed our people by His blood and His death. On this his hair grew again. The carriage she leads doth signify the wheel of fortune for though the carriage goeth on wheels she lays the burdens of the world on the two damsels that follow her. The fairest follows on foot and the other on a horse much broken down and both are but poorly clad. The shield of the red cross that was left at the court of King Arthur doth signify the Cross on which our Lord died and may not be taken up by anyone except with the command of God.'

Of this Gawain knew well for he had oft heard of the shield that hung in the great hall of King Arthur waiting for the Good Knight that should come to take it. Sayeth he to the chief priest, 'Much now do I understand, but I am in great sorrow for a lady that her husband did slay on my account though no blame was in her or in me.'

'Truly there was great significance in the death of the lady. When on the Cross Our Lord was smitten in the side by the spear thus was the old law destroyed. The lady doth signify the old law.'

'Sire,' sayeth Gawain, 'I met a knight in the forest who rode his horse backwards and carried his shield and lance upside down and hath his armour hanging from him. But when he hath seen me he set himself to right and rode as any other knight.'

'The old law had turned to the worst before Our Lord's death upon the Cross. As soon as He was dead God's new law began and all was restored.'

'Also, Sire, a knight with a shield of black and white challenged me to joust within him on behalf of Marin the Jealous who had slain his wife. He I vanquished and he did pay me homage.'

'When the old law was destroyed all mankind that remaineth are subject to the new law and shall be forever more.'

'Sire, I marvelled greatly at a child who rode a most savage lion in a hermitage. None dare to come near the lion save only the child and he was not above six years. The child was the son of the blameless lady that was killed on my account.'

'The child doth signify the Saviour of the world who was born under the old law. The lion doth signify the people of the world and the beasts and the birds that none may be governed save by virtue of Him alone.'

'That, Sire, bringeth me great joy at heart. One day I found the fairest of fountains in the forest wherein was an image that hid beneath the water when it seeth me. A clerk brought a golden vessel as three damsels filled another golden vessel hanging from the main pillar. The three damsels then departed seeming to me to be just one. Thereon the clerk took the golden vessel from the pillar and set the one he carried in its place before departing.'

'This, Sire, cannot be told to you beyond that you already know. For it is a secret of the Saviour and must remain within his bosom.'

'Then, Sire,' sayeth Gawain, 'may I ask you of a King to whom I returned the body of his son whereon he had his son cooked and made to be eaten by the high folk of his land.'

'By your example the King hath turned to Christ, and by Christ's example made sacrifice of his flesh and blood through his son that the people of the land might follow him in his new devotion. And therefore was all evil belief uprooted from the land so that none remain therein.'

Sayeth Gawain, 'Blessed be the hour that God did send me there!'

'Blessed indeed,' sayeth the priest.

On the morrow, when he had heard Mass, Gawain departed and rode in to the fairest land he had ever beheld. The meadows were many coloured with flowers, the rivers flowed clear and full with wholesome fishes, and the forest aboundeth with wild deer and hermitages. One night he came upon a hermitage wherein the good man had not gone forth for forty years When he seeth Gawain the hermit looked forth from the window and sayeth, 'A good welcome to you, Sire.'

'And may God give you joy,' sayeth Gawain. 'Will you give me lodging this night?'

'I cannot, Sire, for none hath entered herein for forty years but myself and I have sworn to allow none other in but God. But, Sire, if you continue but a little further you will see a castle wherein all good knights are lodged.'

'What is the name of the castle?'

'It is the castle of the good Fisher King and is surrounded by plentiful waters and is of the fairest setting under God. But they will only lodge good knights.'

'May God grant that I may be amongst that company. Before I go thither good hermit, will you hear my confession for I must be cleansed of all sin?'

'Gladly,' sayeth the hermit and heard him of Gawain's true repenting.

The hermit then continued to say, 'Sire, if God is willing, do not forget to ask that which the other knight forgot. Be not afraid at what you see at the entrance to the chapel and ride on without fear. Worship at the holy chapel within the castle for there is where the flame of the Holy Spirit comes down each day for the most Holy Grail and the point of the lance that is presented there.'

'As God guides,' sayeth Gawain as he departeth.

It was not above long before Gawain came upon a right fair castle. In his approach he saw a chapel and went in to pray on his knees for the aid of God. He then rode on until he came upon a rich tomb that was enclosed all around. As he rode passed, a loud voice cried out, 'Touch not the sepulchre, for you are not the good knight through whom it shall be known who lieth therein!'

Coming to the castle gate, Gawain saw that it was reached by three great and horrible bridges whereunder flowed most savage waters. And the first bridge was a drawbridge of length a bow-shot but not above the length of a man's foot in width. Narrow seemed the bridge and the waters swift and deep below. And Gawain knew not what to do.

At this, a knight came forth from the castle and crieth above the waters, 'Knight, pass quickly over the Eel Bridge for night approaches and they of the castle are even now awaiting us.'

'But, Sire,' sayeth Gawain, 'how may I pass over the bridge?'

'All I know, Knight, is that this is the only entrance to the castle. If you desire to come in you must come over without hesitation.'

Gawain was ashamed at his delaying and that he had not harkened too well to the hermit who had told him that of no mortal thing need he be troubled at the entrance to the castle. Knowing him to be confessed and so less in dread of death he crossed his breast and commended his soul to God and gave spur to his horse. To his marvelling the part of the bridge on which he rode grew to a width of easy passage and thus he completed his passing without harm. Then, as if by a hidden engine, the drawbridge raised itself full upright.

The next bridge seemed as long as the other and with fearful water beneath. When Gawain came to the bridge it appeared to be made of thin ice. Again he commended his soul to God and ran at the bridge whereon it turned to solid stone and bore him and his horse with ease. Again the bridge was drawn up.

The third bridge was a great and rich bridge with marble column with tops of gold. And he crossed without hindrance but of the knight could nothing be seen.

The castle gate had set above it an image of Our Lord triumphant on the Cross. On one side was His Holy Mother and on the other

Saint John. All were of gold and with precious stones that flashed like fire. On his right hand he seeth a golden image of an angel that pointed towards the chapel wherein the Holy Grail might be seen. At the gate, Gawain seeth a great and fearsome lion that stood on its feet. But when Gawain passed the lion it fell down in to a retreating crouch.

Within the court of the castle Gawain dismounted and put his lance and shield against the wall before mounting a flight of marble steps. The great hall was a marvel to behold with painted images of gold and of red and of green. There also was a high couch next a table. As he looked in wonder, two knights entered the hall and sayeth to him, 'Welcome, Knight.'

On his returning their salute they made him sit upon the couch and take off his armour. They then brought him two golden basins of water to wash him. After that, came two damsels that brought him a rich robe of cloth of gold and who sayeth unto him, 'Knight, be of good cheer whilst you are here, for this is a lodging of good and loyal knights.'

'That shall I do,' he replieth, and thanked them courteously for their service.

Gawain then looked about him in wonder for he knew it to be night, yet the hall was lit with a light so bright it was as if the sun shone within, but there were no candles burning.

Then the knights said to him, 'Do you wish to see the lord of the Castle?'

And Gawain made reply, 'Gladly I would see him, for I wish to present him with a sword.'

They took him to the chamber wherein lay the Fisher King. The chamber was strewn and sprinkled with the sweetest of balm, green herbs and reeds. The Fisher King lay upon a bed held by silken cords from ivory columns. The coverlet was of sable fur. His cap was of sable fur covered with red silk on which was embroidered a cross of gold. Under his head was a pillow smelling of sweet balm and at the four corners of the pillow were four stones that gave off a bright light. By the bed was a silver eagle on a copper column. At its neck it bore a cross of gold holding a piece of the true Cross on which Our Lord was crucified. This the Fisher King much worshipped. At the four corners of the bed were four tall gold candlesticks in which were tall candles.

Gawain entered the chamber and saluted the King. And the King made him right welcome.

'Sire,' sayeth Gawain, 'I present you with the sword whereof Saint John the Baptist was beheaded.'

'Thank you,' sayeth the King. 'I knew full well that you would bring it for neither you nor any other knight would have come here without the sword. And if you had not been without great valour you would not have gained it.'

And in to the chamber came three damsels. Two sat at the foot of the bed, the other at the head. And the King took the sword and kissed it before giving it to the damsel at the head of the bed for safe keeping.

'What is your name?' sayeth the King.

'Sire, my name is Gawain.'

'Gawain, the brightness of light that shines here within comes from God for love of you. For every time a good knight comes thither to lodge at this castle it appeareth as brightly as it now does. For myself, I wish that I could welcome you more cheerily than I do but I have fallen in to a sickness from the moment the knight of whom you have heard lodged here. On account of but small words he delayed to speak did this sickness fall upon me. I pray therefore that in the name of God you remember to speak them for much joyous I should be if you restored to me my well-being. And here beside me is Dindrane the daughter of my sister that hath been plundered of her land and disinherited in such manner that never can she make regain save through her brother whom she seeks. We have been told he is the best knight in the world but tidings of him there is none.'

'Sire,' sayeth the damsel to her uncle the King, 'I thank Gawain for the honour he did to my lady-mother when he came to her castle. He brought peace to our land and gained the keeping of the castle for a year and a day and sent my lady-mother's five knights there with us to keep it. But the year hath now passed and war will be begun again and God helps us not. And I find not my brother whom we have long lost.'

'Damsel,' sayeth Gawain. 'I only helped you as I could and would so do again. More than any knight in the world I wish to see your brother. But no true tidings have I of him save that I was at a hermitage where was a King hermit and he bade me make no noise for the best knight in the world lay sick therein. And he told me that the knight's name was Parluifer. I saw his horse being led before the chapel by a squire and his shield bore a golden sun.'

'My brother's name is not Parluifer. He was baptised as Percival and it is said by them that hath seen him that no more handsome knight was ever known.'

And the King sayeth, 'And such was the knight that lodged herein. None better have I known to be a good knight but I had no good reward for sheltering him for I may not help myself or any other. In the name of God, Gawain, remember me this night for great confidence have I in your valour.'

'If, Sire, it pleaseth God I shall do nought to bring dishonour upon me.'

At this, Gawain was led in to the great hall where he met twelve ancient knights all of whom had lived for more than a hundred years but none seemed above forty years. They sat him at a rich ivory table and sat round about him. They then filled their drinking horns and drank in his honour saying, 'Remember the good King's prayers ere this night is passed.'

And Gawain replieth saying, 'May God help me in my remembrance.'

Then came dishes of venison and wild boar in gold and silver vessels. Golden candlesticks were placed on the table with tall lighted candles but their brightness was dimmed by the light all around the hall.

Thereupon, two damsels entered the hall from a side chapel. They moved upright in silence as if with no steps as mist across a meadow. The first maiden held in her hand the most Holy Grail. The second maiden held the Spear from the tip of which blood dripped in to the sacred vessel. Side by side the damsels came towards the table whereat the knights were sat and a sweet and holy smell fell upon them. Gawain looked at the Holy Grail and the Spear but it seemed to him to be two angels bearing golden candlesticks in which candles burned. The damsels departed in to another side chapel and Gawain's mind was filled with praise of God. The other knights were fearful of what they had seen and looked to Gawain for he had not asked the question.

Again the Damsels issued from the chapel bearing the Holy Grail and the Spear and came again before Gawain. But he saw only three angels of whom one bore a small child. The knights beckoned to Gawain but the knight looked only at the angels. And three drops of blood fell on the cloth before him and he was in such wonderment that he spoke no words. And the damsels left the hall.

Again the damsels entered the hall and the knights were all in dread and looked at one another. Gawain had not taken his gaze from the three drops of blood. He went to kiss them but they vanished away and he was sorrowful that he had not touched them. Then appeareth in front of him the two damsels bearing the most Holy Grail and the Spear. But he saw three angels of whom one carried an image of Our Lord upon the Cross with Crown of Thorns and a deep wound in his side. And Gawain was moved to great pity. And the knights sayeth to him that he shouldst say the words, for if he delay never again would he have the moment. But Gawain heareth them not and looketh upon the image of Our Lord. And the damsels left the hall.

At this, the ancient knights rose and left the hall leaving Gawain alone. Then he seeth the doors to the great hall had been made fast that no one might pass through. Thereon he slept on the couch until the morn was announced by the sound of a loud horn.

Gawain rose and put on his armour and buckleth his sword to his side. It was his wish to take leave of the Fisher King but all the doors remained fast against him. But he could hear the fairest singing from the chapel and was sorrowful that he could not take Mass as was his custom. Then a damsel came in to the hall and sayeth, 'Sire, you may hear the service that celebrates the bringing of the sword that you presented to the good King and great joy would have been made had you been there. But you are not permitted to enter the chapel for you did not ask the question. So holy is that place that no man nor priest may enter from Saturday noon until after the Monday Mass. You alone, Sire, may have entered had you said but a few words.' As Gawain bowed his head in shame, the damsel sayeth, 'May God be you guardian, Sire, for I believe it not to be by your fault that you did not speak the words whereof this castle would have had great joy.' With that she departed.

And Gawain heard again the sound of a great horn and a loud voice heard he saying, 'He that is from without, let him go hence! The gate is open and the lion is in his den and the bridges are lowered. Thereafter the bridges shall be lifted against the King of the Castle Mortal that warreth against this castle, and therein shall be his death.'

Thereupon Gawain left the hall and found his horse all made ready at the mounting stage with his lance and shield. Beyond the gate he found the bridges wide and long and rode until he came to a great river and he passed by its side. He then entered a forest where there came upon him a storm most fierce and the rain compelled him to put his shield over his head. In such manner he continued until, to his marvelling, he saw a knight riding with a bird on his arm on the far side of the river. Behind the knight rode a fair lady dressed in bright silks for no rain did fall on them and the sun did shine brightly. Then he saw a squire on the other side of the river also idling beneath the sun. And he calleth across to the squire and sayeth, 'Squire, how is it that the rain falleth on me on this side of the river, but on the other side it raineth not at all?'

'Sire,' replieth the squire, 'then you must have deserved it, for such is the custom of the forest.'

'Will this tempest that is with me last for ever?'

'No, Sire. At the first bridge you come to it will cease.'

It was as the squire telleth. The storm continued most fierce until he came to a bridge and crossed. The clouds vanished and he saw before him a great castle where many knights and ladies and damsels were at joy in the fields before the gate. Gawain rode there and alighted but could find no one to take his reins. They continue merry around him but all avoid him. At this, he remounted and left seeing nothing but ill-will towards him. As he departed he came across a knight and asked of him, 'Sire, what castle is this?'

'See you not, Sire, it is a castle of joy?'

'As God is my witness, they are not over-courteous for none came to take my reins nor would any speak with me.'

'They have courtesy in plenty, Sire, but this is no more than you deserve. They take you to be as slow in deed as you have proved to be in word for they saw by your armour and your horse that you come from the Forest Perilous whereby pass all the knights of discomfort.'

Gawain rode on in sorrow and shame until he came to a land much parched and barren. There he findeth a poor castle wherein he entered. All around was poor and wasted. And a poorly clad knight came to him and sayeth, 'Sire, you are welcome.'

The knight took Gawain by the hand and led him to the hall that was in condition most poor. Two damsels entered the hall. Both were poorly clad but were fair of feature and made great welcome to Gawain. Thereon he sought to take off his armour when a knight entered the hall with the tip of a lance through his body. And he knoweth Gawain. Sayeth the knight, 'Haste you, Sire! Take not off your armour! It is with great joy I meet you for I have left Lancelot in combat with four knights who think that he is you. They are kindred to the knights you slew at the tent where you defeated the evil practice. I tried to help Lancelot but was smitten by one of the knights as you see.'

At once Gawain left the hall in haste and full armoured and mounted his horse. As he departed the knight of the castle sayeth, 'Sire, I wish to go with you but I may not depart from the castle until it be restored with people and the land be mine again through the valour of the Good Knight.'

Gawain did not make reply but spurred on his horse and entered the forest and followed the trail of blood made by the wounded knight. Afore long he heard the sound of sword and axe upon armour and shield and came in to a clearing where Lancelot was sore beset by three knights and a fourth lay dead upon the ground. Then another knight retired from the combat as he was much wounded by the knight who had brought the message to Gawain. As he left his horse he fell dead upon the ground. But the two knights that remained were full in force and pressed Lancelot greatly. Gawain rode at one of the knights and sent him and his horse rolling to the ground where he lay slain. The other departeth at great speed and Lancelot cheered the arrival of Gawain.

As Gawain gathered up the horses of the slain knights he telleth Lancelot of the poverty of his host at the castle and how ill-clad the fair damsels hath been. 'Shall we give him what we can provide of these knights?' sayeth Gawain.

'Indeed, good friend,' sayeth Lancelot. 'But it grieves me that one escaped and we cannot grant him more.'

'I assure you, my friend, that the poor knight will welcome even what little we can supply.'

They then rode to the castle and gave the poor knight the three horses and armour of the slain knights and he made great joy and thought himself a rich man. And the two damsels helped the two knights take off their armour. At this, the poor knight sayeth, 'Sires, I should provide you with a robe but none I have except my own jerkin.' The knights asked that he hath no concern in the matter but the two damsels took off their torn gowns and their ragged short coats and gave them to the knights who accepted them with grace for to have refused would have been bad grace against the damsels. At this, the damsels had great joy that the knights had accepted their poor clothing.

'Sires,' sayeth the poor knight, 'the knight that brought the tidings of the combat, he that was stricken though by the lance, is slain and now lays in the castle chapel. He confessed himself to a hermit and asked to be remembered of you. He asked also that you should be at his burial for no better knights are there, so he told me.'

'That we will,' sayeth Lancelot, 'for he was a good knight. Sad it is to me that we do not know his name nor of what country he is from.'

The two knights bided at the castle and were lodge by the poor knight as well as he may. In the morn they went to the chapel to hear Mass and to be at the burial of the knight. Thereupon they departed and took their leave of the poor knight and the two damsels.

As they rode, Lancelot sayeth to Gawain, 'They know not at King Arthur's court what has become of you and many believe you to be slain.'

'Then, brother knight, I shall repair there straight way for long have I toiled in my search. There I shall rest until I gain once more the will to seek adventure.'

Gawain then recounteth to Lancelot how he had been in the presence of the Holy Grail at the castle of the Fisher King, 'And even as it was before me, I could not ask the question whom it served. But I am both sorry and glad. Glad for the great holiness that I witnessed, and sorry that I could not answer the prayer of the Fisher King. Much shame did I feel at the castle and my only comfort comes from knowing that the best knight that ever was also failed before me.'

'Truly, brother, there is much ill that you have brought about by your failure to ask the question. But now God tells me where I must go. I shall go to the castle of the Fisher King and to make amends for what has been done.'

At this, the two knights parted without a word but with their hearts joined in goodwill for each other.

Part the VIIth

Riding at great pace through the forest, Lancelot saw a knight come to him well-armed. 'Sire,' sayeth the knight, 'from whence come you?'

'I come, Sire, from the court of King Arthur.'

'Do you have tidings of a knight that bears a shield of green such as I? If so, he is my brother.'

'What is the name of your brother?'

'It is Gladoens. He is a good and brave knight and he rides a strong and swift white horse.'

'Sire,' sayeth Lancelot, 'are there other knights of your land that bear a shield of green as do you and he?'

'For certain, Sire, there are none.'

'Why do you ask of him?'

'For a certain man hath stolen one of his castles for he was not there. And I know that he will return to restore it to him.'

'Is he a good knight?'

'He is the best of the Isles of the Moors.'

Sayeth Lancelot, 'Sire, if you please, raise your helmet visor.'

The knight raised the visor of his helmet and showed Lancelot his face.

'Knight,' sayeth Lancelot, 'truly you much resemble him.'

'Then, Sire, do you have any tidings of him?'

'I do, Knight,' sayeth Lancelot, 'I can tell you all, for long he rode beside me. Never have I seen one look like another as you do to him.'

'This should it be for we were born of the same mother on the same day. My brother saw light before me and is, therefore, the better and more sharp of mind than I. And though my armour be near me, my skin is nearer still, and my brother is closer even than my skin. As well there is a damsel of the Isles of the Moors that loveth him beyond measure who hath not seen him above a year and even now searches in the forests of the world for him. Pray, Sire, tell me where I may find him.'

'I will tell you, Sire, though it causes me great pain.'

'Hath he done you some misdeed?'

'No, Sire. So much hath he done for me that I owe you my service.'

'Please, Sire, tell me what you mean?'

'Knight, this forenoon did I bid his body farewell and help to bury him.'

'Truly, Sire? Is my brother slain?'

'He is, Sire. And much to my grief for he was slain whilst aiding me. Sad am I to tell you this for no knight have I had so much regard in so short a time as I for your brother. He saved me from death, and so I am bound to you in honour of him.'

'This is great grief to me, for I have lost all by his slaying.' And the knight wept in his sorrow.

At this, Lancelot sayeth, 'Gentle Knight, pray put aside your grief for he will not return by it. Instead, I shall ride at your side and together we shall restore your honour.'

'Truly, I have great need of your help and I shall owe you much if so God guides us.'

'It shall be,' sayeth Lancelot, 'as God commands.'

With that, they went their way together the knight taking much comfort from the words of Lancelot. And they rode until they reached the land of the Moors where they saw a castle on a high rock above lands of meadows.

'This,' sayeth the Knight of the Green Shield to Lancelot, 'was the castle of my brother and is now mine through misfortune. And yet it was stolen from him by a knight of such skill at arms that he feareth no other knight that lives.'

At this, a squire rode from the forest with a slain wild boar across his saddle. And the Knight of the Green Shield asked him whose man he was. And he answereth, 'I am the man of the Knight of the Rock that once belonged to Gladoens. And he cometh behind well armed for he is seeking the brother of Gladoens for whom he hath much disregard.'

Then from the forest came the Knight of the Rock and Lancelot saw him and smote his horse with his spurs. The proud and hardy Knight of the Rock did likewise and the two came at each other most swift. So much did they hurtle that their lances broke upon their shields and Lancelot brought down the Knight of the Rock and his horse also. Lancelot drew his sword and came above him and the Knight of the Rock pleadeth for mercy saying, 'What is this to you, Knight? Am I not challenged by the brother?'

'Indeed, you are, Sire, for I am now his brother as by honour bound.' With that, Lancelot cut off the head of the Knight of the Rock and gave it to the Knight of the Green Shield saying, 'Tell me, Sire, now that he is slain doth the castle belong to you of entirety?'

'It does, Sire, for by his death all claim by his family is vanquished.'

Lancelot lodged that night at the Castle of the Rock and in the morning departed, leaving the knight with his lands and people as before. Before he gave spur to his horse, Lancelot sayeth to the knight, 'Sire, you have my most faithful pledge that should you ever be in peril or in any jeopardy whereof I may help you, and I am free and in place so to do, you shall have my help for ever more. For your brother gave his life to help me.'

Again Lancelot rode through the forest until he espied a knight in a sorrowful situation. Bent forward over his saddle-bow the knight groaned with pain. Sayeth the knight to Lancelot, 'Sire, for the sake of God and His angels, turn back for you are going to the most cruel pass in the world where in I was much wounded through the body. I beseech you, Sire, turn back!'

'Of which pass do you speak, Knight?'

'It is the Pass of the Beards. It is named thus for when entered a knight must leave his beard or be challenged. I took the challenge and I believe me wounded unto death.'

'It was gallantly done, Sire, but I shall not take the way of the coward and turn back. I would rather be smitten through the body with honour than lose with shame a single hair of my beard.'

'Then, Sire,' sayeth the knight, 'may God guard you for the castle thereby is more cruel than you think. And may God protect the knight that destroys the evil therein for shameful is the way they treat knights that pass thereby.'

After bringing what comfort he could to the knight, Lancelot rode on until he crossed a great bridge leading to a castle. There he saw two knights holding the reins of their horses and with their lances and shields leaning against a wall. Behind them lay the gate of the castle all covered with beards and the heads of many knights hung therefrom. As he came close the two knights mounted their horses and came before him saying, 'Hold, Sire, and pay your toll!'

'What, Sire? Do you demand a knight pays a toll?'

'All those that have beards. Those without beards have no such obligation. But you, Sire, have a beard most fine and we are sore in need of it.'

'Why do you need my beard?'

'For the forest hermits that make hair-shirts.'

'Then, Sire,' sayeth Lancelot, 'they must do without mine for I shall not give it up!'

'There is no difference, Sire, in your beard to any other. You shall give it up or you shall pay dearly.'

Seeing that they were determined to shame him, Lancelot lowered his lance and raised his shield and ran hard at the first knight. His lance pierced the other's breast and threw him dead from his horse. At this, the other knight ran at Lancelot and breaketh his lance upon his shield whereon Lancelot bore him to the ground with such force that he was right wounded. Thereon the Lady of the castle came forth from inside with two damsels and saw Lancelot stand over the wounded knight with his sword drawn.

'Sire!' the Lady crieth. 'Stand back from him and harm him further not. Come and speak with me without harm.'

'My Lady,' sayeth one of the damsels. 'I know this knight well for he is Lancelot of the Lake, the most courteous knight at the court of King Arthur.'

Lancelot came before the Lady and sayeth, 'Lady, what is your pleasure?'

'I desire,' sayeth she, 'that you lodge in my castle and that you make me amends for the shame that you have done me.'

'Lady, no shame have I done you but it was a shameful business your knights were on. They were minded to take the beards of stranger knights by force.'

'Very well,' sayeth she, 'I will forego any ill-will I may have if you will lodge in the castle tonight.'

Then sayeth Lancelot, 'Lady I have no desire for your ill-will, therefore will I lodge in the castle tonight.'

Lancelot entered the castle and his horse was brought in to the courtyard after him. And the Lady had the dead knight brought to the chapel and buried. The other she had disarmed and commanded that his wounds be mended. Then Lancelot was disarmed and given a rich robe and the Lady telleth him that she knows full well who he is. He replieth, 'Well it is for me that you know who I am.'

Thereupon they sat at table to eat. The first course of foods was brought in by knights in chains that had their noses cut off. The second course was brought in by knights led by squires. The knights were in chains and had their eyes put out. The third course was brought in by knights who had but one hand. The fourth course was brought in by knights that had but one foot. The fifth course was brought in by knights that were tall and fair of feature. When they had delivered their course of food they gave the Lady their swords and kneeled down whereon she cut off their heads.

The Lady then took the hand of Lancelot and led him to her chamber and sayeth, 'Lancelot, you have seen the manner in which I rule my castle. All the knights you have seen were defeated at the gate of my castle.'

'And, Lady,' sayeth he, 'they have been treated most foully by the chance that hath befallen them.'

'Such a mischance would have befallen you but for your being a good knight. And greatly have I desired for such as you to pass by this way for I will make you Lord of this castle and of me also.'

'Lady,' sayeth Lancelot, 'I am willing at be at your service and I have no wish to refuse the Lordship you offer. I thus hold you to this Lordship of the castle and of you.'

'Then, Sire, you will abide with me in this castle for I love you more than any other knight that ever lived.'

'I cannot,' sayeth Lancelot, 'for I may abide not in any castle above one night until I have been to where I must go.'

'Where are you bound?'

'To the castle of the Fisher King.'

'Full well I know this place. The Fisher King doth languish on account of two knights who lodged at his castle but did not ask the question. Is that where you wish to go?'

'Yes, my Lady,' sayeth Lancelot.

'Then pledge me by your faith that you will return to me to tell me that you have seen the most holy Grail and that you have asked of whom doth it serve.'

'This I promise,' sayeth Lancelot, 'even if you were beyond the sea.'

But then a damsel entered the chamber and sayeth, 'Sire, your promise is of nothing worth, for the Holy Grail will not appear to one of such wanton behaviour as you. You, Sire, love the Queen Guinevere, the wife of your Lord, King Arthur. While such an unworthy love remains in your heart, you will never behold the Holy Grail.'

At this did Lancelot feel his face much burn.

'Lancelot,' sayeth the Lady, 'do you love other than me?'

But Lancelot would only reply that the damsel must speak as she was minded.

That night he lodged at the castle and was greatly angered by the damsel who sayeth that his love for the Queen was as if disloyal to his King. After hearing the Mass he took his leave of the Lady of the castle whereon she constantly besought him to keep his covenant. And he replieth that he would so do without fail.

After riding all day, Lancelot found the trail goeth through a burial ground surrounded by a hedge of thorns. Therein were many tombs and sepulchres and a chapel wherein candles were lighted. There he set himself and passed a dwarf digging a grave and did not speak with him. 'Lancelot,' sayeth the dwarf, 'you are right not to salute me for of all the men in the world you are the one I most hate. May God give me vengeance of your body, and soon for you will be stricken down now that you are come here.'

Lancelot looketh hard at the dwarf but did not make reply. He entered the chapel putting his lance and shield without. Within he found a damsel wrapping the body of a knight in a winding sheet. But as she did so the wounds on the body opened up and began again to bleed. At this, the damsel sayeth to Lancelot, 'Now I see that it was you that slayeth this knight that I prepare for his tomb.'

Thereon two knights entered the chapel each bearing the body of a dead knight which they set down in the chapel. And the dwarf cried out unto them saying, 'Now shall we see you avenge yourself on the enemy of your friends.' For one of the knights was the knight who had fled from Lancelot and Gawain and had gone to the place for the bodies of his companion knights. And he sayeth to Lancelot, 'You are our mortal enemy for by you were these three knights slain.'

'And well they deserveth it,' sayeth Lancelot. 'But whilst within this chapel I am in no peril of you. And I stay here until the dawn for I know not the forest hereabouts.'

When the day broke the two knights were outside. And Lancelot did take up his lance and shield and did mount his horse. At this, the dwarf cried out to the two knights saying, 'What ails you? Will you let your mortal enemy depart thus?'

Thereupon the two knights mounted their horses and rode one each to the two entrances to the burial ground. Lancelot rode in slow manner to the unknown knight and faced him at the entrance he had chosen. The knight delayed in response and Lancelot thrust his lance through the knight's body and he fell from his horse dead. On seeing this, the other knight who had fled from the first combat turned and fled to the forest in great fear.

Lancelot took the horse of the knight he hath slain and rode into the forest until he came to a hermitage with a hospitable hermit where he heard Mass and did sleep. On the morrow as he mounted his horse a knight with a squire rode up to him and sayeth, 'Sire, to where do you travel?'

'I go, Knight as God commands. And you, Sire, where do you go?'

'I go, Sire, to see my brother and two sisters who I hear have fallen on such misfortune that he is known as the Poor Knight for which I have much sorrow.'

'I know of him, Sire, and poor he is, more is the pity. Sire, will him you take a message from me?'

'Willingly, Sire,' sayeth the knight.

'Then, Sire, present him with this horse and tell him that it is from Lancelot that lodged with him.'

'Gladly I will, Sire, and blessed may you be for it for he that doth a kindness to a worshipful man will not lose by it.'

'Salute the damsels for me,' sayeth Lancelot.

'As you command, Sire,' sayeth the knight and gave the horse to his squire as they departed from the hermitage.

Lancelot also departeth from the hermitage and entered a waste land where lived no beast nor bird nor anything to eat. Before him he saw a city of much great size and he entered and seeth that the walls were broken down and the gates ruined. Inside the Waste City there were no folk of any sort and he wondered at the sight of palaces in much decay and graveyards unkempt. Churches were fallen down and markets abandoned. He came to an ancient palace and stood outside whereupon he heard much sorrow coming from within. Voices of knights and ladies sayeth in much grief, 'May God have pity on you that you must die in such a manner and that your death may not be stayed. How we hath hatred for him that giveth you such a death.' But nothing could Lancelot see.

Then looked he in to the great hall and seeth a young knight come in to the hall clad in a red jerkin. About his waist was a great band of gold and a rich clasp at his neck flashed with many precious stones. On his head he wore a great cap of gold and in his hand he held a mighty axe. And the knight sayeth to Lancelot, 'Alight from your horse, Sire!'

'As you wish, Sire,' sayeth Lancelot, and he alighted and tied his horse to a silver ring by the mounting stage and he put aside also his lance and shield. 'What is your pleasure?'

'Sire,' replieth the knight, 'you must take this axe and cut off my head for so it hath been ordained. Should you not so do, I will cut off your head.'

'But why?' sayeth Lancelot, 'For you have harmed me not and I do not wish the blame of your death.'

'For, Sire, you will not leave until you have done that which I demand.'

'But, young Sire, you appear gentle and of good form. Why do you take you death so graciously? You know full well that in combat I shall slay you before you slay me.'

'It is as true as you say but there will be no combat. I wish you to promise me before I die that you will return to this city within a year and you will set your head at the same peril without challenge as I now do.'

'Sire,' sayeth Lancelot, 'betwixt dying here now and living for another day I choose to live as would any man. But tell me, Sire, why are you so dressed so grandly to meet your death?'

'Ere long, Sire, I shall be before the Saviour of the World and I should dress as richly as I may. I am purged of all wickedness and misdeeds by confession and I repent me truly thereof.'

At this, the knight gave the axe to Lancelot and the knight saw that it was of good sharpness.

'Sire,' sayeth the young knight, 'pray hold your hand towards yonder church as a sign of fidelity.' And Lancelot did as he was bidden. 'Thus, then, will you swear upon the holy relics within that church that on this day at this hour and within a year you will come to this place and put your head in the same peril as I have placed mine, without neglect?'

'This I swear and give you my most solemn pledge.'

With that, the knight did kneel and Lancelot took up that axe and sayeth, 'May God have mercy upon you.'

And he did let fall the axe and cutteth off the young knight's head with such force that it did fly far from the body. Lancelot cast aside the axe and left the hall and mounteth his horse and taketh up his lance and shield. He looked back in to the hall and saw that the body and head of the knight had disappeared and there was the sound of much sorrow from unseen knights and ladies. They cried of vengeance within a year. And Lancelot departed from the Waste City.

Part the VIIIth

Though Gawain had failed to ask the question of the Holy Grail at the castle of the Fisher King, there had been another good knight who had done likewise. And much to his sadness and sorrow for his failing, great misfortune had fallen upon the knight. In time, wearied of much soreness and down at heart, he came to the hermitage of his uncle, King Pelles, and retired for long within to restore his faith and courage. King Pelles gave him the name of Parluifer and told passing knights that his nephew was in poor times and could not meet them. But one day as King Pelles had gone in to the forest the knight took himself to be quit of his illness and felt himself to be sound and lusty. At this, he raised up and armoured himself and mounted his horse taking his lance and his shield with the golden sun thereon. Now he heard the birds sing and saw the green of the forest and right joyful was he. And he prayeth unto God to find him an adventure wherein he might be tested for he did not know where his courage lay.

And the knight came to a clearing in the forest and rested beneath a shading tree. There he heard the sound of a horse and prayeth that it might be a knight against whom he might be tested. He sayeth unto God, 'Grant that there be a brave knight on that horse that I may prove whether there be any valour of knighthood within me. For I know not what strength I have nor whether my heart is sound. And it is only by trial against a good and brave knight that I might find my courage. Dear Saviour, bring such a knight before me and grant that he slay me not nor I him.'

And from the forest came a knight well armed and bearing a white shield whereon was a golden cross and he came at a swift pace with his lance low. And in great joy the knight from the hermitage put his lance low and smiteth his horse with his spurs shouting, 'Knight! Raise your shield as I do mine for I defy you on this side of death. May you prove to be a good knight who shall try me hard. I am not as I once was and better I shall learn of a good knight than of a bad.'

With that he struck the knight full hard on his shield and making him lose his stirrups. And the knight sayeth, 'Sire, what misdeed have I done you?'

But the knight from the hermitage sayeth nothing for he had no joy that the other knight had not been set low. Again they hurtle together that their lances splintered and their shields full battered and their faces ran with blood. And they drew their swords whereon the Knight of the Cross of Gold calleth out, 'Gladly I would know who you are and why you hate me for you have wounded me sorely and I have found you to be of great strength.' But no answer came and they fell on each other with their swords and the forest rang with the sound of their swords on armour as though neither bore any wounds.

At this, the hermit King Pelles came from the woods with a damsel and rode between the two knights crying to the Knight of the Golden Cross, 'Hold, Sire! Great shame be on you for you have much wounded a knight who hath long lain sick in this forest.'

But the knight replieth, 'No more than he hath wounded me, Sire. Never would I have run at him had he not challenged me. Nor will he tell me who he is or why he challenged me thus.'

Then asked the hermit, 'And you, Sire, who are you?'

And the knight replieth, 'I am Lancelot of the Lake, son of King Ban of Benoic. And who is this knight?'

'This, Sire, is your cousin, Percival, the son of the Widow Lady.'

The hermit King then made each knight take off his helmet and embrace as kin.

And the damsel washed their wounds right tenderly and speaketh of Lancelot to the hermit King, 'Sire, this knight must rest awhile for his wounds places him in peril.'

'And Percival?'

'He, Sire, will soon be healed.'

All returned to the hermitage where the damsel tended their wounds to make them whole. There within lay the true shield of Percival with a white hart on a field of green. This shield was well known to Lancelot and he would not have accepted the challenge had that shield been borne. Now he lay in much discomfort as his wounds were tended.

Part the IXth

And a squire came before King Arthur and kneeled saying, 'Sire, I am the son of the Knight of the Red Shield of the Forest of Shadows who was slain by the son of the Widow Lady. His shield hangs upon the column. Do you, sire, have tidings of this knight?'

'Gladly I would have tidings of him,' sayeth King Arthur, 'for I wish no evil to come to him. Of all the knights in the world he is the one I most desire to see.'

'Yet, Sire, it is an honour for me to hate him for he slew my father. He that should bear that shield was a squire when he did that foul deed and I am much in sorrow that I did not find him when he remained a squire. Now must I be a knight to challenge him and I pray, Sire, that you make me a knight as you have done others.'

'How are you named?' sayeth the King.

'I am called Clamados of the Forest of Shadows.'

Then stepped forward Gawain who was in the great hall. Sayeth he unto the King, 'Sire, if this squire be the mortal enemy of the good knight who should bear that shield, it will not be well for us if you advance this squire to be a knight and thus to be the equal enemy of the good knight. For the bearer of that shield is the most chaste and best knight in the world and of holy lineage. Long have you waited, Sire, for his coming. I say this not to hinder the advancement of the squire but nought should you do that will give the good knight cause for complaint against you.'

At this, Queen Guinevere spoke saying, 'Gawain, well do I know you guard the honour of the King, but much blame will come upon him if he does not make him a knight for he hath never refused any who are with knightly grace. Nor will the good knight bring complaint for he knoweth well that those who are so advanced take on the knightly virtue of slowness in taking offence and are sober in their deeds. I tell you, Sire, that he will listen to reason and I commend the King to make him a knight and thus avoid the blame of false delay.'

'Lady,' sayeth Gawain, 'if this be your wish, then let it be so.'

The King then maketh Clamados to be a knight. Robed as such, all the court declared him to be the fairest knight they had seen in memory. Clamados did then wait and was on constant watch for the good knight that should come for the shield, but the hour and the place were not yet upon them.

At length Clamados wearied of his wait and determined upon an adventure to prove his knighthood. He rode long and hard in to the forest bearing a red shield as had done his father before him. And he came upon two mountains whereof a narrow pass went between. At the entrance to the pass he espied three damsels one of whom had been shorn of her tresses and beside them stood a carriage drawn by three fair harts. And he knoweth of their story from the court and sayeth unto them, 'Damsels, do you have tidings of the knight who should bear the white shield with the Cross of Red?'

'He is the one we seek,' sayeth the Damsel of the Carriage, 'and we pray God that we shall soon find him.'

'Amen to that,' sayeth Clamados. Then sayeth he, 'Why wait you here?'

'We wait, Sire,' sayeth the damsel, 'for a knight who will guard us through this narrow pass. For within is a lion of most ferocious and horrible nature that none dare enter therein unguarded. The lion abideth with a good knight who hath control of him, but oft the knight is on adventure and then the lion doth bestir himself most savagely.'

'Damsels,' sayeth Clamados, 'as you are in quest of the same knight as I, I will gladly guard you through the pass.'

And they entered the pass most narrow until they came to a castle with a fence and a lion sat at the gate. And the lion saw them and put up his ears. He then rose to his height and ran full speed at Clamados with his jaws agape and with a roar that shaketh the forest trees. At this the damsels crieth to Clamados not to meet the lion whilst on his horse for the lion would destroy the horse. And Clamados alighteth and braced himself with his lance whereupon the lion did run and was pierced right through. Clamados drew back his lance and thinketh to strike again but the lion raised him up on his hinder legs and put his fore feet on the shoulders of the knight and hugged him towards him as one man does another. And the armour of the knight was torn asunder and his flesh torn most grievously. At this, Clamados doubled his valour and heaved the lion over and drew his sword and thrust it in to the heart of the lion whereon the lion gave a great roar that shook the mountains and he fell slain.

Clamados cut off the head of the lion and hung it by the gate. And he mounted his horse all bloody and the damsels cried, 'Knight, you are sore wounded!'

'Pray God,' sayeth he, 'that it is as of but small hurt.'

Thereupon a squire came forth of the castle and came to them full pace. 'Hold, Knight,' sayeth he, 'for you have done a foul deed. You have slain the lion of the most courteous and valiant knight that was ever known. And you have done great outrage by hanging the head at his gate!'

'My friend,' sayeth Clamados, 'well may it be that the knight is most courteous, but the lion was most wretched and foul and would have slain me and others that passed by. If your lord loved this lion he should have had him chained. For better I thinketh that I slay him than he slay me.'

'But, Knight,' sayeth the squire, 'this is a land forbidden to travellers for there are those who would plunder the lands and castle of my lord. It was against the coming of his enemies that he allowed the lion to be unchained.'

'What is the name of your lord?'

'It is, Sire, Meliot of England, who even now has gone in quest of Gawain of whom he holds this land and is most dear to him.'

'But Gawain abides at the court of King Arthur. Tell your lord to depart thence and there he shall find him.'

'If only my lord knoweth that you hath slain his lion, then, Sire it would be hard on you should you meet him or Gawain.'

'If he be as courteous as you say, my friend, no offence would he hold against me for defending myself and others. May God forbid that I should meet any that would do me evil for so doing.'

Thereupon Clamados and the damsels departed and went safely through the narrow pass. Ere long they came upon a rich castle set amongst meadows, high forest, and great waters, but of people there were none. Nonetheless, they intended there to go when they met a squire who told them that better it would be if they continued to where there were people in plenty. Thus they went on and came beyond a forest where they saw a great abundance of bright tents surrounded by a long wall of white linen. Within they heard the sound of great joy. They entered and saw ladies and damsels in great numbers and all of great beauty. The damsel of the shorn hair and her companions were greeted with much cheer and two damsels led Clamados to a tent where they took off his armour and washed his wounds. They brought him a rich robe and led him before the Lady of the Tents who made great joy of him.

'Lady,' sayeth she of the shorn tresses, 'this knight hath saved my life for he hath slain the lion which barred many from coming. Pray make great joy of him.'

'Damsel,' sayeth the Lady, 'none can make greater joy than I or the damsels herein, for we wait the coming of the good knight and there is none in the world that we would more desire to see.'

'Lady,' sayeth Clamados, 'who is this good knight?'

'The son of the Widow Lady of the Valley and Castles of Camelot.'

'Tell me, Lady, do you say that he will come hither presently?'

'I believe this so to be.'

'Then, Lady, also shall I have great joy thereof. May God lead him here soon.'

'Knight,' sayeth the Lady, 'what is your name?'

'It is Clamados, my Lady. I am the son of the lord of the Forest of Shadows.'

At this, the Lady threw her arms around the neck of Clamados and kissed him. 'This is joy indeed. For you are the son of my brother and I have no one close in family as you are. You, dear nephew, should be the lord of all my land and of me as is right.'

When they heard this the damsels of the tents make great joy of him. And he bided there until his wounds were whole. And the damsels wondereth much why the good knight did not come, for in their midst was the damsel who hath tended his wounds from his conflict with Lancelot. For she telleth them that he was healed but Lancelot lay still within the hermitage.

Bound of a promise to Lancelot that he would return as soon as God willed, Percival rode in to the forest and came upon a castle wherein he would seek lodgings for the night. He was met by a tall knight with face much scarred. Other than his household no others lodged in the castle. Upon making his salutation, Percival heard the knight say to him, 'Now shall you have the reward you so richly deserve. Never shall you leave this castle for you are my mortal enemy and you have thrown yourself in to my keeping. For I am Chaos the Red, brother of the Knight of the Red Shield whom you slew. I now war against your mother and this castle have I taken from her. Now I shall wring the life out of you.'

'Sire,' sayeth Percival, 'you are bound as a brother knight to afford me safe lodging for the night. In the morning let us see what the break of day should bring.'

'No!' crieth Chaos the Red. 'Only as a dead man will you lodge here!' And he thereupon ran in to the hall and taketh up his sword and ran at Percival who cast aside his lance and ran at Chaos the Red. And Percival was in great anger that the other did war against his mother and had taken this castle. So fierce did Percival strike the other that his sword cut through his armour and deep in to his flesh. But Chaos the Red brought his sword against the helmet of Percival such that sparks flew therefrom and his shield was cut through. Bewildered by the might of his opponent, Percival brought his sword down and cleaved through the sword arm of Chaos the Red. Bereft of his arm and sword, Chaos the Red ran at Percival who struck him on the helmet with such force that he fell dead.

At this, a cry went up from the castle household who had witnessed the combat from the hall balcony. 'Sire! You have slain the strongest and most redoubtable knight in England. We knoweth that this castle is by right your mother's and will offer no challenge.

Kind Sire, may we take up the body of our lord and take it to the chapel for the sake of his knighthood?'

Percival assented and they took the body away and wrapped it in a shroud and gave it seemly burial. After which they came to Percival and sayeth, 'Sire, here are the keys of the castle which you have won for your mother. All the doors are barred and none within but we servants and two damsels.'

Percival sayeth, 'What is the name of this castle?'

'It is known, Sire, as the Key to Wales.'

'Thus I command you to go to my mother, the Widow Lady, and tell her of what has passed. Salute her for me and tell her that I am sound and whole and that she shall see me as soon as God commands.'

On the morn, Percival departed and came to the bright tents behind the wall of linen. But there was no sound of joy as when Clamados arrived with the shorn lady. There was the sound of much sorrowing. On alighting amidst the tents a damsel from the castle came unto him saying, 'For shame, Sire, have you come to this place.' She then crieth out to the Lady of the Tents saying, 'Lady! Behold here he who hath slain the best knight of your family.' Then she crieth out to Clamados who was within the tent saying, 'You, Clamados, here is the knight that slew your father and uncle! Now shall we see what you shall do!'

At this, the Damsel of the Carriage appeared saying, 'Sire, you are indeed welcome. Let others sorrow, but I make great joy of your coming!' She took him into her tent and made him lie on a rich couch as her companion damsels removed his armour. She then took him to the tent of the Lady of the Tents who was in much sorrow and sayeth, 'Hold your sorrow, for here is the good knight on whose account these tents are pitched and on whose account you have been making great joy until this day.'

Sayeth the Lady, 'Is this then the son of the Widow Lady?'

'It is.'

'But he hath slain my family's greatest knight and the one who protected me from mine enemies.'

'Lady,' sayeth the damsel, 'this is the best knight in the world and will be able better to protect and defend us.'

The Lady took the hand of Percival and made him sit next to her. 'Sire,' she sayeth, 'whatever the road you have taken here, my heart bids you welcome.'

'Thank you, my Lady. Truly Chaos the Red would have slain me within his castle and caused me to defend myself with all my power.'

And the Lady looked in to his face and felt a passion within her that grew strong and fervent. 'Sire,' sayeth she, 'if you will grant me your love, I shall pardon you of the death of Chaos the Red.'

'Willingly your love would I have, as you have mine.'

Then sayeth the Lady, 'How shall I know your love?'

'For there shall be no knight in the world that shall desire to do you a wrong, but I shall be at your side to defend you.'

'But such a love is no more than a knight ought to bear to a lady. You would surely do as much for another.'

'That may well be, Lady,' sayeth Percival, 'but a knight may do more to help one than another.'

The Lady desired greatly to hear from Percival of his inward love but he would say no more. She looked upon him deeply with her heart unrestrained but he would not give a greater pledge of his love for her despite her great beauty. She could not move her eyes from him nor diminish her desire and the damsels looked upon her with wonder that she had so soon forgotten her mourning.

Then entereth Clamados in to the tent and beheld the knight who, when only a squire, had slain his father and had now slain his uncle. And he saw that the Lady looked upon him with great sweetness.

'Lady,' sayeth he, 'this is a great shame that you do bring upon yourself. For seated at your side is your and mine mortal enemy. Never again shall anyone trust in you.'

'Clamados,' she replieth, 'this knight hath just arrived and I shall do him no evil but give him lodging and harbour him safely. Nor has he done ought that might be adjudged as murder.'

'Lady, he slew my father in the Lonely Forest without challenge and smote him through with a spear. Therefore I pray you that you give me my right of avenge, not for being one of your kin for that I no longer give regard, but as a stranger who gives this appeal.'

Percival looked at Clamados and saw him to be an upright knight that stood with dignity. 'Sire,' sayeth he, 'you should not hold me guilty of evil towards your father for I had no mind towards evil. May God defend me from such a shame and grant me the strength to defend myself from such blame.'

But Clamados stepped forward as if to issue a challenge to Percival. 'Hold, Sire!' sayeth the Lady. 'There shall be no challenge in this tent. We shall wait until the morrow and take counsel that right shall be done to each.'

Clamados went his way saying that no man should put his trust in woman. But he understood not the great love that the Lady bore for Percival. Meantimes, the Lady was in much sorrow for Percival did not show her any measure of love beyond that already said.

On the morrow Mass was sung when in to the chapel came a knight all armed and bearing a white shield whereon was a golden lion. He came before the Lady and sayeth, 'Lady, I am in search of a knight that hath slain my lion. If you shield him from me, I shall do you as much or more harm as I would have done to him for I must have my vengeance on him. Therefore, I pray you, for the love of Gawain whose man I am, that you do me right.'

Sayeth the Lady, 'What is the name of this knight that you seek so vengefully?'

'He is called Clamados of the Forest of the Shadows.'

'And what, Sire, is your name?'

'It is Meliot of England.'

At this the Lady crieth, 'Clamados! Do you hear what this knight sayeth?'

And Clamados sayeth, 'I do, Lady. But again I pray that you do right by me in the matter of the knight who slew my father and my uncle.'

To which Meliot sayeth, 'Lady, I know not of this other knight. I am here to right the foul deed done to me and to my lion and I wish it to be done straightway for I must depart. If you do not give me the right, it is you I shall challenge.'

'Clamados,' sayeth the Lady, 'do you again hear what this knight sayeth?'

'I do, Lady. Truly I did slay his lion, but not until he had come upon me and given me the wounds of which I am barely healed.

Percival hath done me much more wrong and I pray that you will let me take vengeance of him first.'

'But you see that he is armed in full and wishes to depart forthwith. Meet him first, Sire, then we will talk of the other.'

'Thank you, my Lady,' sayeth Meliot, 'for Gawain will think well of this. This knight hath slain my lion that defended me from all my enemies, but worse, he insulted me greatly by hanging the head of the lion at my gate.'

And the Lady sayeth to Meliot, 'You have no true quarrel with him in the matter of the lion for he was defending himself. But the insult he did you can be seen at this court and if you desire to deliver battle, no blame shall befall you.'

Clamados then went and armed himself and mounted his horse. A tilting ground was made in the midst of the tents and the ladies and damsels gathered there all around.

Sayeth the Lady to Percival, 'I wish that you should be Marshall of the field.'

He replieth, 'As my Lady commands.'

Meliot and Clamados charged at each other at great pace and met in such collision that their shields and armour were both pierced and much blood both gave. Again they came at each other and both horses fell to the ground. Now they drew their swords and fell to pounding each other most fiercely.

The Lady sayeth to Percival, 'Go you and part these two knights that they may not slay one another for they are both sore wounded.'

And Percival sayeth to the knights, 'Withdraw yourself back, you have done enough!'

The Lady came to Clamados and sayeth, 'Fair nephew, are you wounded badly?'

'I am,' he replied.

'I never saw braver knight and all for a misunderstanding. A man need not always stand upon his rights but allow for natural justice.'

The Lady had Clamados placed on his shield and taken to a tent where his wounds were searched and found to be sore perilous.

And Clamados sayeth to the Lady, 'Do not let the knight that slew my father depart unless it be with a good hostage that he may come back when I am healed.'

'I shall do as you request, nephew.'

The Lady then went to Meliot and had his wounds searched and they were less than Clamados. She commanded the damsels to tend upon him with much kindness. To Percival she sayeth, 'You should abide here until such time as my nephew be healed for you know he has complaint against you. Nor would I wish that you depart with no being cleared of the blame.'

'Lady,' sayeth Percival, 'I have no wish to depart without your leave. But I shall clear my name whensoever and wheresoever God shall decide. I do not wish to abide here for I must be elsewhere. This, then, I pledge to you, that I shall return hither within a term of fifteen days from the time Clamados shall be made whole.'

Then up spoke the Damsel of the Carriage and sayeth, 'Sire, I shall remain here in hostage for you.'

But the Lady then sayeth, 'No! You must pray that he remaineth here with us.'

And Percival sayeth, 'Lady, I may not stay. For I left Lancelot sore wounded in the hermitage of my uncle.'

'Sire,' sayeth the Lady, 'I had prayed that remaining here might have pleased you as well as it would have pleased me.'

'Lady,' sayeth he, 'remaining with you would please everyone, but I have given my word that I would tend to Lancelot and I have to keep my bond as a worthy knight.'

'Then you will promise as a worthy knight that you will return the soonest you may? That you will return within the term appointed by you after you have learned that Clamados is healed, to defend yourself against his accusations?'

'And what if he should die?'

'Then, Sire, it is my fervent wish that you would return for love of me. For right well should I love your coming.'

'Lady, be assured that if I am in place so to do, I shall never fail you or your need.'

At that he departed with the Damsel of the Carriage commending him to God. He came full pace to the hermitage of his uncle thinking to find Lancelot therein. But his uncle telleth him that Lancelot had healed of his wounds and was all sound. And he had departed.

Part the Xth

Lancelot had ridden through the forest a long way when he chanced upon a castle. On approach to the gate he saw an old knight and two damsels who greeted him right well and bid him alight and go in to the hall. The joy of the damsels was exceeding great as they took off his armour and bid him rest.

Then sayeth the old knight, 'Sire, I beg your pity upon these damsels, my daughters. On the morrow comes a knight to rob them of this castle and they have no defender other than me. And I am too old and feeble. We have no kin to aid us nor have I found a knight willing to take up his arms on our part. You, Sire, seem of such great valour that we pray you will defend us on the morrow.'

Sayeth Lancelot, 'What is this you say, Sire? I have barely come beneath your roof and yet you wish me to engage in battle?'

'Sire,' sayeth the old knight, 'hereby you may prove your valour to be as great in deed as it appears in display. Thus may you defend my daughters in their right of claim and win the love of God and the praise of the world.'

At this, the knight and his daughters pleaded with Lancelot to take up their cause, and he raiseth them up for he had great pity.

'Sire, damsels,' he sayeth, 'I will aid you to the uttermost of my power. But I would wish not to remain here overlong.'

Sayeth the damsels, 'Sire, the knight that would rob us of our claim comes on the morrow and without a brave knight to defend us we shall be lost. Our father is old and our family is fallen and decayed.'

'Why doth this knight come to rob you of your castle?'

'On account of Gawain, whom we gave harbour here.'

Lancelot lay within the castle that night. On the morn he went to Mass and armed himself and looked from the castle windows at the gate barred and shut. Then he heard the loud blast of a horn three times beyond the gate.

'The knight is come,' sayeth the father of the damsels, 'and he thinketh there is no defence.'

'May it please God,' sayeth Lancelot, 'that there is.'

And there was another loud blast from the horn. And the old knight sayeth, 'Sire, the knight without thinketh that no one will come forth to accept his challenge.'

At this, Lancelot did mount his horse and with the damsels at each stirrup went to the gate. The damsels then prayed of him that he save the honour of the castle without which they must flee as beggars.

There was another blast of the horn and Lancelot rode from the gate with shield up and lance lowered. There he saw the other knight and rode at him with full pace. The knight seeing him come cried out, 'Knight! What is this? Are you here to do me evil?'

'Yes,' replieth Lancelot, 'for that evil you would do I defy you in the name of the knight and the daughters therein.'

Both delivered lance to shield with great might but none were unhorsed. Lancelot drew his sword and thrust it at the knight and pierced his arm and side whereon the knight's horse tumbled and fell to the ground. Lancelot alighteth right quickly and ran to the fallen knight with sword in hand.

'Hold, Knight!' sayeth the fallen knight. 'Pray withdraw from me and slay me not. What, Sire, is your name?'

'My name is for those on whom I choose to bestow it.'

'I would gladly know your name for a good knight you seem to be as I am taught by this encounter.'

'I am called Lancelot of the Lake. And what is your name?'

'I, Sire, am Marin of the Castle Gomeret, the father of Meliot of England. Again, Sire, I pray you do not slay me.'

'So shall I do unless you withdraw you enmity towards this castle.'

'By my faith,' sayeth Marin, 'do I withdraw it for ever. Never again shall they be troubled by me.'

And Lancelot sayeth, 'I cannot accept your pledge unless you enter the castle to repeat it.'

'Alas, Sire, I cannot mount my horse for my wound.'

Lancelot helpeth Marin to mount his horse and led him in to the castle where the knight gave his sword to the old knight and his daughters. He yielded up his shield and lance and made vow upon the holy relics that never again would he make war on them. He then returned to Castle Gomeret as the old knight and the damsels made great joy.

And Lancelot departed with the damsels and the old knight commending him to God and rode many a long time until he came to a city in a wide plain. Over the city there rose much smoke and from its gates came forth a multitude making great joy with much music. And when they saw Lancelot their joy redoubled. Many approached him, with the lords and provosts of the people, and sayeth, 'This joy is because of you, this sound of gladness is for your coming.'

'But why?' sayeth Lancelot.

'For, Sire, this city began to burn on the death of our King, nor might the fire be quenched until we have a new King crowned in the midst of the fire. And we know of you, Sire, and would grant you the crown for we know you to be a good knight.'

'Thank you, Sire,' sayeth Lancelot, 'but I have no need of a kingdom. Indeed, I pray to God that he defend me from such a want.'

'But, Sire,' sayeth they, 'would you see this great city burned away by the refusal of a single knight? To be King here carries much in riches and you would save the city and the people and thereof you shall have great praise.'

And the people led his horse in to the city and the ladies and damsels looked from the high windows upon him saying, 'Look at the new King they are leading in. Now will the fire be quenched.'

But many sayeth, 'What a great pity it is that so fine a knight shall end thus.'

Yet others sayeth, 'Be quiet! It is better that there should be great joy that the city be saved by his death. For ever prayers will be made throughout the kingdom for his soul.'

Lancelot was taken to the palace which was a fair and rich place hung with curtains of silk and the people came to do him homage in their finest clothing. But he refused to be their King or their lord. Thereupon a dwarf leading a horse which beareth a most beautiful lady entered the city. And they tell him of Lancelot and his refusal to be King and the story of the fire.

At this, the dwarf entered the palace and called the provosts and lords about him saying, 'My lords, since this knight is not willing to be King, give me the crown and I will govern this city as you wish.'

And they replieth, 'In faith, since the knight refuseth the honour and you desire it we will grant it to you and permit the good knight to leave.'

Therewith they set the crown on the dwarf's head and Lancelot maketh great joy thereof. Commended unto God by the people of the city who saw him leave, they sayeth that he did not wish to be King for he did not want soon to die.

As the sun fell beyond the trees of the forest, Lancelot came upon a hermitage and chapel all builded new. The hermit young and without beard came out and sayeth, 'Sire, you are welcome here.'

And the knight sayeth, 'And may God be with you. But I have never seen a hermit so young.'

The hermit replieth, 'My only regret, Sire, is that I dallied for so long.'

With the horse of Lancelot stabled, the hermit led the knight in to the hermitage where he was disarmed by the squire and set at ease. The hermit then sayeth, 'Sire, have you any tidings of a knight that lay sick for a long time in the house of a hermit?'

'It is not long, Sire, since I saw him in the house of the good King Hermit, who hath tended me and healed me of wounds that the knight gave me.'

'And is the knight healed?'

'He is, God be thanked. Why do you ask?'

'For my father,' sayeth the hermit, 'is King Pelles, and the mother of the knight is my father's sister.'

'Then all the more do I love you, for I have never found any man who hath done me as much kindness as King Pelles. Tell me, Sire, what is your name?'

'My name is Joseus, and, Sire, what is your name?'

'I am Lancelot of the Lake.'

'Then, Sire, we are close in kin.'

'And right glad am I so to be.'

At this, Lancelot looked in to the chamber and saw shield, lance, and armour. 'Sire,' sayeth he, 'why do you have these arms?'

And the hermit, Joseus, sayeth, 'This is a lonely part of the forest and none but my squire and I do live here. So, when robbers come, we defend ourselves.'

'But hermits neither assault, nor wound, nor slay.'

'Sire,' sayeth the hermit, 'God forbid that I should wound or slay.'

'How then, do you defend yourselves?'

'When robbers come, we arm ourselves and if any come to me I catch hold of him and my squire slaith him or wound him in such manner that he will not return.'

'In God's name, were you not a hermit you would be a truly valiant knight.'

And the squire sayeth, 'Truly do you speak, Sire, for I know of none more strong or hardy throughout the Kingdom of England.'

That night as they slept, four robbers came to the hermitage for they knew that a knight abideth therein. They were seen by the hermit as he gave prayers in his chapel and he woke his squire and bid him arm himself and bring arms for the hermit. 'Shall I awaken the knight?' sayeth the squire.

'No, for he is our guest,' sayeth the hermit.

Taking a coil of rope, the hermit and his squire went to the stable where the robbers were intent on taking the horse of Lancelot. With a great shout the hermit beareth one robber to the ground and bound him tightly. At this, the other robbers thought to rescue their fellow and Lancelot awoke and went to the stable sword in hand. There he found the hermit and squire had all four robbers bound tightly.

The hermit sayeth to Lancelot, 'Sire, it grieves me to find you awakened.'

'But no, Sire, I am grieved that you did not wake me sooner.'

'Such assaults happen oftentimes and are not worthy of your disturbance.'

The robbers asked for mercy but Lancelot sayeth that God would not permit thieves to flourish. With the light of day, the robbers were taken deep in to the forest by Lancelot and the squire and hanged in a place wasted by fire.

On his return, Lancelot telleth the hermit that the world had lost a good knight on account of his becoming a hermit. But the young hermit sayeth that many men were now alive that he hath so done and that was a good thing.

Lancelot mounted his horse and received the hermit's commendation to God. And the hermit did bid him to salute his father and cousin for him and also Gawain. And Lancelot departed.

He rode for many days until he came to a land of broad meadows wherein ran a wide river. And Lancelot seeth a man rowing a boat on the river. In the boat were four knights. Two were sitting and one lay with his head in the lap of a damsel. He was covered with a rich covering of ermine and another damsel sat at his feet. The fourth knight was fishing with a golden rod and put his fish in a small cockle-boat that came behind. Lancelot came to the river and saluted the knights and damsels and they returned his salutation with great courtesy.

'My lords,' sayeth Lancelot, 'is there a castle nigh, or other lodgings?'

'Yes, Sire,' they replied, 'beyond the mountain there is a fair and rich castle and this river floweth all about it.'

'Whose castle is it?'

'It is the castle of the Fisher King, and the good knights lodge there when he is in this country. But he has found much fault in the knights that have lodged there of late.'

And Lancelot rode to the foot of the mountain and espied a hermit in his chapel. Thinking to rid himself of sin before entering the castle wherein the Holy Grail appears Lancelot confessed him to the hermit saying that he repenteth of all sin save only one. And the hermit asked him what it was that he would not repent.

'Sire,' sayeth Lancelot, 'I can admit the sin of my arm and of my lips but never of my heart. For my love for the Queen is deeper than any in the world and yet she is the wife of a good and honourable King. My love for her is such that I cannot withhold it for it is rooted deep within my heart and it seemeth to me not to be a sin but the highest and finest of duties. All I do in my knighthood I do only as an obligation to her.'

'Alas!' sayeth the hermit, 'You tell me of a mortal sin and you tell me that your deeds of knighthood are done in the shadow of such a sin. You, Sire, are a traitor towards your earthly lord and you have turned against Our Saviour. Of all the seven deadly sins, you have committed the one whereof the delights are the most false. Dearly shall you be punished unless you straightway repent.'

'No, Sire. For she hath in her such beauty and worth and wisdom and nobility that no one who ever loved her can take it to be a sin.'

'But, Sire, you talk of a blessed and anointed Queen that hath taken her vows before God. Yet now she is given over to the Devil for her love of you and your love of her. Knight, my fair friend, abandon this cruel folly and repent of this sin. Do this and I will take the penance upon myself and pray to the Saviour every day that as He pardoned him who pierced His side with the spear, so may He pardon you of this sin.'

'Thank you, Sire, but no. I have no wish to renounce it as a sin. Happily will I do penance but I will serve my Lady the Queen for as long as it is her pleasure, and long may I have her goodwill. So dearly do I love her that I have no desire for repentance. I know that God is merciful, and may He have pity upon us for no treason have I done to her, nor she toward me.'

Then sayeth the hermit, 'Plain it is, Knight, that I cannot avail against you whatsoever I say. Therefore, may God grant the Queen and you the desire to able to do the will of Our Saviour. Until then I tell you that however long you remain in the castle of the Fisher King you will never see the Holy Grail for the mortal sin that remaineth in your heart.'

And Lancelot departeth from the hermit and came unto the castle of the Fisher King. There he saw the bridges that Gawain had seen but they were broad and long and he crossed them at ease. There also did he see the likeness of Our Lord upon the Cross above the gate and two lions that guardeth the entrance. The lions were unchained but he passed between them without heed and entered the courtyard and alighteth before the great hall. He was greeted by two knights and taken in to the hall where he was disarmed by servants and given a rich robe by two damsels. About him he saw the hall clothed in silken curtains and adorned with images of the saints.

The knights led Lancelot to the chamber of the Fisher King where he lay upon the richest bed known in the world. At his head sat a damsel and another at his foot. The chamber was lit as though by sunlight even though it be night and no candles could Lancelot see. Lancelot saluteth the King most nobly and the King replied as though to a worthy knight.

'Sire,' sayeth the Fisher King, 'have you tidings of my sister's son, that was the son of Alain le Gros of the Valleys of Camelot, whom they call Percival?'

'I have, Sire,' sayeth Lancelot. 'It is not long passed since I saw him in the house of the King Hermit, his uncle.'

'Then tell me, Sire, is he a good and worthy knight?'

'He, Sire, is the best knight in all the world. I know this well for I felt his valour and knighthood cause me much wounding before we knew of each other.'

'And what is your name?' sayeth the King.

'I, Sire, am called Lancelot of the Lake, son of King Ban of Benoic.'

'Then, Lancelot, you ought to be a good and worthy knight as I have heard witness. Close by is the chapel wherein abides the most Holy Grail. The sacred vessel hath appeared to two knights that have been herewithin. I know not the name of the first knight, but never saw I any so gentle and quiet, nor any that had better likelihood to be a knight. Yet it was through him that I have fallen in to decay. The second knight was Gawain.'

'Sire,' sayeth Lancelot, 'I know the name of the first knight.'

'Then,' sayeth the King, 'pray tell me for I would dearly wish to know.'

'It was, Sire, your nephew, Percival.'

The King started as if burned by a cinder. 'Have a care, Sire, of what you say!'

'I speak truly, Sire, for I know him well.'

'Then why did I not know him? Through him I have fallen in to this decay. Had I known then I should be whole of my limbs and my body. Pray, Sire, when you see him again tell him to come to me or I shall die. And he will wish to aid his mother whose men have all been slain and whose land has been robbed and cannot be regained but by his aid alone. Even now, his sister searches for him throughout all kingdoms.'

'Gladly will I do so, Sire, should I encounter him. But it is difficult for he oft changes his shield and conceals his name from all that are with him.'

And they honoured Lancelot right richly and gave him meats on a table shining with gold and silver vessels. But the Holy Grail did not appear, for though Lancelot was one of the three most valiant knights of renown he bore in his heart the sin concerning the Queen. And two damsels took him to his bed and remained with him until he was asleep.

He rose on the morrow with the light of day and went to hear Mass before taking his leave of the Fisher King and departing by the lions at the gate. In his heart he thought of nothing but the Queen for great was his desire to see her again. Great also was his desire to see Percival but no tidings came of him except that he was far distant.

Lancelot rode in to the forest in great mind to find Percival. Therein he came upon a knight and a damsel clothed in rich robes of silk and gold of such splendour as he had never seen before.

The damsel wept constantly pleading with the knight to have mercy upon her. But the knight stayed silent and spoke not.

Upon the approach of Lancelot the damsel sayeth to him, 'Sire, I beg you, please speak to this knight on my behalf.'

'On what account do you wish I should speak with him?'

'Sire,' sayeth she, 'for a year he hath urged his love upon me and hath made a covenant that I would be his wife, and thus I am dressed to be. But my father will not allow the marriage for he is more rich than this knight. Yet I have come to him for I love none other, nor can I. But now he will not honour his covenant for he loves another better than me. This hath brought me great shame.'

And Lancelot looked upon this fairest of damsels with great pity and sayeth to the knight, 'Sire, this you shall not do. You shall not shame so fair a damsel with whom you have made covenant. For there be not a knight in all of England or in Wales that would not be well pleased to have so fair a damsel for wife. I pray, Sire, that you honour your covenant with her. This would be of such rightness that I would hold it a favour to me and my honour.'

But the knight sayeth, 'No, Sire, I will not for I have no desire so to do.'

'Then, Sire,' sayeth Lancelot, 'I have never seen so base or lowly knight and no lady nor damsel ought again to put trust in you for the disgrace you intend upon this damsel.'

'Sire,' sayeth the knight, 'I have a greater and more worthy love than this damsel. And no more shall I have to do with her.'

'But what do you intend to do with her?'

'I shall take her to my house and give her in charge of a dwarf who dwells therein. Then I will marry her to a knight or some other man. Hungry dogs will eat dirty meat.'

'As God doth witness,' sayeth Lancelot, 'this is the most foul manner I have ever beheld. Had you been armed as I am you would already feel my wrath.'

At this the damsel sayeth, 'No, Sire, harm him not I pray you for I truly love him. Just make him honour his covenant to me.'

Lancelot looked upon the knight and sayeth, 'Knight, will you honour your covenant with this damsel?'

'No, Sire, I shall not. Nor shall I under duress.'

'By my God, Sire, you shall so do or bring death upon yourself. For I say this not for the damsel alone but for the honour of all knights who would honour their word. This, Sire, is my covenant to you, if you do not honour her as should a true knight I shall slay you so your manner remaineth not as a reproach to other knights.'

At this, Lancelot drew his sword but the knight sayeth, 'No, Sire, slay me not. What would you have me do?'

'You must take this damsel in true and honourable marriage.'

'Then if the choice is death or marriage, Sire, I will take her for my wife.'

Then Lancelot sayeth to the damsel, 'Is this your wish?'

'It is my sweetest wish, Sire, but yet further may I pray you to stay with us until we are married?'

'As you wish, damsel.'

Together they rode through the forest until they came to a chapel by a hermitage and the hermit wedded them with much joy. Upon the end of the Mass Lancelot wished to depart but the damsel asked that he should go with them to her father to witness to him that she was rightfully wed. 'Sire,' sayeth she, 'the castle of my father is close by.' And Lancelot agreed.

And soon they came upon the castle of the old knight who Lancelot had defended against Marin the Jealous Knight and the old knight was in great despond for he knew not of his daughter. But Lancelot told him of her wedding and great was the joy of the old knight. At this, Lancelot bade farewell and departed again to the forest.

Thereupon he saw a damsel and a dwarf riding at great pace and they came to him and the damsel sayeth, 'Sire, from whence come you?'

'I come, damsel,' sayeth he, 'from the castle of the old knight that is in this forest.'

Sayeth she, 'Did you meet a knight and a damsel on your way?'

'I did,' sayeth Lancelot, 'and he hath wedded her.'

'Is this true?'

'It is true. But had I not been there he would not have married her.'

'Then shame and misadventure upon you,' sayeth the damsel, 'for you have robbed me of the one thing in the world that I love the most. You should know, Sire, that she shall never have joy of him, and that had he been armed as you are he would never have bowed to your will. Yet again, Sire, you have harmed me. You and Gawain have slain my uncle and two cousins in the forest. Those whom you had me put in to their graves in the chapel where you watched, the chapel where you saw my dwarf was making the graves in the burial ground.'

Sayeth Lancelot, 'Damsel, it is true that I was there but I departed from the grave-yard with my honour safe.'

And the dwarf sayeth, 'But only for the knights were craven and failed.'

'My friend,' sayeth Lancelot, 'I would rather they would be cowards than knights of courage.'

And the damsel sayeth, 'Sire, you have done much outrage for you slew the Knight of the Waste Manor whence the hound led Gawain. Had he there been known he would not have departed so soon for he was loved no better than you. May God grant that you meet a knight that may avenge the evil in your heart and that of Gawain. That, Sire, would bring great rejoicing for many a good knight have you slain. Be assured, Sire, any trouble I may bring you I shall so do as quickly as I may. And, Sire, may you always have the wind in your face.'

But Lancelot would not answer the reviling so the damsel and the dwarf departed henceforth.

And Lancelot rode through the forest until he arrived at the house of the good King Hermit who made great joy of him. And the King Hermit asked if he hath come upon Percival but he hath not. And the King Hermit asked him if he hath seen the most Holy Grail but he hath not.

Thereupon the King Hermit sayeth, 'Well do I know why this was so. Had you the same desire to see the Holy Grail as you had to see the Queen then the Holy Grail would have been revealed unto you.'

'Sire,' sayeth Lancelot, 'my desire to see the Queen is for no other reason than her wisdom, her courtesy, her grace and her precious worth. This every knight is bound so to do for in her lives every honourable virtue that a Lady may have.'

'Then may God grant you safe passage through life, and may you do nought that will deserve His wrath on the Day of Judgement.'

On the morrow, Lancelot departed after hearing Mass and journeyed straightway to the court of King Arthur where the King and Queen sat with many knights and barons.

Part the XIth

As Lancelot returned to the court of King Arthur, Percival rode at great pace through the forests of England to the land of the Queen of the Tents. Therein had he left the Damsel of the Carriage as hostage for his return to accept the challenge of Clamados whose father and uncle he had slain.

But as he came night to the land of the Queen of the Tents he came upon the Damsel of the Carriage who greeted him with great joy. The Damsel sayeth to Percival that Clamados hath died of the wounds given him by Meliot of England and that Meliot was all healed.

'Sire,' sayeth she, 'the tents and the linen wall are all come down and the Queen has taken herself and her maidens to her castle. By my joyous meeting with you, you may know that you are no longer bound by your bond. Also, Sire, you should know that your sister, Dindrane, goes in search of you for your mother hath much need of you. Never again shall your sister know joy until she hath found you. Even now she searches for you in all the kingdoms of the world in great sorrow for none hath she found who can give her tidings of you.'

Bidding the damsel the protection of God, Percival rode to Wales until he came upon the Castle of Tallages which is seated high over the sea on a great rock. Thereon a knight rode from the castle gate and Percival asked to whom the castle belonged and the knight telleth him that it belongeth to the Queen of the Maidens.

He entered the castle and alighted at the mounting stage and rested his shield and lance. Before him rose the steps to the great hall and on each step were many knights and ladies but none greeted him. All were silent. At this, Percival saluted them all and ascended the steps to the door of the great hall which was shut. Taking the ring that hung thereon he struck the door and made a great sound that echoed within the hall. The door was opened and a knight stood at the door and sayeth, 'Knight, you are welcome.'

'Thank you, Sire,' sayeth Percival, 'and may God look well upon you.'

At this, Percival took off his helmet and the knight leadeth him to the chamber of the Queen. She rose to meet him and made great joy of him and made him sit next to her all armed.

With that a damsel entered the chamber and sayeth, 'My Lady, this is the knight who saw first the Holy Grail. He did I see at the court of the Queen of the Tents, where he was accused of treason and murder.'

The Queen turneth to her knight and sayeth, 'Haste now, and let sound the ivory horn.' And the knight hastened away to do her bidding.

When the sound of the ivory horn was heard throughout the castle the knights and ladies on the steps to the great hall rose upon their feet and made great joy and sayeth that their penance is now done. Thereupon they entered the hall and did meet the Queen who came from her chamber leading Percival by the hand.

And the Queen sayeth, 'Look upon the knight through whom you have the pain and trouble and by whom you are now released.'

And the knights and ladies cried out, 'And welcome may he be!'

'Welcome he is,' sayeth the Queen, 'for no other knight in the world had I more desire to see.'

At this, the Queen had Percival disarmed and had him brought a rich robe of silk and gold for his comfort. Then sayeth she, 'Sire, four knights and three ladies have been upon the steps of the hall since the time you were at the castle of the Fisher King and you did not ask the question of whom the Grail served. Since that time they have had no other place to be, nor to eat, nor to drink. And they have had no joy since that time. Therefore you need not marvel at their great joy at your coming. Nonetheless, Sire, we have another great need of your coming. For a foul knight wars upon us yet he is the brother of the good Fisher King. He is known as the King of Castle Mortal.'

'My Lady,' sayeth Percival, 'the knight of whom you speak is my uncle, as is the good Fisher King and the good King Hermit. But truly, Lady, there is none more foul and cruel than the King of Castle Mortal. Nothing deserves he of love or good fortune for he wars also against my uncle the Fisher King and means to take the Castle of the Holy Grail and the Spear.'

'Sire,' sayeth he Queen, 'it is for the aid I have given the Fisher King that the King of Castle Mortal doth challenge me for my castle. Oftentimes he comes to an island by this castle and he hath slain many of my knights and damsels. May God grant us vengeance upon him.'

At this, the Queen took Percival by the hand and leadeth him to the windows of the great hall and sayeth, 'Sire, there you may see the island where goeth your uncle to lay his plans for his assaults upon this castle. And see below the ships I hold for our defence.'

In the days that followed, the Queen gave great honour to Percival and made great joy of him. But though she loved him the Queen knew that never may she have her desire of him, nor should any lady nor damsel thereabouts for he was a good and chaste knight.

Ere long it came about that Percival heard that his uncle had arrived at the island and was intent on challenging the Queen for its possession. And the Queen would send many knights against the King of Castle Mortal but Percival prayed her not so to do for he would stand alone. With this, Percival had him rowed in a barge to the island full armed. And the King of Castle Mortal marvelled at this for no knight had before come from the castle to meet him in challenge.

And when the barge took the ground of the island Percival issued forth. Above him watched the Queen, the knights, ladies and damsels from the castle hall and seeth the approach of the nephew and the uncle.

The King of Castle Mortal was tall and strong and hardy and he knoweth not the knight who came upon him body to body, sword to sword. But Percival knew his uncle and came at him with sword drawn and shield raised and dealt him a great blow upon his helmet that maketh his body bend. And the King replied with many blows that caused the knight's helmet to bend and crack. And the King searcheth Percival with his sword with many blows that nought but the armour of the knight saved him from great wounds. And the Queen and all those at the windows marvelled that Percival could receive such blows yet yield not. Then Percival layeth another great blow against the King but his sword fell upon the shield of the King and near split it asunder.

And the King took him back and looked upon the shield that Percival carried and sayeth, 'Knight, from whence did you obtain this shield? On behalf of whom do you bear it?'

'I bear it,' sayeth Percival, 'on behalf of my father.'

'Was your father Alain of the valleys of Camelot? A knight who bore a shield of red whereon was a white hart?'

'He was indeed my father, a man without blame for he was a good and loyal knight.'

'Then you are my nephew for his wife was Yglais, who is my sister.'

Sayeth Percival, 'And therein I find no worth nor honour for none of my kindred lack loyalty as you do. I know that on reaching this island I should meet you and that you make war upon the good Fisher King and on the good Queen of this Castle. And may it please God that the Queen shall have no further need to guard her castle against you, nor shall the good Fisher King defend the sacred vessel and spear that God hath placed in his keeping. For God loves only those who regard highly loyalty and honour. You know nothing of either, therefore I do the work of God in defying you and holding you my enemy.'

The King now knoweth well that his nephew stood against him and Percival came to him with sword raised and in great rage as a lion. At this, the King ran full fast to his ship and leaped therein and pushed from the shore. Percival followed him to the beach and cried, 'Tell me evil King that I am not of your family! No knight of my mother's family did ever flee from another knight! You should know that this island is conquered and never will you here be seen again!'

And the King sailed from the island with no mind to return.

Percival returned from the island in his barge and went in to the castle of the Queen where he was met with great joy. And the Queen asked him if he was harmed.

'Lady,' sayeth he, 'no wound have I thank God.'

At this, she disarmed him and gave him great honour commanding all there to obey his wishes. For now the evil King had so meanly departed they know he will not return for dread of his nephew.

Part the XIIth

At the castle of King Arthur there was great joy at the arrival of Lancelot and Gawain. And the King asketh of them if they have seen his son Lohot but they say they have seen nought of him in the forests or islands.

The King sayeth, 'Much I marvel for I know not where he is nor have I tidings beyond those brought by Kay who slew Logrin the giant and brought me his head. For this I did most willingly increase the lands of Kay. And I love him greatly for he hath avenged me of the evil done by the giant.'

But had the King known truly of Kay and his deeds he would not have so highly honoured his chivalry and courage.

One day the King sat with the Queen and meat when a damsel of great beauty alighteth before the castle. She was Dindrane, the sister of Percival. And she came up the steps of the hall where sat the King and sayeth, 'Sire, I come before you as the most dismayed damsel ever you have known. I come, Sire, to ask the help of your brave and noble heart.'

'Damsel,' sayeth the king, 'I shall do as much for you as God permits for I cannot allow the plea of such a damsel as you to go unheeded.'

At this, the damsel looked at the shield that hung in the midst of the great hall and sayeth, 'Sire, it is my wish beyond all other that you allow me the aid of the knight that comes to take this shield.'

'Damsel,' sayeth the King, 'insofar as it be the wish of the knight I shall be most pleased to grant your request.'

'Sire, if he is as good a knight as his fame brings before him he will not refuse your request nor mine should I be here when he cometh. For had I found my brother whom I have long sought then no aid should I need. But I have sought him in many lands and could find nothing of him. To my sorrow I have had to ride through many lands at great danger to my body but God did ride beside me and I lived.'

'Damsel, I shall refuse you nothing for a right cause troubleth me not.'

'Sire,' sayeth she, 'may God be thanked for your great worth.'

And they sat her down at meat and gave her much honour. On the tables being cleared the Queen took the damsel to her chamber where she and her maidens make great joy of her. And the hound that was come with the shield lay on straw in the chamber and he would not stand for the Queen nor the knights but when he seeth the damsel he came to her and made great joy of her and the others did marvel at this for none before had he done this.

And the Queen asked the damsel if she knew the hound and she sayeth, 'No, Lady, for as I understand, I knoweth him not.' But the hound now staith with her and will leave her not.

Every day the damsel entered the chapel and wept before the image of the Saviour and prayed to His Mother for she was sore afraid of losing her castle. And the Queen sayeth to her, 'Damsel, who is your brother?'

'My Lady,' sayeth she, 'I have heard throughout the lands that he is one of the best knights in the entire world. But he departed from my father and mother a young squire. Now my father is dead and my lady mother is without help or counsel and a foul knight intends to rob her of her castle and slay her men. The castle would have long been taken were it not for Gawain that made her safe for a year and a day but the term is now nigh to its end and my mother lives in dread for she has nought but her castle. Thus hath she sent me to search for my brother whom she hath heard to be a good knight. But I cannot find him and so I am here to ask the King for the help of the Knight of the Shield if he hath pity upon me.'

And the Queen sayeth, 'Damsel, my wish is that you hath found your brother for it would bring great joy to me that your mother hath found his aid. May God grant that the Knight of the Shield come quickly and give him the courage and wisdom to help your mother.'

'May God so grant Lady, for never was there a good knight that hath not pity.' And the damsel told the Queen of her father and mother and how a great sadness did hang about her.

One night as the King lay with the Queen he awoke and could not return to sleep. He arose and looked out upon the dark sea that was quiet and without wind. Far off the King saw a light as if of a candle and much marvelled at what it might be. And the light came closer until the King saw that it was a ship that came towards the castle. He saw that it came near the shore and went to see it. At the helm was an old man who allowed the King to come thereon. When the King entered the ship he found a knight that lay full armed upon a bed of ivory. Candles in golden candlesticks were lighted at the head of the knight and his feet and when the King drew nigh he saw that the knight was of great comeliness.

And the old man sayeth to the King, 'Sire, pray draw back and let the knight rest for he hath had much to endure these many days.'

'Sire,' sayeth the King, 'who is the knight?'

But the old man sayeth, 'Only he can tell you that, Sire.'

At this, the King departed and returned to his Queen who he told of the strange knight. And the Queen rose and dressed in silk and ermine and went to the great hall with the King.

And the door of the great hall opened and there entered the old man from the ship bearing a tall candle in a golden candlestick. He was followed by the knight all armed and with his sword in his hand. And the queen sayeth, 'Knight, you are indeed welcome.'

'Lady,' sayeth the knight, 'I thank you and may God witness your kindness.'

And the Queen sayeth, 'Knight, have we aught to fear of you?'

'No, Lady, you have nought to fear of me.'

The King then seeth that the knight bore a shield of red whereon was a white hart and the hound that heareth the voice of the knight came in to the hall and made great joy around the legs of the knight.

And the knight went to the main column of the hall and took down the shield of white with the red cross and hung in its place the shield of red with the white hart. He then went to the door of the hall as if to depart.

The King sayeth unto him, 'Knight, pray do not leave so hastily.'

But the knight sayeth, 'Sire, no time have I to linger, but you shall see me again.' And he entered his ship with the hound and left the shore.

As the sun rose and hearing of the visit of the knight the Damsel Dindrane came to the King and sayeth, 'Sire, did you talk of me and my fears to the knight.'

'I did not,' sayeth the King, 'for to my sorrow he departed before I could.'

'Pray God that you are so good a King that you will not forget your covenant with a damsel so forlorn as I.' With that she left the court to continue her search for her brother and the King was most sorrowful that he hath not remembered the damsel when the knight came.

At this, Gawain and Lancelot entered the hall and when they heard the tidings of the knight and the shield they were both much grieved to have not seen him.

Gawain sayeth, 'This is ill-chance that I have not seen him.'

And Lancelot sayeth, 'I have seen him at close quarters and none have I faced body to body that hath wounded me so. And I him, and we lay together at the house of the King Hermit until I was healed.'

'Lancelot,' sayeth Gawain, 'I would gladly suffer wounds to have known him for as long as you.'

The King sayeth, 'It is our duty to seek this knight for a damsel needs his aid and such tidings must quickly reach him.'

The Queen sayeth, 'Sire, this will be a great service to the damsel for she is the daughter of Alain le Gros of the Valleys of Camelot. Her mother is named Yglais and her own name is Dindrane.'

'Lady,' sayeth Gawain, 'she is the sister of the knight that hath borne away the shield. I know her from the time I lodged at her mother's castle.'

'That,' sayeth the Queen, 'gives account of why the hound loveth them both.'

And Gawain sayeth, 'I shall go in quest of this knight, Lady, for I have great desire to see him.'

'And I also,' sayeth Lancelot, 'for I would gladly see him.'

The King sayeth, 'Pray do not forget, Sires, the damsel who hath great need of tidings of her brother and to whom I am bound in covenant so to find.'

'Sire,' sayeth Lancelot, 'we shall tell him that his sister hath been at your court and that she seeks him most urgently.'

The two knights left the court and rode together through the forest until they came to a high Holy Cross where all the roads did meet. Gawain sayeth, 'Lancelot, choose which road you will that we may go our way alone. Thus we may sooner hear tidings of the Good Knight. Let us meet here at this Cross one year hence to tell each other how we have fared. For, may it please God, let one path lead to him.'

And Lancelot taketh the way to the sunset, and Gawain to the sunrise. And they departed commending each other to God.

Part the XIIIth

Gawain rode until the decline of day and lodged well in the house of a hermit. And the hermit sayeth unto Gawain, 'Sire, whom do you seek?'

'I, Sire, am in quest of a knight that I would find with great gladness.'

But sayeth the hermit, 'Sire, there are no knights that dwell in this land.'

'No knights, Sire? Why not I pray you?'

'At one time there were many. But now all are gone save for one knight who lives alone in a castle and another who lives alone upon the sea. It is he who hath slain all the others.'

'And who, Sire, is the Knight of the Sea?'

'I know not, Sire,' sayeth he hermit, 'all that is known unto me is that his ship goes by the sea to an island that is beneath the walls of the castle of the Queen of the Maidens. From that island he chased an uncle that made war upon the castle. Any knight that came to the aid of his uncle was slain until none remained and the castle was safe.'

Sayeth Gawain, 'Sire, since when did he begin his life upon the sea?'

'Scarce twelve months, Sire.'

'And how far is the sea from us?'

'It is close by, Sire, and easily reached. Often have I walked there and seen his ship pass by. I have seen him also, full armed, of great comeliness and as noble as a lion. Never, Sire, has any knight been more dreaded. Had it not been for him the Queen of the Maidens would have been robbed of her castle. But he goeth not there but searcheth the islands and seas for the boastful and the arrogant to bring them down. The Queen is in great sorrow that he goeth not to the castle for she hath great love of him and would willingly make him a prisoner of her desire.'

'Sire,' sayeth Gawain, 'do you know the shield that this knight beareth?'

'I know nought of such things, Sire. I know nought beyond the dismay throughout this land caused by this knight.'

After Mass, Gawain departed and found the sea. Nothing could he see of the ship and he rode along the shore until he came upon the Castle of the Queen of the Maidens. The Queen made great joy of him and showed him the island that Percival had taken from his uncle. She sayeth, 'Sire, this knight doth cause me much pain in my heart for he will not enter the castle. He has not come within its walls since he made his uncle flee but stays upon the island or upon the sea.'

'And where is he now?' sayeth Gawain.

'As God may witness,' sayeth the Queen, 'I know not nor may any other for he comes and goes as he wish.'

And Gawain felt deep despond at not knowing of the whereabouts of the knight. After Mass he departed to continue his search and rode along the shore but of the ship there was nought. He then came upon a great forest in which he entered and saw a knight riding at a great gallop as though to flee from someone who would slay him.

'Hold, Sire,' sayeth Gawain, 'why do you ride so fast?'

'I flee, Sire, from the knight that hath slain all the others.'

'And who is this knight?'

'I know not who he is, Sire, but should you go towards him you will soon discover him.'

'It seems to me, Sire,' sayeth Gawain, 'that we have met before.'

'We have, Sire, for I am the Knight Coward whom you met when you defeated the Knight of the Black and White shield. I, Sire, am the man of the Damsel of the Carriage. I pray you therefore, Sire, that you do me no hurt for the knight from whom I flee looks so fierce that I thought I would die when I saw him.'

'You need not fear me, Sire, for I know your damsel well.'

'If only other knights would say as you do, Sire, for no fear have I save for myself alone.'

With this, both departed from the other and Gawain turned to seek the knight from whom the Knight Coward had fled. And he came upon a sand hill by the shore and saw a knight all armed and on a fine horse and he beareth a shield of gold with a green cross. And Gawain sayeth, 'God grant that this knight may give me tidings of him that I seek.'

And he came upon the knight and made salute and sayeth, 'Sire, have you tidings of a knight that beareth a shield of white whereon is a red cross?'

'I have, Sire,' sayeth the knight, 'for he shall be at the assembly of the knights within forty days.'

'Where will the assembly be held?'

'In the Red Land. Many knights shall be there and he will be found without fail.'

And Gawain thanked the knight and felt great joy at such tidings. He then departed for the Red Land and saw not the knight of the gold shield and the green cross return to the shore and enter in his ship and put to sea.

Gawain rode until he came upon a fair castle. Close by he saw a damsel following two knights who bore the body of a dead knight on a litter. And Gawain saluted the damsel and sayeth, 'Who is the dead knight?'

And she replieth, 'Sire, he was a knight who hath been slain in great outrage.'

'And where do you take him?'

'I take him, Sire, to the Red Land.'

'Why there, damsel?'

'For whomsoever is best at the assembly of the knights shall avenge the death of this knight.'

With this, the damsel departed and Gawain went to the castle close by and found none therein save an old and feeble knight and a squire who waited upon him. The old knight lodged him well and made the castle door be made fast shut. On the morrow,

Gawain was want to depart but the old knight sayeth to him, 'Sire, I granted you lodging last night and hope that you may reward me by defending me against a knight who would slay me for granting lodging to the King of Castle Mortal, he that wars against the Queen of the Maidens.'

'What shield doth he bear?' sayeth Gawain.

'He bears a shield of gold with a cross of green. And he is a hardy and true knight.'

'Have you tidings of another knight whom I seek? He is called Percival and hath carried away from the court of King Arthur a shield of white that beareth a red cross.'

At this, the old knight looked from his window and saw a knight near the castle bearing a shield of gold with a green cross. Gawain did arm himself and mounted his horse and issued forth from the castle with lance lowered and shield raised. But the knight moved not nor did he prepare for battle and Gawain marvelled at this. But the knight had no ill intent towards the old knight and had come thither to meet knights that sought adventure. And Gawain looked behind him and saw that the castle door was closed and the drawbridge raised. To the knight he sayeth, 'Sire, do you intend to do harm here?'

'No, Sire, I do not,' replieth the knight.

At this, the damsel of the dead knight came riding at a great pace and came to the two knights saying, 'In the name of God, shall I ever find a knight to take my vengeance to the evil knight that lives in the castle?'

'Is he evil? sayeth Gawain.

'He is the most evil you ever saw,' crieth the damsel. 'He gave lodging to my brother and made him swear he would defend the old knight against a knight that would appear before the castle. When the knight appeared my brother set out to keep his covenant. They met in combat so fierce that their lances thrust through their shields and pierced their hearts and both were slain. With this, the old knight issued forth from the castle and took away their armour and horses leaving their bodies to the beasts and the birds. But for my coming with two knights just such would have come about.'

'Then,' sayeth Gawain, 'the Lord God must surely be thanked for protecting this knight and me from such harm.'

And the knight sayeth, 'It seemeth to me that the old knight would have knights slay each other. How can this be?'

'For, Sire,' sayeth the damsel, 'he covets their armour and horses.'

'Damsel,' sayeth Gawain, 'whither go you?'

'To join my dead knight that lieth upon a litter.' With that, she departed at great pace.

And the knight sayeth his farewell to Gawain. And Gawain sayeth to him, 'Sire, forgive me my churlishness for I have not asked your name.'

But the knight sayeth, 'Pray, Sire, do not ask my name until I ask you of yours.' He then rode to the forest and Gawain continued on his way. As he rode he met many knights and damsels and asked them of the Knight of the White Shield with the red cross and all told him that the knight would be found at the assembly in the Red Land.

One night he lodged with a hermit who asked whence he had come. 'Sire, I have come from the land of the Queen of the Maidens.'

And the hermit sayeth, 'Have you seen Percival the Good Knight that took the shield from the court of King Arthur?'

'To my great sorrow,' sayeth Gawain, 'I have not. But a knight that bore a shield of gold with a green cross told me that he would be found at the assembly at the Red Land.'

'Then, Sire,' sayeth the hermit, 'the knight of which you speak was none other than the knight for whom you search. Indeed, he hath lodged here and has left me his hound that I might care for it.'

'But,' sayeth Gawain, 'the shield he bore was not the shield by which he may be known.'

'This he doth,' sayeth the hermit, 'so he may not be known. The shield from the court of King Arthur awaits him at the hermitage of Joseus the son of the King Hermit. It is the very hermitage where Lancelot lodged and did hang the four thieves who tried to rob the hermit.'

And Gawain sayeth, 'Such great misfortune have I found for should I have known his name I would have laid before him the message I bear from King Arthur. Even now, Lancelot searches throughout England for him. Twice I have seen him and spoken to him only to lose him.'

'Sire,' sayeth the hermit, 'he is a knight that keeps close to himself and is wary of others for he will not waste a word, nor will he be untruthful, nor will he speak a word that he would not want to be heard. Nor will he do shame of his body for he is chaste and will not commit outrage upon anyone.'

'This I know well,' sayeth Gawain, 'that all the valour and purity that should be in a knight is abundant in him. Therefore, I am of great sorrow that I am not amongst those he knows for to know such a knight brings great worthiness upon others.'

Gawain departed the next morn after Mass not knowing that the hermit with whom he had lodged was Josuias, the brother of the wife of the King Hermit and the uncle of the hermit Joseus and, as was his nephew, a brave and noble knight who had renounced all his power and possessions for the love of God.

And Gawain rode until he came to the Red Land where he seeth the assembly of the knights with many tents and pennants. All had their shields outside their tents but nowhere could Gawain see the shield for which he made search. He did not know, that the knight had changed his shield to blue barred with gold that none may know him. There did Gawain find the damsel that waiteth for the knight who shall have mastery of the tournament.

As Gawain watched he saw a knight that bore a blue and gold barred shield that sendeth to the ground all knights he challenged. Desirous of taking part in the combat until he should find the knight whom he sought Gawain rode on to the field and came before the Knight of the Blue and Gold Shield. They met with such force that both were all but felled from their saddles. Again they met and their lances broke apart at the hurtle and the handles of their shields came apart from their fastenings. Once more they came at each other with the fury of lions and many marvelled that their bodies were not pierced or broken. But God would not allow good knights to slay each other but to know instead the worthiness of each other. Even their armour did not protect them but only the love of God in whom they had faith and to whom they prayed for their salvation. But the knights then fell upon each other with their swords and dealt one the other with mighty blows until the many knights did part them for they had fought as had no other.

And the damsel that brought thither the slain knight sayeth to them all, 'Sires, declare for me the knight who hath done the best that I might seek vengeance and thus bury this noble knight.' And they sayeth that the Knight of the Shield of blue barred with gold and the Knight of the Red Shield that bore a golden eagle hath done better than all of them. But the Knight of the Blue and Gold Shield had fought longer than the other and thus he was judged best.

The damsel then sought the Knight of the Blue and Gold Shield but could find him not for he had departed. She then sayeth to Gawain, 'Sire, as I cannot find the Knight of the Blue and Gold Shield I now come to you to avenge the knight that lieth slain upon the litter.'

But Gawain sayeth, 'Damsel, it would bring great shame to me to do such a thing for only the best knight at the assembly can do it with honour. The Knight of the Shield of blue and gold has been chosen and it is he who must avenge your wrong. I know him to be the best and cannot bring shame upon me by pretending his place.'

'But, Sire,' sayeth the damsel, 'he hath already entered the forest and I have lost the aid of the best knight in the world.'

'How know you him to be the best knight in all the word?'

'Well I know it,' sayeth she, 'for it was to him that the most Holy Grail did appear in the Castle of the Fisher King for he only was of the goodness of mind and body. But he forgot to ask whom the Grail served and thus sore harm hath befallen the land. He it was that came to the court of King Arthur to take the shield which he alone can bear. To this time I have known him but now he hath changed the colours of his shield and I know him not.'

'Damsel,' sayeth Gawain, 'the tidings you bring me cause me much pain for I also seek him. But he will not tell me his name and he changeth his shield often. It seems I shall only know him from the blows he lays upon me for never in arms have I known a knight of such strength and valour. But such would I gladly suffer that I might be known unto him.'

'Pray, Sire,' sayeth the damsel, 'will you give me your name?'

'I am called Gawain.' And with that he commended the damsel unto God and did depart from her. As he rode he prayed to God that the Saviour might lead him to such a place where he might find Percival that he might be his brother knight.

Part the XIVth

The good knight Lancelot rode to the hermitage where he hanged the four thieves and was greeted with great joy by the hermit, Joseus. But the hermit knew not of the son of the Widow Lady. The knight had been to the hermitage once since he left the court of King Arthur but the hermit knew not whither he had gone.

Lancelot entered the chapel and saw the shield of white with the cross of red and sayeth, 'Sire, but this is his shield, do you hide him from me?'

'I do not,' sayeth the hermit, 'for he hath taken another shield of gold with a green cross.'

Nor had the hermit seen Gawain but sayeth to Lancelot, 'Sire, you have earned the enmity of the kin of the four robbers you hanged and they search for you in this forest. I pray you greatly that you be on your guard against them.'

'As it pleases God,' sayeth Lancelot.

After lodging in the hermitage for the night, Lancelot departed after Mass and rode through the dark forest until he saw a strong and well-made castle whence came a knight with a hawk upon his wrist. The knight came to Lancelot and sayeth, 'Welcome, Sire, may God attend you.'

'And you also,' sayeth Lancelot. 'Pray tell me, Sire, what castle is this?'

'It, Sire, is the Castle of the Golden Circlet. I am come today for it is the day ordained for the adoration of the Gold Circlet.'

'What, Sire, is the Golden Circlet?' sayeth Lancelot.

'It is the Crown of Thorns that Our Saviour wore upon His brow when He was put upon the Cross. The Queen of this castle hath set it in gold and precious stones and once a year allows the knight and ladies of the kingdom to see it. But it is said that the first knight to achieve the most Holy Grail shall come to take it. Thus it is that no stranger knight shall be allowed in to the castle. But, Sire, if you will allow it, you may lodge with me at my dwelling nearby.'

'Thank you, no, Sire,' sayeth Lancelot, 'for I must go forward whilst the light of day remains.' At this, he departed from the knight and rode past the castle and thought to himself, 'What honour should come to a knight who by his valour should take the Golden Circlet from a place so strong.'

At this, he came upon a damsel escorting the body of a knight upon a litter. 'Damsel,' sayeth he, 'may God be with you.'

'And with you also,' sayeth she.

'What, damsel, do you do with this body of a knight?'

'I, Sire, am made to keep this body of the knight with me by the hatred I bear for the knight that hath killed him. Also I have no liking for the knight who should avenge him for him I cannot find.'

'Who hath slain this knight?'

'The Knight of the Dragon.'

'And who say you should avenge the slain knight?'

'The knight who was held to be the best at the assembly in the Red Land. The same that fought with Gawain and was judged best for he had fought the longer.'

'Surely,' sayeth Lancelot, 'he must have been a knight of exceeding great valour to have bettered Gawain. What shield did he bear?'

Sayeth the damsel, 'At the assembly he had a shield of blue and gold but before he hath carried a shield of green and a shield of gold with a green cross.'

'And Gawain did not know him?'

'No, Sire, and he is much sorrowful for not knowing that he hath fought the son of the Widow Lady, Percival.'

'Do you know, damsel, whither they have gone?'

'No, Sire, neither one nor the other.'

With this, Lancelot commended the damsel unto God and departed from her. It was the time of the setting sun and the rocks and forest grew dark and Lancelot was much alert to the dangers and cast his eyes to both sides of the trail but he saw not the dwarf who spied upon him from the trees. The dwarf then went at great pace to a house wherein lived a damsel of great beauty but who had a heart of evil for she had grown amidst robbers and was nurtured by wrongdoing. Full many knights had she drawn to their slaying by her beauty and her evil ways.

And the dwarf sayeth unto her, 'Damsel, here cometh through the woods the knight that did hang your uncle and three cousins.'

'This day have I long waited,' sayeth she, 'for I intend to have the better of him both for my share in his wealth and for the slaying of my kin. Look now to your arming for I may need your aid.'

'And you shall have it, damsel, for he shall not pass by without being slain for his misdeeds.'

And the damsel went right quick to put herself on the track by which Lancelot was to pass. And she stood there of great beauty and with her dress parted and not held in a seemly manner.

Thereupon, Lancelot came and saw the damsel who saluted him and sayeth, 'Sire, the night is dark and I have a house which my forefathers built for the lodging of knights that pass through this forest. And you should know that there is no other lodging nearby.'

'Damsel,' sayeth Lancelot, 'I thank you heartily of this kindness for I seek lodging and would willingly accept such an offer from so fair a maiden.'

On their coming to the house there were none there save the dwarf who stabled the horse of Lancelot and did wait upon him.

When they entered the hall Lancelot did feel a darkness about the place that did not settle his mind. At this, the damsel sayeth, 'Sire, disarm yourself and be at ease for you have full assurance of safety.'

But Lancelot sayeth, 'Pray do not concern yourself for no trouble do I have with my armour.'

And the damsel sayeth, 'But, Sire, no knight hath ever been armed within here. Are you fearful of something for you are quite safe? Do you have enemies hereabouts?'

'No knight is loved by everyone,' sayeth Lancelot, 'and many do cover their hatred with disguising flattery.'

At this, the table was set and Lancelot sat at meat with the damsel. She then took him to a rich couch where he lay but had brought to him his helmet, shield and lance. But on the soft couch his eyes closed and he did fall asleep. With this, the dwarf mounted the horse of Lancelot and rode to the dwelling of the five robbers who raged to slay the knight that had hanged their kin.

And the dwarf sayeth in great excitement, 'Up, Sires! Avenge your kin! He is with the damsel and I bring his horse as a token of this truth.' And the robbers are in great joy and arm themselves and set forth to the house of the damsel.

As Lancelot slept the damsel did creep upon him and silently draw his sword from its scabbard. Holding it aloft she circled the knight to mark the place she might strike him for to slay the knight would bring her great worship amongst her robber kin. But as she held the sword high the door to the hall opened and there came therein the five robbers and the dwarf.

With this, Lancelot did jump up and the damsel ran to the robbers. The chief of them came at Lancelot and he took up his lance and thrust it through the body of the robber. He then ran at the four remaining robbers thinking to slay one but the damsel came at him with his own sword. Letting his armour take the blow he held the sword and pulled it from the hand of the damsel. Now with sword in hand he ran to the nearest robber and brought the blade down right heavy, but the damsel ran beneath and the sword struck her on the head and she fell slain. Lancelot was sore grieved by this for a knight does not kill damsel nor lady but he reckoned it to be the work of God against the evil in the damsel.

Then the robbers pressed their attack and he dealt two of them wound for wound until they withdrew to the door of the hall. At this the dwarf did cry loudly, 'You cannot retreat from a single knight! Stand, I say, and avenge your kin!' And Lancelot felled him with a single stroke of his sword and he lay slain. The knight then advanced to the door where stood the robbers but they went outside as though to wait in ambush. But Lancelot closed the door and barred it so that none may enter. And he took the bodies of the slain, even that of the damsel, and threw them out of the window so that they lay by the robbers that waited outside. This done, he rested his wounds as the robbers made plan to keep him inside until he starve or has need for water. But the hall had plenty of meats and drinks. Only the need for a horse held Lancelot within for he knew not what the dwarf had done with his horse for a knight must be mounted to defend him against other knights and brigands.

As the sun did rise and the birds began their song Lancelot placed himself in the hands of God and prepared to meet whatever the day may bring.

Part the XVth

Gawain was heavy with sorrow that he had thrice met Percival but had known him not. He went to the High Cross to meet Lancelot but of him could find him no sign. To return to the court of King Arthur without success could not be done. Gawain, therefore, returned to the search for Lancelot or Percival. And he came upon the hermitage of Joseus who gave him great welcome. And Gawain asked him of tidings of Percival but the hermit answered saying that he had not seen the good knight since before the assembly in the Red Land. Nor did he know where Percival may be found. As they spoke thus, a knight bearing a blue shield rode to the hermitage. After a good welcome by the hermit Gawain asked of him if he had seen a knight with a blue and gold barred shield in the forest.

'I have, Sire,' sayeth the knight, 'I spoke with him this day. He asked me if I have seen a knight that bore a shield of red with a golden eagle and I could but tell him I have not. When I asked why he sought for this knight he telleth me that such a knight had shown great valour at the assembly in the Red Land and he wished to make acquaintance with him for he was a good knight.'

Sayeth Gawain, 'His desire cannot be more than that of the knight that he seeketh for there is none in this world that he would more gladly meet than the Knight of the Blue and Gold Shield.'

And the knight seeth the shield of Gawain and sayeth, 'You, Sire, seemeth to be that knight whom he seeks.'

'Truly do you speak, Sire. Pray, can you tell me where I can find him?'

At this Joseus the hermit sayeth, 'He will not have gone forth from this forest for this hermitage is his safe refuge and he hath brought here the shield he took from the court of King Arthur.'

And Gawain made great joy at the sight of the shield. And the knight sayeth unto him, 'Sire, are you Gawain?'

'I am, Sire.'

Then, Sire, long have I sought for you. I bear a message from your man, Meliot of England, whose mother was slain on your account. Now his father hath been slain by Nabigant of the Rock on your account and who challenges for the land of Meliot. He prayeth that you go to his aid as a lord is bound so to do.'

But Gawain was sore troubled by these tidings. He was a good knight and a good lord to those in his service and under his protection. But nought could he do but say to the knight, 'Pray, Sire, tell Meliot that I will hasten to his aid as soon as I may but I am bound by the enterprise I am now on and I cannot leave it with honour until it is achieved.'

And the knight departed on the morrow after Mass. Gawain put on his armour ready to mount his horse when he saw a knight riding a tall horse and bearing a shield of gold with a green cross come forth out of the forest. And he sayeth to the hermit, 'Sire, know you this knight?'

And the hermit replieth, 'Truly I know him well, Sire, for he is Percival, the knight whom you seek.'

'May God be praised,' sayeth Gawain. And he set off on foot with the hermit to greet the knight. And Percival dismounted as Gawain sayeth, 'Right welcome are you, Sire.'

And Percival replieth, 'And may God smile upon you, Sire.'

The hermit sayeth to Percival, 'This, Sire, is Gawain, nephew of King Arthur.'

'Then right glad am I to see him for all who speak of him do so with honour and joy.' To Gawain he sayeth, 'Sire, can you tell me of a knight that was at the assembly in the Red Land?'

'What shield did he bear, Sire?'

'A shield of red with a golden eagle. He was the most sturdy knight I have met save only for Lancelot.'

'Sire,' sayeth Gawain, 'that was the shield I bore when I fought against the Knight of the Blue and Gold Shield, a knight who held within him all that knighthood shall mean amongst the valiant.'

And Percival sayeth, 'All that I may have done that day was shown in equal measure by you, Sire.' And he came to Gawain and they clasped each other by the hand in manly brotherhood.

In the hermitage, Gawain sayeth to Percival, 'Sire, when you took the shield from the hall at the court of King Arthur your sister, Dindrane, also was there. She hath prayed most fervently that she should have the aid of the knight that bore the shield away. But the King failed to tell you and your sister is greatly troubled thereof. At this, the King was want to search for you to tell you of the woes of your sister but Lancelot and I did undertake to search for you. This, Sire, is the fourth time I have encountered you and now make great joy at giving you the message for your mother gave me the fairest of lodgings at Camelot. Now she hath been robbed of all her castles save Camelot and has but few knights to defend her. Your father, Sire, is dead and your widowed mother looks to you for aid and comfort. Pray, Sire, honour your mother and go to her defence.'

And Percival sayeth, 'I thank you, sire, for your tidings. I shall do as you say for none other do I bear thanks as I do my mother, now a widow.'

'And you shall have much deserved praise,' sayeth Gawain, 'for God knows that which is right throughout all worlds.'

And the hermit sayeth, 'And so speaketh God through the scriptures for he that honoureth not his father and mother neither believeth in God nor loveth Him.'

With this, Percival sayeth, 'What tidings are known of Lancelot?'

'He but lately lodged herein,' sayeth the hermit, 'but before then he lodged here when we were set upon by robbers and he hanged four of them in the forest. Whereof he is much hated by their kinfolk who have taken oath to make him suffer for their loss. And they abound in this forest. I told him of this but he made much light of it and sayeth that he will do to them as he hath to their kin.'

Then Percival sayeth, 'This, Sire, I shall not allow for even the best knight may not prevail against much greater force. I shall not leave this forest until the well-being of Lancelot is assured.'

And Gawain sayeth, 'And I shall be at your side, Sire, for as he would not turn aside a plea for aid, nor shall I abandon him when he needs my sword.'

Percival and Gawain departed from the hermitage. And Percival bore the shield of white with the cross of red. As they rode through the forest they came upon a knight riding at great pace as if in much fear of what followed him. And Percival sayeth, 'Hold, Sire. Why do you ride as if in much dread?'

And the knight sayeth, 'Sire, I have come from the forest of the robbers. They have chased me to slay me but they are now gone to the house wherein they hold a knight who they say hath done them great harm. This knight hath hanged four of their kin, slain another and a dwarf in their service and did also slay a damsel who deserved to be slain for her part in the deaths of many good knights who came to her for lodging.'

'And know you the knight?' sayeth Percival.

'No, Sire, I do not. But he hath been wounded and lives only on what remains of food in the hall where he is entrapped. Nor hath he a horse on which to fight or escape.'

'Thank you, Sire, for these tidings,' sayeth Gawain, 'but we must go fast to this place to aid Lancelot.'

And the knight sayeth, 'Sires, if you will permit me I would accompany you to the house to see the justice of God brought to these robbers. I am the cousin of the Poor Knight of the Waste Forest that hath two poor damsel sisters where Gawain did joust with Lancelot and the knight that brought you tidings thereof died in the night.'

'Indeed, Sire,' sayeth Gawain, 'well remember I that courteous knight and the courteous damsels. May the Lord God grant them much good.'

And the knight led Percival and Gawain towards the house where Lancelot lay trapped. But as they came night they heard the sound of sword on armour and they spurred their horses to a gallop. On sight of the house they saw Lancelot under great combat from three robbers. Another robber lay slain upon the ground for

Lancelot had issued sword in hand from the hall and fought the robber for his horse. Now the three remaining robbers pressed sore upon Lancelot.

At this, Percival and Gawain lowered their lances and ran at two of the robbers and knocked them from their horses such that they were slain. The third robber tried to flee but the knight who was cousin to the Poor Knight took courage from the actions of Percival and Gawain and pierced him through with his lance until he be slain also.

With this, there was great joy at the meeting of Lancelot with Percival and Gawain. And they held council and decided that the horses of the robbers should go to the Poor Knight and the houses of the robbers and all the treasures therein should be given to the sisters of the Poor Knight. And right gladly did the cousin knight depart to bear this message to those in receipt.

Then sayeth Percival, 'Brethren, I must now depart in search of my sister and go to the aid of my widowed mother. Pray salute the King and Queen for me and give them word that I shall attend the court as soon as God permits.' And Percival went in to the forest as Lancelot and Gawain turned towards the court of King Arthur.

Percival then entered a forest that was unknown to him. It was a waste forest with no people and only wild beasts could be seen. And he came upon a hermitage in a valley by a mountain and alighted without the chapel. When he looked in he saw the hermit singing a requiem Mass over the body that lay before the altar covered with a shroud. He would not enter the chapel for he was armed and listened at the door with great reverence. Thereon the hermit did come to him and Percival sayeth, 'Sire, for whom have you done this service?'

And the hermit sayeth, 'I have done it, Sire, for Lohot, the son of King Arthur.'

'Who hath slain him?' sayeth Percival.

'I will tell you, Sire,' sayeth the hermit. This forest is part of the realm of England and hereabouts lived a horrible and cruel giant named Logrin who hath wasted this forest and the land hereabouts. And it pleased God to send Lohot in search of adventure. The son of the King did not retreat from the giant but fought him long and hard with much courage until Logrin was defeated and fell slain. At this, Lohot, in great weariness from the combat, fell in to a deep sleep by the slain giant. Thereupon came Kay, a knight from the court of King Arthur, who came silently upon Lohot and struck off his head. The traitor then struck off the head of the giant and tied it to his saddle-bow. Kay then repaired to the court of King Arthur and presented the king with the head of the giant. And the King is right joyous at this and gave Kay much honour and new land. Then came a damsel to my hermitage and led me to the body of Lohot. She asked me for the head of the knight in reward and I this granted. She then set the head of the knight in a casket of gold and precious stones wherein were many sweet scented herbs. She then departed I know not where.'

Percival sayeth, 'A great sore pity is this for I have often heard that Lohot was growing well in chivalry. The King should know of this for Kay begs a fate that is right and just for his evil actions.'

Percival departed on the morrow after Mass and rode in search of tidings of his mother. At noon he heard the sound of a damsel in great distress crying to herself. He looked and saw in a clearing the Damsel Dindrane kneeling with her arms stretched out in prayer. And she sayeth, 'Sweet Saviour of the World and your precious Mother pray hear my plea. I have searched through all the land of Greater Britain yet I can find no tidings of my brother whom it is aid is the best knight in all the world. But what avail him of his knighthood if we cannot have his aid and comfort? His most gentle and loyal mother hath great need of him for if she loses her castle we must be wanderers and beggars in a strange land. Her brother the good Fisher King languishes and her brother King Pelles serves Our Saviour as her other brother, the King of the Castle Mortal makes war on her with the Lord of the Moors and would rob her of her castle and land. All of the brothers of my father have died and can no longer give us aid.'

On hearing this, Percival rode from the trees and the damsel seeth him come and seeth also the white shield with the cross of red. And she clasped her hands to heaven and sayeth, 'Dear sweet Lady that did bear the Saviour of the World, you have not forgotten me for now here comes the knight who will bring aid and comfort to my mother and to me. Lord God, grant him the strength to do thy will. Give him the might and courage to protect us.'

At this, Percival came upon her and she took his stirrup to kiss his foot but he sayeth, 'No, damsel! I am a knight of the Round Table and will act as God doth command. No need have I for such from any damsel.'

And the Damsel Dindrane sayeth, 'Sire, have pity on my mother and on me as the Holy Mother had pity on Our Saviour as He hung upon the Cross. There is none other to whom we can fly for aid for I am told that you are the best knight in the world. I have been, Sire, to the court of King Arthur and throughout all manner of lands in search of my brother who is a knight also but I have not found him. Also King Arthur did forget to tell you of my troubles when you took the shield from where it did hang in the hall.'

And Percival who knoweth this to be his sister but sayeth nothing of it sayeth to the damsel, 'So much hath the King done for you, damsel, that he did send his two best knights in search of me that I might come to you. And be assured, damsel, that in the sight of God I shall do all that I may to aid you and your mother.'

With this, Percival helped the damsel to remount and they rode together through the forest. And the damsel sayeth to Percival, 'Sire, I must go on alone to the Perilous Graveyard.'

And he sayeth, 'Why do you go thither?'

And the damsel replieth, 'A holy hermit did tell me that my uncle the King of Castle Mortal that warreth upon us may not be overcome by any knight save I bring him some of the altar cloth from the chapel of the Perilous Graveyard. I have therefore vowed to the Holy Mother that I will obtain some of the cloth for it is the holiest cloth in Christendom being that which Our Lord was covered in the Holy Sepulchre. Yet none may enter the Perilous Graveyard except alone. Thus I go this night and may God protect me for the place is fearful and full of dread. Pray, Sire, you continue towards the Castle Camelot where awaits my mother, the Widow Lady. There you shall see how we need your aid and comfort.' Then she sayeth, 'Sire, this is the path I must take. You may see it is little frequented for no knight hath the courage to take it beyond here. May our lord have you in His keeping and may He remember me also this coming night.'

Percival knew full well that he could not forbid nor aid his sister in her trial for such she had to do alone. And he sayeth, 'Know you well, damsel, that I shall do all that I can under God to aid you and your mother. And may He be at your side this night.' And he departed knowing that save for the King of Castle Mortal none of his family would knowingly be disloyal nor fail in their word nor do any base deed.

The Damsel Dindrane went on alone in great dread until she came upon the gate to the Perilous Graveyard. As the sun set she saw a tall Cross whereat she knelt and kissed the image and prayed to the Saviour of the World that He would bring her forth from the burial-ground with honour.

The Perilous Graveyard was wide and ancient and contained many knights who had died in the forest but only those who had repented of their sins could be buried therein. And Dindrane entered the dark burial-ground and saw that it was full of tombs and coffins and fear settled upon her as a dark cloak. But no evil spirit could abide in the graveyard, for it had been blessed by Saint Andrew, yet no hermit could remain therein after the sun had set for it was soon beset by the shades of knights that had died in the forest but did not lay in the blessed burial ground.

And soon the Damsel Dindrane heard the sound of the shadow knights and then seeth them as they ran back and forth roaring beyond the graveyard wall. Such spectral knights there were in multitudes and they fought one with the other with lances and swords of fire until the forest resounded thereof. Yet none could enter the burial ground. And the damsel did almost swoon in fear. But she made the sign of the Cross and commended her spirit to the Saviour and His Holy Mother. Then she saw a chapel small and ancient and alighteth and entered wherein she found a great brightness of light. Within stood an image of Our Lady to whom the damsel prayed that she might survive the night. On the altar she saw the Holy Cloth and could smell the sweet scent that came from it as of no other scent in the world. As she came unto the cloth it rose from the altar and went so high that she could not reach it. And she wept and crieth, 'Dear God! Is it my sins that cause the cloth to be raised beyond me?'

Then the damsel fell to her knees and sayeth, 'Holy Father, I pray you, never did I evil to anyone, nor did I shame to myself, nor have I knowingly done against your will, but rather I serve you and your Holy Mother with love and fear. All the trials I have suffered I have done so in your holy name, nor have I set myself against ought that should please you. I pray you, Dear Lord, that you should release my mother and me from the great grief which is set upon us for she is a Widow Lady without comfort. You, Lord, who hath the world at Your command, grant me tidings of my brother and let him be alive that he might come to our aid in Your holy name. Grant also Lord, Your blessing on the knight that is gone to aid my mother. Remember, Lord, Your pity and compassion on that dear Lady's woes. Pray, Dear God, remember also that I am of the family of Joseph of Arimathea who spurned gold to take the body of Our Saviour from the Cross and did lay him in the Holy Sepulchre. Let it be Your pleasure, Lord, that You help a Lady of virtue and her forlorn daughter.'

At this there was the sound of rending as the cloth above her head parted, the greater part going upon the altar and the lesser part into her beseeching arms. Thus it was since the death of Our Lord that the Damsel Dindrane was the only one ever to touch the sacred cloth or did God grant a piece thereof. And she kissed the cloth full reverently and put it next to her heart.

Still yet the noise of combat was sounded without the graveyard and flames lighted the dark sky from the clashing of their swords and the damsel was sore afraid. Then spoke a voice from above to the spirits of the dead knights at rest in the burial ground. And the voice sayeth, 'Prepare for lamentation for sore loss hath befallen you. The good Fisher King who made Our service every day in the chapel of the Holy Grail is dead. And his castle is taken by his brother the King of Castle Mortal. No more shall the Mother of God enter the chapel on the Lord's Day and no more shall the most Holy Grail appear. Gone are the Guardian Knights, gone are the priests, gone are the damsels that attended the Holy Grail and the Holy Spear.' Then the voice spoke to the Damsel Dindrane and sayeth, 'And you, damsel, may depend no more upon stranger knights for none save your brother can bring you aid.'

And a great wailing went up from the graveyard and amongst those that fought beyond the walls. Such was the sound that it was as if the world itself did tremble.

And the damsel near did swoon and sayeth, 'Dear God, we have lost the good Fisher King and I can no longer turn to the good knight for aid and comfort.' She then stayed in prayer in the chapel until the light of dawn did bring quiet upon the lands thereabouts.

The damsel then rode to the Valley of Camelot where she came upon Percival looking upon the castle that he had not seen since he departed as a squire long years before. And she sayeth, 'Sire, I have tidings of the worst kind for my uncle the good Fisher King is dead and my uncle, the King of Castle Mortal, hath taken the castle wherein is sheltered the Holy Grail.'

And Percival sayeth, 'Can this be true? Is he dead?'

And she replieth, 'So help me God, it is true.'

'This then is evil tidings indeed for I had hoped to see him again and bring an end to his troubles.'

'Alas, Sire,' sayeth the damsel, 'for you I also bring yet more bad tidings for I also know now that none may help my mother nor I but my brother for whom I have sought these many years. The castle will soon be lost, for soon the Lord of the Moors will begin warring upon us again and we will have to abandon it and go to my uncle the hermit King Pelles.' Thus weeping in great sorrow that her long search for her brother had been in vain she rode beside Percival through the valleys, mountains and castles that were all robbed of her mother by the Lord of the Moors.

As they drew night the castle the Widow Lady therein looked out and saw her daughter with a knight. 'Fairest God,' she sayeth, 'grant that this knight may be my son without whose aid I shall lose this castle and his inheritance.'

And Percival remembered the chapel built on four columns of marble that lay between the castle and the forest and where his father did teach him of the story of knights and how there be none of greater worth than a good knight. Also remembered he of the coffin therein that would not open for any save the best knight in the world. And Percival made to ride past the chapel but the damsel sayeth, 'Sire, no knight should pass the chapel but should enter to see the coffin.'

At this, he alighted and lay down his sword and lance and entered the chapel. Therein he came to the rich coffin and lay his hand upon it. The coffin did then open to show him that was inside. And the damsel fell at his feet for pure joy. With this, the Widow Lady entered in to the chapel with her five ancient knights. She seeth that the coffin was opened and her daughter was full of great joy and she knoweth that this knight was her son and ran to him to kiss and embrace him. 'Know I now well,' sayeth she, 'that our Lord God hath not forgotten me but hath brought me my son.' And then sayeth she, 'My beloved son, none may doubt that you are the best knight in the world. Only for you hath the coffin opened.' All therein then prayed as the Widow Lady sent for her chaplain who came and did read letters from within the coffin, and he sayeth that the body inside was that of one of the good men who took our Lord down from the Cross. This was true for within the coffin were iron pincers all bloody with the sacred blood that had pulled the nails from the Cross. And they saluteth the Lord with full reverence before leaving the chapel whereon the coffin did close up again.

And the Widow Lady did take Percival to her castle and telleth him of the shame that hath befallen her and of how Gawain did gain her the grace of one year and a day from the warring of the Lord of the Moors, which was soon to end. But she sayeth, 'Now I know that I shall be guarded well by you against him that coverts this castle. He is a knight most horrible and without due cause hath robbed me of my valleys and castles. Now I claim none of this land save only enough for my tomb. The land is yours and you may avenge yourself and your family as you may and as God may permit. Remember, Son, you do no wrong if you hurt an enemy of your family but remember also that the scriptures sayeth that none should do evil to their enemies, but pray to God that He amend their ways. Now you are come I have no anger against my enemies but wish them to return to righteous ways. As the scriptures sayeth, "To curse a sinner is to curse yourself." My son, before I go to face the Guardians of Heaven's gates it is the greatest wish of my heart that you amend for the shame that you have earned by not asking the question of the Holy Grail. Since you did not ask the question the Fisher King fell into great ailment from which no respite could he find. But such could have only been at the command of God and we must all yield to His will and pleasure.'

On hearing this, Percival felt courage flow through him and he determined upon a path of honour for the sake of his family and his name before God.

On the morrow, one of the ancient knights of the Widow Lady was in the forest hunting when he came upon the Lord of the Moors, an evil knight who had robbed the Widow Lady of much of her land and now waited for the time but a few days distant that would end the year and a day promised to Gawain before he would fall yet again upon the Widow Lady. And the Lord of the Moors asketh the knight why he hunted in his forest. And the knight replieth that the forest did not belong to the Lord of the Moors but to the Widow Lady, and her son, Percival, was come to obtain the return of the land. At this, the Lord of the Moors knew much anger and did slay the knight with his sword.

When the body of the slain knight was returned to the castle the Widow Lady sayeth to her son, 'This is the manner of gift I receive from the Lord of the Moors. He taketh my land and put my knights to the sword. Since before you were born he hath robbed me of my land and you were baptised with the name "Percival" to remind you of the valleys that he hath taken.'

At this, Percival took two of the ancient knights and rode in to the forest until they came upon a castle from whence issued five knights all full armed. And Percival sayeth, 'Whose men are you?'

And they sayeth, 'We are men of the Lord of the Moors and we go to seek the son of the Widow Lady. If we shall find him we shall have great reward from our lord.'

'Then, Sires,' sayeth Percival, 'look no further for I am he.' With this his spurred his horse and rode at the first knight and thrust his lance though him that he fall to the ground slain. The ancient knights did also ride forward and knocked two knights from their horse wounding them grievously. The two knights remaining tried to flee but Percival faced them and they did lay down their weapons. Thereupon did Percival take them prisoner and took them with the wounded knights to the castle of his mother. There he sayeth to her, 'Lady, here are four prisoner knights in exchange for the knight you did lose. Also is there another knight who lies slain upon the ground as did your knight in giving message to the Lord of the Moors.'

And the Widow Lady sayeth, 'Thank you, my son, but rather would I have peace than another slain knight and prisoners.'

'Lady,' he sayeth, 'I can only act as God provides. Where he sendeth warriors I can only fight them as a warrior. When he sendeth peaceable knights I shall be at peace with them.'

When the Lord of the Moors heard that Percival had slain one of his knights and taken four others his wrath grew greatly and he gave command that he would grant a castle to any knight that would take the son of the Widow Lady. And thus came eight knights all armed and did chase the deer in the forest near the castle of the Widow Lady that they might be seen from its walls.

After Mass, the Damsel Dindrane did say to Percival, 'Sire, by the grace of God I have a piece of cloth from the most Holy Shroud without which this castle and the land may not be reconquered. Pray hold it full reverently for it is as a shield of God.'

And Percival did hold the cloth with much reverence and kissed it and put it to his forehead before placing it next to his heart.

Percival did then arm himself fully as did the four ancient knights. They then mounted their horses and issued from the castle like lions unchained. And they came to the eight knights and asked of them whose men they were and they answered that they were men of the Lord of the Moors and were come to take the son of the Widow Lady. And Percival sayeth, 'Not unless God wills it!' At this, Percival and his knights ran at the others and knocked five from their horses. The remaining knights did run upon Percival but were brought down in a great tumble.

And the noise of combat did sound through the forest and did fall upon the ears of the Lord of the Moors who hunteth nearby and he came at full gallop.

As the prisoners were taken to the castle one of the ancient knights did say to Percival, 'Look, Sire! Here cometh the Lord of the Moors, the knight who hath robbed your mother of many castles and much land and hath slain many of her knights.' And Percival turned and looked upon the Lord of the Moors as he came at full gallop at him.

The good knight made the sign of the Cross upon his breast and commended his spirit unto God and run full hard at the Lord of the Moors. They did hurtle with much violence and the lance of Percival did splinter as he brought down the knight and his horse together. As the Lord of the Moors lay upon the ground Percival alighted and drew his sword whereupon the Lord of the Moors sayeth, 'Hold, Sire! Would you slay me?'

'No, Sire, not yet, for there is more for you to do before I send you to the pit of Hell where you belong.'

And the Lord of the Moors then jumped up with his sword and sayeth, 'I go nowhere at your command or that of your mother who this day shall find shelter only with the beggars.' With this, he ran upon Percival and struck him hard upon the helmet. But Percival stood beneath the blow and did strike back wounding the Lord of the Moors so that he was disarmed.

The Lord of the Moors was taken in to the castle where Percival did say to his mother, 'Here, Lady, is the Lord of the Moors that would take this castle from you for this he intended to do today as the year and a day grace obtain by Gawain is now ended.'

And the Widow Lady sayeth, 'God be praised!'

Then the Lord of the Moors sayeth, 'Lady, though your castle should be mine by conquest, your son hath taken me and my knights. I therefore yield to you this castle on condition that you let my knights and myself go free.'

But before the Widow Lady could answer, Percival sayeth, 'No, this will not be! For it sayeth in the scriptures, even in the Old and New Laws of God, that murderers and oppressors shall suffer His justice. You have done my mother great shame and slain her knights. No pity did you show her or her daughter. And I will not disobey the command of God but shall do His work and bring you His justice.' With this, Percival had brought forth all the prisoner knights and had their heads struck off and their blood poured in to a large cauldron. And he then drowned the Lord of the Moors in the blood saying, 'You wanted the satisfaction of the blood of the knights of my mother, now know the satisfaction of the blood of your own knights.'

The heads and bodies of the knights and the Lord of the Moors were taken to a bone pit and cast therein and the blood was taken and poured in to a stream which did turn red.

And when tidings of this spread throughout the land, many knights did return to the Widow Lady and many brought keys to the castles that had been robbed of her so that now she hath much contentment save for the loss of her brother the good Fisher King.

One day as the Widow Lady sat at meat with Percival and the Damsel Dindrane, the Damsel of the Carriage and her two companions came in to the hall and saluteth them with honour. And they sayeth to Percival, 'Sire, God be praised that right speedily did you bring comfort to your mother. Now, Sire, may you bring equal haste to your destiny and go to the castle of the Fisher King for there the law of God is denied. The King of Castle Mortal doth rule there and sayeth that he shall give aid to those who deny the law of God but will destroy those who keep their faith.'

And the Widow Lady sayeth, 'Fairest son, great sorrow am I in that this evil man is of my family.'

And Percival sayeth, 'Lady, no longer is he your brother or my uncle since he hath denied God. For this we should hate him more than any infidel.'

'My son,' sayeth the Widow Lady, 'I pray that you never will forget or neglect the laws of Our Saviour for no better Lord can you serve, nor one that will give you reward as will He. Remember, son, that none can be good knights who do not serve and love the Lord. Always be swift in His service and delay not His work. Be forever at His command whether it be eventide or morning so that you shall honour your family. May He grant you the courage to go on to the end even as you have begun.'

And the Widow Lady and her daughter did rise and go to the chapel there to pray for Percival that he might receive long life for he was known throughout the world for his wisdom and his courtesy as well as for his valour.

Part the XVIth

King Arthur and Queen Guinevere were sat at meat with Lancelot and Gawain at Castle Cardoil when two knights entered the great hall. They carried before them the bodies of two knights that were full armed even though the knights were slain. And the knights sayeth to King Arthur, 'Sire, the loss of these two knights has come about through your most fearful enemy. This shame will further lose you many knights unless God shall show you great mercy.'

And the King sayeth, 'What hath brought this evil about?'

'Sire,' sayeth they, 'the Knight of the Dragon has entered your realm and destroys your knights and castles. None may contend with him for he is of greater height than any that live and carries a sword that is three times longer than any sword carried by other knights. His lance is more heavy than a knight may carry and two knights may shelter under his shield. On that shield is the image of the head of a dragon which sends forth flames at his adversaries. None may stand against him for he destroys all that so do.'

Sayeth the King, 'from whence doth such a knight come?'

'He comes from the Land of the Giants and is sore displeased for the death of the giant Logrin, the head of whom was brought to you by Kay. He is come, Sire, to take vengeance on your body or on the knight that you love best.'

'Then we must look to God for our protection,' sayeth the King. But he was sore afraid inside and asked Lancelot and Gawain for their counsel. And Lancelot sayeth that he and Gawain should depart and meet this fearful enemy and bring him down. But the King sayeth, 'No. Not for a King's ransom would I allow you to go. For methinks that this is not a knight but a fiend from Hell. Truly, any knight that conquers him will win great renown, but you are my best knights and I will not place you in peril. You shall stay by my side and come the day we shall face him together.'

But there was great dismay in the court that no one would go forth against the Knight of the Dragon.

Part the XVIIth

Percival departed from his mother and sister and entered the forest and came upon a wide clearing wherein stood a tall red Cross. On one side of the clearing was a young knight dressed in white robes and bearing a golden dish. On the other was a fair young damsel in white also bearing a golden dish. As Percival did look a strange and beauteous beast, the like of which he had never before seen, ran from the woods crying piteously. The beast, all white and with eyes as green as emeralds, ran to the young knight as if for aid but comfort there was none. The beast then ran to the damsel but again could find no comfort. It then ran to Percival who reached from his saddle as if to pick the beast up and give it comfort but, at this, the young knight cried out saying, 'No, Sire! Do not hold him for he must endure his fate.'

The beast then ran to the Cross and within its shade twelve small dogs came through its mouth from the inside of the beast where they had been biting and clawing. The beast then tried by showing signs of submission to crawl to the Cross but the dogs did leap on it and tear it apart and then ran howling into the forest. With this, the young knight and the damsel came to the Cross and picked up the parts of the beast and put them on the golden dishes with the blood thereon. They then kissed the ground and the Cross full reverently before entering the forest.

Percival came to the Cross in wonderment at the mystery he had seen and in like manner kissed the Cross in adoration. At this, a voice called to him in great agitation saying, 'Stand back from that Cross, Sire! You have no right to be near it!' He looked and saw two priests coming from the forest and the first priest fell to his knees at the foot of the Cross and began to adore it in a most worshipful manner. But the second priest did push the first one to the side and began to beat the Cross with a large rod whilst weeping loudly.

Percival looked on in anger and sayeth sharply, 'What sort of priest are you, that you behave in such a manner?'

And the priest sayeth, 'Who we are, Sire, or what we do is no concern of yours!'

And Percival was much angered but would not cause harm to a priest. Therefore he did ride into the forest where he came upon a knight full armed who rode towards him saying, 'For God's sake, Sire, look to your safety!'

'Who are you?' sayeth Percival.

'I am the Knight Coward, Sire, and I am a man of the damsel of the shorn hair.'

'But, Sire, if you are a coward, why are you dressed as if for combat.'

'For I hope to delay any knight that would come at me, Sire, and thus escape being slain.'

'Are you truly a coward, Sire?'

'I am, Sire, and much more.'

'By the wounds of Christ, Sire, no knight should have a name like yours. Come with me, Sire, and I shall have it changed for you are a knight of brave appearance.'

'Dear God, no!' sayeth the Knight Coward. 'Do you wish to see me slain? I have no wish to change my courage nor my name for no good knight will do me harm when he knoweth me to be a coward.'

'Then, Sire, you will be slain for not all knights are good. Now ride ahead of me so that I may see you and that you may not retreat.' And the Knight Coward did so with much grudging.

Not far had they ridden when they heard the cry of two damsels bewailing loudly and they did seek out the sound and saw a tall man full armed driving two damsels before him with a large rod and they had blood on their faces. And Percival came up to them and sayeth, 'Hold, Sire. Why do you treat these damsels thus?'

And he sayeth. 'These damsels have taken mine inheritance which was given to them by Gawain.'

And the damsels sayeth, 'In God's name, Sire, come to our aid for this is a robber who lives in the forest and is the last of his family. The others were slain by Gawain, Lancelot, and another knight and the victor knights gave our father the robber's horses and to us they gave the robber's house and treasures. Now he is come to slay us. Pray, Sires, help us in the name of all that is Holy.'

Percival sayeth, 'This is true what they say, for I was there when they were given the house and the treasures.'

'Then,' sayeth the robber, 'you it was that did slay my kindred. Now I shall have my vengeance.'

And the Knight Coward sayeth to Percival, 'Take no heed of what he sayeth, Sire. Let us withdraw and leave this place unharmed.'

'No, Sire,' sayeth Percival, 'we cannot leave these damsels thus with honour.'

'Indeed, Sire,' sayeth the Knight Coward, 'I can.'

And Percival sayeth to the robber, 'I have here mine own champion who will defend the damsels on my behalf.' And he took his horse back to leave the Knight Coward facing the robber. The Knight Coward looked all ways to flee but could not with Percival behind him.

With this the robber did run hard at the Knight Coward and broke his lance against the knight's shield, but the Knight Coward sat all straight and did not fall from the saddle. And Percival cried out, 'Knight! This is my honour you defend and the honour of the damsels.' But the knight remained unmoved still seeking flight.

The robber then drew his sword and ran hard at the Knight Coward and struck him hard upon his helmet but the knight moved not. Thereon the robber did strike him many times about the helmet and body until blood ran from the Knight Coward's mouth. With this, the Knight Coward sayeth, 'Sire, I am now wounded and it seemeth to me that you intend to slay me. Such is truly the act of a coward that he would harm another who doth not harm him.' And the Knight Coward drew his sword and ran full hard at the robber and knocked him from his horse. He then alighted and struck the head off the robber and gave it to Percival saying, 'This, Sire, is the trophy from my first combat.'

And Percival sayeth, 'I thank you, Sire. Remember now that you are a knight and fall not back in to the ways of the coward for it is too great a shame to be born by a knight.'

The knight replieth, 'Nor will I, Sire, and greatly do I wish I had done this long back for never would I have been treated with contempt when I should have earned honour.'

And Percival sayeth, 'Knight, I commend these two damsels to your care. Take them back to the house from which they have been removed by the robber and see them safely therein. Also, Sire, from this time forth you shall be known as the Knight Hardy for it is a more honourable and true name than that you did come here with.'

The damsels thanked Percival and rode off with the knight they now did name Knight Hardy.

Percival crossed mountains and forests until he reached the land about Cardoil, the castle of King Arthur. And the land was spoiled and laid waste and Percival asked the people why this was so and they say unto him that a knight did war upon the King and the knight was such that no other knight could endure against him. Percival rode to the castle and alighted before the great hall. There he was met by Lancelot and Gawain who made great joy of him as likewise did King Arthur and his Queen. All the court that know of him were in great joy and those who knew him not gazed upon him in wonderment for his valour went before him.

As the court sat to meat the door of the hall opened and four knights came in each bearing the body of a slain knight. All the slain were as if struck by lightning. And the knights sayeth to the King, 'Sire, again great shame is put upon this land by the Knight of the Dragon. He comes and destroys as is his want and sayeth that none in this court dare face him.' And Lancelot and Gawain are much troubled that the King will not allow them to meet the Knight of the Dragon. And the many knights in the hall did murmur that there was none amongst them who could meet such a knight.

At this, the damsel who bore the body of the knight on the litter entered the hall and sayeth to the King, 'Sire, I beseech you that you give me your aid. For there beside you sits Gawain and the Knight of the Blue and Gold Shield that did contend at the assembly in the Red Land. And both were known to be brave knights but the Knight of the Blue and Gold Shield endured the longer. But he did leave the field and I have not found him to ask that he should fulfil the wish of my heart.

Percival then sayeth to Gawain, 'Sire, it seemeth to me that you were the best knight at the assembly.'

But Gawain sayeth, 'I thank you, Sire, but it is your courtesy that speaks. The knights assembled all gave you the prize, and rightly so.'

And the damsel sayeth, 'Nor should he deny me that which I ask for the knight whose body I bear is the son of his uncle, Elinant of Escavalon.'

With this, the countenance of Percival did change and he sayeth, 'Make sure you say the truth, damsel, for well I know that Elinant of Escavalon was the brother of my father, but of a son I know nothing.'

'He, Sire,' sayeth the damsel, 'was Alein of Escavalon and well deserve he for his deeds to be known for he was of much valour and, had he lived, would have been among the best knights in the world. The Damsel of the Circlet of Gold did love him greatly and sayeth that upon whoever doth avenge him shall she bestow the Circlet of Gold although she hold it great regard for it is most Holy. There can be, Sire, no greater reward for any knight.'

'Damsel,' sayeth Percival, 'know you where the Knight of the Dragon now is?'

'I do, Sire. He is on the Isles of the Orchards where he hath committed great outrage on a land that was once among the fairest. Even now he is close by the Castle of the Damsel of the Golden Circlet and it grieves her heart to see her knights taken by him and slain.'

And Percival thinketh to himself that God has put this adventure upon him and thus it was the command of God that he should seek out the Knight of the Dragon and put an end to his outrages. And so he departed from the castle in company with Gawain and Lancelot as the King gave his command that all the hermits around Castle Cardoil should pray to God for his safe protection for no knight had ever faced such danger as he. And he was followed by the damsel who brought the slain knight.

They came upon an open land before the forest and saw there a great castle surrounded by running waters and girdled with high walls. And the castle did turn as doth a potter's wheel. It turned faster than the wind and the knights marvelled much for such a castle they had not seen and the damsel sayeth that it was the Castle of Great Endeavour. At the gate were many chained lions and bears all roaring and the sound of great copper horns made the ground shake. On the walls were seen many bowmen with arrows of copper that no armour could withstand. And the damsel sayeth that Lancelot and Gawain should not go near for they would fall to the bowmen. She sayeth to Percival that she should take his shield and lance and go to the castle walls to announce him, for none save the knight who go to battle with the Knight of the Dragon and seek out the Golden Circlet and the Holy Grail may be received into the castle. And Gawain and Lancelot were sore grieved that they may not give their fellowship to Percival who took his leave of them with great sorrowfulness saying, 'I commend you to the Saviour of the World.'

And they replied, 'May he that died upon the Cross defend your body, your spirit, and your life.'

With that he rode after the damsel who showed his shield to the castle. He rode over three bridges that raised behind him and showed such courage that the lions and bears did hide from him and the castle stopped its turning as he entered.

When Gawain and Lancelot saw the castle had stopped its turning they rode close as if to enter in aid of their brother knight, Lancelot. At this, a knight came to the castle wall and cried, 'Hold, Sires! If you come closer the bowmen will let loose upon you, the castle will turn again and the bridges be lowered.' They did stop and heard from the castle the sound of much joy and the people saying that the knight had come who would save them from the knight who bore the spirit of the Devil. And the two knights turned away in great sorrow and rode into the forest.

Ere long had passed, Gawain and Lancelot came unto the land wherein lay the Waste City. And Lancelot sayeth to Gawain, 'Now, Sire, it seemeth that God hath ordained that I am to be slain.'

Gawain sayeth, 'No, Sire. This cannot be. Why should God so ordain?'

'For he hath directed me here.' And Lancelot told Gawain of the young knight whose head he had struck off at the knight's request, and how he should return to the Waste City within a year to meet the same fate.

'Then, Sire,' sayeth Gawain, 'I shall stand by your side and do all I can to end this foolishness for neither the world nor the King nor, Sire, even I, can allow the unworthy death of so good a knight.'

'But I know full well, Sire,' sayeth Lancelot, 'that you would follow your word with your honour had the eye of God fallen upon you, and thus must do I.' And Lancelot raised his hand in salute and turned to the city.

As he did so, a knight was seen issuing from the Waste City and, upon coming near it, was seen that he was none other but the Poor Knight of the Waste Forest, who sayeth to Lancelot, 'Sire, that you have done much good by me and by my sisters I have come to an accord with the people of the Waste City that you shall not be bound by your promise to return until forty days after the most Holy Grail shall be achieved. That, Sire, is all the further life I could obtain for you. Pray remember, Sire, this loyalty you have found in me.'

'I shall never forget it, Sire, and I thank you for putting off the day until after I shall rejoice at the achievement of the Sacred Chalice.'

And the Poor Knight returned to the Waste City and Lancelot and Gawain rode towards Castle Cardoil wherein was King Arthur.

Part the XVIIIth

And the people of the Turning Castle are in such joy as was unknown before. It had been prophesied that the castle would not cease its turning until a knight should come who was golden haired, who had the look of a lion, and a heart of steel. He had to pure and chaste, be without taint of wickedness, be of great valour, and firm in his belief in God. Also he had to bear the shield of Joseph of Arimathea who had taken Our Saviour down from the Cross. Such a knight was Percival and no other. Now released of their dread of the Knight of the Dragon they saved their souls by being baptised in the laws of God.

Percival was right glad when he saw the people turn to God. And the damsel sayeth unto him, 'Sire, now you must finish that which you are started on. And it must be finished soon for the Knight of the Dragon doth destroy much of the land and many knights are slain.'

After Mass on the morrow, Percival rode from the castle in company with the damsel who took the body of the knight Alein of Escavalon, the cousin of Percival. They rode until they came to the Isles of the Orchards wherein lay the Castle of the Golden Circlet. They entered the castle and did find the Queen of the Golden Circlet in great sorrow, and she took them to the castle wall and there did show them the Knight of the Dragon sat on his horse with four slain knights on the ground. The Queen sayeth, 'There, Sire, is the cause of great misery through the land for no knight shall conquer him.' But Percival looked upon him silently and sayeth nothing. And the Queen sayeth, 'Four of my best knights hath he slain this day. But you, Sire, who have no force nor aid from other knights, if you can defeat him I shall give you right willingly the sacred Golden Circlet for I can see from your shield that you are a Christian knight. Should you defeat him it will show that the true God was born of man and liveth in Heaven.

At this, Percival was right glad. He crossed himself and touched his forehead and left the castle followed by the damsel. As they reached the open ground beyond the castle gate, the damsel sayeth, 'I have carried the body of this knight to the site where he was slain. Now, Sire, you may have your cousin for I have done all that was right in the sight of God.' With this, she returned to the castle to stand by the side of the Queen.

Percival looked to the Knight of the Dragon and seeth that the knight was of height greater than any he had known or heard of. He held before him a great black shield which bore the image of a dragon that turned its head and sent forth a stream of flame that carried a great stench.

And the Knight of the Dragon seeth Percival and was in great scorn for Percival came to the field alone. Thus the Knight of the Dragon took not up his lance but his sword that was long and burned with red heat.

Percival couched his lance and raised his shield and gave spur to his horse that he ran at full pace at the Knight of the Dragon thinking to smite him through the breast. But the knight raised his shield and the dragon thereon breathed a fire that burned the lance of Percival to the very gauntlet. At this, the knight brought his sword down upon the helmet of Percival but the good knight raised his shield and the blow fell upon the red cross made by Our Saviour's blood and harmed him not. And the Knight of the Dragon looked upon this in wonder for none he had faced had so survived such a great knock. He then rode to the body of the knight brought by the damsel and sayeth to Percival, 'Have you charge of the burial of this knight?'

'I have,' sayeth Percival.

And the Knight of the Dragon turned his shield against the body of the slain knight and burned it to ashes and sayeth, 'Now you have nothing but ashes to bury, how think you now?' And Percival was in great wroth at this discourtesy and ran hard at the knight and did bring his sword down upon the black shield and cleft it almost to the head of the dragon. But the Knight of the Dragon did hit Percival on the shoulder and cut him most deep. As they parted, Percival saw that his sword now burned red from the flame of the dragon. He ran again at the knight and thrust his burning sword down the throat of the dragon and the dragon did roar with a great loudness and turned its head away from Percival and sent a river of fire at its bearer. And the Knight of the Dragon was burned to ashes. The dragon now free from the shield went to the sky as if returning lightning and could not be seen.

And the Queen came to him and had him taken in to the castle and had his wounds cleaned and cared for, and the damsel took up a handful of the ash of the Knight of the Dragon and put it on the wounds of Percival that they heal the quicker. The Queen then sayeth that all her knights should be at the command of Percival and she returneth Percival his sword and sayeth that those who would not be baptised should die by it. She then placed the Circlet of Gold upon his head and he baptised her in the name of the Lord and she took the name of Elysa in His name. Many came to be baptised in the name of Our Saviour. And they knew Percival by the name of the Knight of the Golden Circlet and his name was spread through the land and when it came to King Arthur and Gawain and Lancelot at Castle Cardoil they knew not which knight it was that had destroyed the Knight of the Dragon.

When he was made whole, Percival departed from the Castle of the Golden Circlet leaving the sacred Circlet under the protection of the Queen, now known as Elysa. And he rode long in to the forest until he came upon a mighty castle known as the Castle of Copper. In the castle was a great copper bull that was worshipped most horribly by the people and it bellowed most mightily that it could be heard throughout all the land. At the gate of the castle were two giants made of copper who fought each other with great iron hammers, and no one could enter the castle for they would be crushed by the hammers or the feet of the copper giants.

And Percival did come close to the castle gate and saw the copper giants. As he did so a loud voice from above sayeth that he might go past the giants in safety and, believing in our Lord, he came to the gate and the giants did stop their fighting and allowed him to enter without harm. Inside he found many people who worshipped the bull and did not follow God and His laws, and none were armed for they believed that strangers could not enter the gates past the copper giants. And Percival seeth that they kneel down in adoration of the bull that bellowed loudly and he knew them to be wrong in their worship. The voice then told him to gather up the people in the great hall which he did. He then made them all pass through the gate to see which of them would believe in the true God. One thousand and five hundred put he through the gate but thirteen only did escape the iron hammers. And the copper bull did melt and the Devil therein fled. The thirteen believers were baptised and put the bodies of the unbelievers in to the waters known as the River of Hell which flowed to the sea as a great pestilence. They then departed for the forest where they built hermitages and did penance for the rest of their lives for the time they had spent worshipping the copper bull.

Percival then repaired to the house of the King Hermit who greeted him with great joy. In telling of his adventures the knight asked of the King Hermit if he knew the meaning of a strange sight he had seen in a clearing in the forest. And he told the King Hermit of the white beast which had disgorged twelve dogs. And the King Hermit sayeth unto him that the white beast signified our Lord Jesus Christ and the dogs were the twelve tribes of Israel who had not followed the laws of God and did set our Lord upon the Cross where His body was torn and rent. And the twelve dogs were scattered throughout the forest as the twelve tribes were scattered throughout the world, where they live without the protection of God until they give full reverence to our Lord. And the knight and the damsel signify the divinity of our Lord and they did collect the torn beast in their golden dishes, for as the scriptures say that he was raised to Heaven to join His Father.

'But what, Sire, of the two priests? One of whom did worship the Cross most reverently but the other beat it with a rod as he wept most piteously.'

And the King Hermit sayeth that the first priest, whose name was Jonas, worshipped the Cross for on it God had died for our sins and he was indeed much grateful for the sacrifice of our Lord. Alexis, the second priest, did believe the Cross to be the giver of great pain and suffering to our Lord and he had deep wroth that our Lord should suffer pain so.

Percival told also of the Knight of the Dragon and sayeth that he had never seen a knight so big and horrible. The King Hermit sayeth that only a most pure knight could have overcome such a devil and it was a good thing for now that devil hath returned to other devils who do nought but torment each other. The devil had burned the body of the slain knight but it had no power to burn his soul. And the Turning Castle was also the work of a devil and Percival had stopped it turning and converted the people therein by his goodness, for nothing can prevent the will of a pure and good knight.

And Percival sayeth that he had sore missed the fellowship of Gawain and Lancelot for they would have been full in his aid. But the King Hermit sayeth that they could not for though they be good and hardy knights who worshipped the true God, they were not pure and chaste.

And the King Hermit sayeth to Percival, 'Since you were made a knight you have done much good work in the name of Our Saviour. Had you not destroyed the copper bull and its believers they were have remained so until the end of the world. You have had much suffering but you must endure it willingly for no honour comes without pain. Now, Sire, you are ready to do the one thing for which God cries out. All of those that live in the land of the Fisher King no longer live in the laws of God for fear of the King of Castle Mortal who hath taken the Castle of the Holy Grail. Though he be your uncle and my brother, you are the only mortal who can claim the castle by right for the good Fisher King was your uncle and brother of your mother. Now it is in the hands of a man who is disloyal to God and a traitor to his family. You should know that the castle is strengthened by nine bridges each guarded by three strong knights. The knights and priests of the Fisher King are scattered and the chapel of the Holy Grail is empty. No other enterprise, Sire, should God so willingly see carried out in His name.'

'So you commend, Sire, so shall I bend my will. There is no reason why he should have the castle. Of better right is my mother that was next-born to the Fisher King of whose death I am most sorrowful.'

'As indeed you must be, fair nephew. For it was on your account that the good Fisher King fell into languishment when you failed to ask the question of the Holy Grail. Had you returned it is said that you could have ended his suffering but I believe that God chose the way you have taken. I have with me a white horse that I wish you to have. Let your banner fly above her when you come upon the castle and you shall be availed of the power of God, for you will face twenty-seven knights guarding the bridges. No single knight can overcome them save by His power. I pray that you always have God and His sweet Mother in your mind. If you do and you face great danger let fly your banner as a messenger of the power of God and your enemies will lose their valour, for nothing will confound a foe more than the virtue and might of God. It is well known that you are the best knight in the world but rest not alone upon your knighthood or your strength but stiffen them with the virtue of God. And you should know that there are two lions at the gate, one is red, the other white. Always put your trust in the white for he takes the side of God, and if your might should fail, look him in the eyes and he will look at you and you shall know the will of God. When you know His will, do as He directs for then may you overcome those who combine against you and you shall pass the nine bridges and the knights that guard them. And may God grant that you pass them safe in body and set right the laws of our Lord where they have been trampled by your uncle.'

Percival departed after Mass and rode towards the castle of the Holy Grail whereupon he came across a hermit riding full fast, but the hermit did join him when he saw his shield. And the hermit sayeth, 'I see from your shield, Sire, that you are a Christian. None other have I seen this many days for the King of Castle Mortal hath driven them from the land. No men who worship God and His sweet Mother dare stay.'

And Percival sayeth, 'But you shall stay, Sire, for the honour of God was not won in retreat. He shall lead you and I shall ride with you. Are there more hermits in the forest?'

'There are, Sire, twelve in number and they assemble by the Cross at the edge of the forest. We are minded to go to another part of England and there do penance for we must abandon our chapels for fear of the dread King that hath seized the land. This King doth demand that we live not under the laws of God.'

They rode to the Cross and found there the hermits amongst whom was Joseus, the son of the King Hermit, and Percival and Joseus did greet each other well and with great joy. Percival sayeth to the hermits, 'Sires, you are holy men and the bearers of God's message on Earth, to you the people from kings and knights to soldiers and ploughmen look for guidance in this life. God has now granted you a test of your holy valour wherein others may reflect their own courage on behalf of God. Shall you be seen to be wanting in holy hardiness? Will you allow the enemy of God to prevail? Will you stand with me in the service of God?'

And the hermit Joseus stepped forward and sayeth, 'I shall stand with you.'

And the other hermits stepped forward also and sayeth they will stand with him also.

Percival sayeth, 'God be praised that He hath such good men in His service. Follow me, Sires, and pray as never before that God's work may be done.'

And they went their way to the Castle of the Holy Grail and came upon a chapel like unto that before Camelot. Percival put his shield and lance at the door and entered, whereon a tomb before the altar did open of its own accord and the hermits were struck with wonderment for the tomb had never before opened. And inside lay the sweet smelling body of one of the good men who had taken the body of Christ from the Cross as at Camelot, and the company of hermits prayed with full reverence at the discovery and sayeth that God had sent them the best knight in all the world for their protection.

Their devotions completed, Percival led them to the castle where they beheld the nine bridges each guarded by three hardy knights. The knights had heard that the tomb had opened for Percival and were sore afraid but the King of Castle Mortal sayeth to them that Percival was but one knight and could fall from the blows of another single knight.

Percival crossed himself and commended his life unto God as the hermits knelt in prayer. He then lowered his lance and raised his shield and ran full tilt at the knights guarding the first bridge. The knights all fell upon him and broke their lances on his shield. One knight he knocked from the bridge with his sword and, though the others fought long and hard, they fell slain also in to the river below.

He then came to the second bridge and the three knights came at him with great hardiness. One he struck slain from his horse but the others gave many blows in reply to his. At this, the hermit Joseus asked of the other hermits if to go to the aid of Percival would be a sin. And they sayeth that God's work can never be a sin. He then threw back his grey cloak and showeth his armour beneath. He unsheathed his sword and rode across the first bridge and fell upon one of the knights and sent him to the ground slain. Percival then sent his enemy to the river below where he drowned. And Percival was greatly tired by the combat and knoweth that he had not the strength for the knights guarding the next bridge. But he looked up and saw the eyes of the white lion and he heard the voice of God saying to go back across the first bridge. Taking Joseus, he obeyed God's command and returned to the hermits. As he did so he looked back and saw the first bridge rise up that would have entrapped him but for the eyes of the lion. And the lion seeing the bridge raise up broke its chains and ran with a great roar across the bridges and did bring the first bridge down again that Percival may continue his way to the castle gate.

And Percival made to spur his horse on again but met the eyes of the lion and he then crieth to the hermit Joseus, 'Take up my banner and follow me!' And Joseus took up the banner with its field of white and the cross of red and rode beside Percival. And the knights of the third bridge were sore afraid at their coming. The first knight received the lance of Percival though his breast and fell slain. The others put their arms aloft and did plead for mercy which the hermit Joseus sayeth to Percival to be a good thing. And so their lives were spared. Thus it was with the knights of the fourth bridge and they promised to be good Christians from then on.

Percival did then think in him that the virtue and might of God was most powerful, but a good knight should do the work of God from his own valour. Surely God would be much pleased with a knight who suffered on His behalf as He had suffered for mankind. At this, Percival sent the hermit Joseus and the banner back across the bridges they had taken.

Percival rode at the knights guarding the fifth bridge and found them to be of much hardiness. None would be knocked from his horse nor would they bend before his lance. With this, the hermit Joseus took up the banner once again and rode to join Percival. Ere long all the knights at the fifth bridge were slain and Percival came to understand that trying to do the work of God without God's aid was for the foolish, not for the worthy.

The knights guarding the sixth and seventh bridges saw the work of God and threw down their arms and begged for mercy which, on the advice of the hermit Joseus, Percival did grant. At this, the red lion did burst from its chains and in great rage did fall upon the knights of the eighth bridge and slay them that they should not set like example to the knights of the final bridge. And the white lion did attack the red lion and tear it to pieces. The white lion did then raise it up to its hind legs and looked at Percival who understood that the banner should be retired with the hermit Joseus and that no mercy should be shown to the knights of the ninth bridge, for they were hard in their condemnation of God and were foremost in the service of their master.

The hermit Joseus returned to the other hermits and bade them mount their horses. He then stayed at their centre and raised the banner, but in accordance with the wishes of Percival did not go beyond the eighth bridge. At this, the knights guarding the ninth bridge think to them that they should plead for mercy but only in falsity for they may then slay Percival in treacherous manner. But Percival knoweth in his mind the guidance of the white lion and bore down upon them full armed. But they cast aside their weapons and did not flee and Percival was most confounded for it was not seemly for him to slay knights who had disarmed themselves. As he came to them his knightly virtue came firm upon him and he raised up his lance and reached not for his sword. The white lion saw this and understood and fell upon the knights and did slay them for the treachery they bore in their hearts.

Then they heard a great cry from the walls of the castle and they did look up to see the King of Castle Mortal. The King drew his sword and thrust it in to his own body and did fall from the walls to the deep and fast water beneath. And they did wonder at this for they knew not why a King should die thus rather than in courageous combat. And they wondered more that the King should be the brother of the good Fisher King, the King Hermit and the Widowed Lady who had all lived virtuous lives. For wickedness is hard and beguiling and harmful to the soul, whereas goodness is kindly and simple and humble before God. But it seemeth to all that God hath ordained that evil men shall meet evil ends and that good men shall have their reward at the right hand of God.

Percival and the hermits did enter the castle and found the chapel of the Holy Grail was empty whereon the hermits did fall to praying to God for the return of the sacred objects once there within.

And the good knights who had served the Fisher King and had fled before the King of Castle Mortal heard of the arrival of Percival and returned all joyous and Percival made much welcome of them. And soon it was known that the Saviour of the World was well pleased with Percival and his deeds for a bright light as if of many candles was seen in the chapel and when the door was opened the Holy Grail and the Sacred Spear were seen within by the hermits with the sword by which Saint John the Baptist was beheaded and many other relics and images all bright with precious stones. And the tomb of the Fisher King was covered with a cloth of silver and gold and no one knew who had done this save only that it was done by command of our Lord.

Part the XIXth

That Whitsuntide King Arthur sat with his Queen and his many knights in the great hall at Castle Cardoil. And the King seeth that the light doth come in the windows at both sides of the hall. He sendeth a knight without the hall to enquire why this should be and the knight came back and sayeth, 'Sire, the sky now shows two suns, one in the east and one in the west.'

And the King thinketh that such be not possible but a great voice came in to the hall and sayeth, 'All is possible to the Lord God for now he showeth His great joy that the good knight who took the shield from this hall hath conquered the land that truly belonged to the Fisher King. The King of Castle Mortal is defeated and slain and the Holy Grail is now returned to the chapel. And the Lord God now demandeth that you make pilgrimage to the Castle of the Holy Grail, for when you return your faith shall be doubled and the people of Greater Britain shall thus give high and noble service to the Lord.'

At this, a richly clothed damsel of great beauty entered the hall carrying a golden box brightened with many jewels. She saluted the King and Queen most courteously and sayeth, 'Sire, I have come to your court for it is the most high in all the lands and I bring you this golden box as a gift. It has inside the head of a knight, but none may open the box save him that did slay the knight. I therefore pray you, Sire, that you may attempt to open the box, and if you fail, that your knights shall do likewise until he who hath slain this knight is revealed. And further, Sire, that the revealed knight may be given grace of forty days after you have made your pilgrimage to the Holy Grail.'

'Damsel,' sayeth the King, 'and shall we know who the dead knight is?'

'Truly, Sire, for inside are letters declaring his name and the name of the knight that did slay him.'

And the King placed his hand upon the box as if to open it but he could not. Then Gawain and Lancelot and all the knights followed and all tried but none could open it. At this, Kay entered the hall all boastful and sayeth, 'What is this? I have slain many knights and struck off their heads. If this knight be of much hardiness then he must be one who hath fallen to me. If this hall were filled with knights heads that I had struck off you would see that I am the knight most able to open the golden box.'

And the King sayeth, 'Come, Kay, we need not to hear of your boldness. Prove yourself with the opening of the box.'

Kay did take up the box and as soon as it felt his hand the box did open and reveal the head inside. And Kay sayeth, 'So I have sayeth, none other could do it but me. Even those you prize most high did fail. Therefore, Sire, you should think the more high of me.'

The King sent for one of his chaplains and sayeth to him that he should read the letter within the box. And the chaplain did look upon the letter and gave a great sigh and sayeth, 'Sire, my Lady, these letters sayeth that the head therein is that of the knight named Lohot, the son of King Arthur and Queen Guinevere. He had slain the giant Logrin and, tired from his endeavours, did fall asleep. Then upon them came Kay and he struck off the head of the sleeping knight and of the giant and took the head of the giant to the King in false claim that he had slain the giant.'

At this, the Queen fell into a swoon and the King near fell down in horror for he had thought that his son had been the good knight whom had defeated the King of Castle Mortal and caused the return of the Holy Grail and the sacred relics. Kay fled and the court fell in to deep mourning. And all were in despair that the damsel had made covenant that he who had slain the knight might not meet God's justice until forty days after King Arthur made the pilgrimage to the Holy Grail.

When the King could be raised from his mourning, Lancelot sayeth to him, 'Sire, the time hath come when you should make a pilgrimage to the Castle of the Holy Grail for you have made a covenant with God so to do.' And the King was ready but the Queen could not be roused from her mourning for her son.

And the King sendeth the head of his son to the Chapel of Our Lady at Avalon where there was a hermit that was much loved of our Lord. Then the King departeth in company of Gawain and Lancelot and a squire to carry their arms.

Kay did leave England and went to Lesser Britain where he lodged with Briant of the Isles. And Kay did tell Briant of the woe that had befallen King Arthur and that the King was on pilgrimage to the Castle of the Holy Grail. Briant was a knight of much hardiness and many knight and castles and who had no love for King Arthur. Thus he began to war against King Arthur and his land and his castles.

Part the XXth

King Arthur in company with Gawain and Lancelot and a squire rode long in to the forest but could find neither house nor castle for their lodging that night. And they sent the squire up a tall tree to see if such lodging is in sight and he sayeth that he can see a ruined house where a fire burned therein. And they go there and pass over a wattle bridge into a courtyard and can see the fire burning hot in the house. They entered the house and sat by the fire all armed, and the squire did go in to a chamber and did prompt issue forth crying unto the Holy Mother. And they asked him what aileth him and he sayeth that the chamber is full of many dead men. Lancelot rose from the fire and entered the chamber and saw a great heap of dead men. But when he returneth Gawain sayeth that there is nought to be feared from dead men, and God would save them from the living.

At this, a damsel of great beauty entered the house lamenting and saying, 'Dearest God, how long must I suffer this penance, when will it come to an end?' The damsel wore clothes all torn and her feet were not shod and did bleed and she carried the body of a dead man and took it to the chamber with the others. When she seeth Lancelot she made great joy and sayeth, 'At last! My penance is finished.'

And Lancelot sayeth, 'Damsel, are you a creature of God?'

'I am, Sire, and nought should you fear. I am the Damsel of the Castle of Beards that did treat knights with great cruelty. You did away with the toll I demanded from the passing knights but made covenant with me that when you achieved the Holy Grail you would return to me, but you saw it not. Instead a penance was laid on me for the cruelty I did the knights, for never a knight came but I cut off his nose, took out his eyes or struck off his hands. Now I needs must to bring to this house all the knights that have been slain in the forest. Now, thanks to God and to you, I am relieved of this penance and may return with the daylight.'

And Lancelot sayeth, 'And glad I am, damsel, so to do, for I have never seen such a penance placed upon so beautiful a damsel as you.'

'Alas, Sire, there is yet more for which you must prepare yourself and may God shield you from it. Every night cometh a band of black knights from where no one knows and are right foul and hideous.

'The black knights then fight each other in long and arduous combat. But a knight who came passing as have you drew a circle around us with his sword and we sheltered therein in good remembrance of Our Saviour Lord and His Precious Mother. You, Sire, should do likewise for our protection.'

And Lancelot drew a circle around them with his sword and they waited inside and bore in mind the Saviour and His Mother.

Thereupon, a great band of black knights came through the forest at great pace and entered the house and fell upon each other. They also tried to fall upon the King and the two knights but the black knights could not enter the circle drawn by Lancelot. And Lancelot was sore raged that he might not go against them and drew his sword but the damsel sayeth that he should stay within the circle for safety. But Lancelot was not a knight to let a challenge go unheeded and he leapt from the circle and fell upon the black knights. As he did so, the King and Gawain joined him and they did cause much harm upon the black knights until they were all slain. And when the black knights fell to the ground they turned into ashes and the ashes became ravens and fled the house.

They then rested within the circle but ere long another band of black knights fell upon the house carrying the bodies of slain knights, and they demandeth that the damsel put the bodies within the chamber but she sayeth, 'No! I am finished with my penance. Never again shall I be at your command.'

And in great rage the black knights ran with their lances upon the damsel and her companions but they could not breech the circle. With this, the King and the two knights did leap from the circle and fell upon the knights but they were soon sore pressed, for the black knights were in great number and were of greater prowess than their earlier brethren. And the moment came when it seemed that the King and his knights would be defeated but the sound of a ringing bell was heard and the black knights fled with a great noise to the forest and all was silent. With this, the damsel sayeth, 'This is the sound I have heard every night and it hath saved my life for the black knights then flee to the forest. If it had not sounded yet more black knights would have come such as could not be defeated.'

And this is a great wonderment for at that time in Greater and Lesser Britain the bell was unknown and only the horn or clappers of steel or wood gave forth a great sound. And the King marvelled much for he thought the sound of the bell could only be that of God.

On the morrow they departed from the ruined house and the damsel went her way to her castle. The King and the two knights then met three hermits who sayeth that they were to bury the slain within the house and there place a hermit to restore the house and build a chapel for the needs of the faithful. And the King was right pleased at this and bid the hermits well. Also the King for the term of the pilgrimage did hear the sound of a bell every hour and it brought him great joy for he knew it to be of God.

And the King did say unto his knights that henceforth on the pilgrimage he was not to be declared their King but he wished to be concealed as a brother knight. And thus they followed his accord.

That evening they came upon a fair house in the forest and the lady therein came to greet them well and took them inside and they disarmed and were given fair robes to wear. Then she sayeth that she knew Lancelot and sayeth, 'Sire, once you saved me from great dishonour whereof I am now in much unhappiness. But it is better that I have unhappiness in honour, than find pleasure in dishonour and shame, for shame endures whilst sorrow is passing.'

At this, the knight of the house entered from hunting and seeth Lancelot and sayeth, 'By my beard, Sire! I know you. It was you that robbed me of my happiness by making me marry this lady. But she hath never had joy of me, nor shall she.'

'Then, Sire,' sayeth Lancelot, 'you do not your duty as a husband. Truly I did make you marry her but did so only that you would not bring disgrace upon her and her family.'

'That mattereth not, Sire, for I still love the one you made me give up and she hateth you and now hath great power in this forest.'

'I know, Sire,' sayeth Lancelot, 'for I have spoken with her and know of her feeling to me.'

At meat the King asked the Lady to sit by him but the knight sent her to sit with the squires and sayeth, 'Now you may see the way I treat her and so shall I continue so to do, for this I have promised the one I do truly love.'

And Lancelot seeth that the knight is not overburdened with courtesy and sayeth quietly to the King that if he should meet the knight in the forest he would use his sword to teach him to show less churlishness to the lady.

They departed the next morn and rode through a land that was quiet and without people until they came upon a small castle by a deep valley and they saw that much of the castle had fallen into the chasm. They came to the gate and saw an old priest and asked him the name of the castle. And he sayeth to them that it was Tintagel.

The King sayeth to him, 'How did much of the castle fall into the chasm?'

And the priest sayeth, 'It came about, Sire, when King Uther Pendragon held a court to which came the king of this castle whose name was Gorlois. And he took with him his wife, Ygerne, who was the fairest Lady in all the kingdom. And King Uther was mightily smitten with her. At this, King Gorlois departed and took his Queen with him for dread of the intentions of King Uther. Then King Uther laid siege to this castle until King Gorlois had to leave in search of aid. With this, King Uther demanded that his sorcerer Merlin give him the resemblance of King Gorlois which the sorcerer doth. And that night King Uther did lay with Ygerne who hath in mind that it was her husband. And that night the seed was planted that was to become King Arthur, for his mother was

Ygerne and his father was Uther. For that sin, the bedchamber and much of the castle fell in to the chasm.'

Of this King Arthur knew nought and was discomforted in front of Gawain and Lancelot but they were both his subject knights and, to the priest, he was but a brother knight. And both knights through loyalty and brotherhood made neither opinion nor question of his lineage but held him in honour and regard.

And the King sayeth, 'What became of King Gorlois?'

The priest sayeth that he was slain by King Uther who then married Ygerne. And so King Arthur was brought about through sin but is yet the best King in the world.

They then went to the castle chapel which was right rich and within lay a fair tomb which was the tomb of Merlin the sorcerer. But the priest sayeth that the body of Merlin was not therein for when the coffin was brought in to the chapel the body was taken, but whether by God or the Devil was not known.

That night they lay at the castle and departed on the morn. They passed through many strange lands and islands and in journeying Lancelot brought to his mind that the time was nigh when he must return to the Waste City and fulfil his covenant to set his head at risk. And he telleth the story of the knight he had struck the head off on the vow that he would return and place his own head in peril. And he sayeth, 'The time is come when I must go thither, for I must meet my covenant or else be considered unworthy. Should God allow me to live, I shall join you again on your pilgrimage.'

With this, they held his hand in parting and wished him God's speed and commended him to the Saviour of the World. And his heart was heavy, not for the challenge he must face but that he could not ask the King to salute the Queen on his behalf, for he would not that the King nor Gawain should know of his love for that Lady.

When he came to the Waste City he found it as before, in ruin and much disordered. And he heard the lamentations of many ladies and damsels who sayeth, 'We have been betrayed for the knight doth not come as he vowed. This day is the day when he should redeem his pledge. Never again should trust be placed in a knight. As the others before him he hath betrayed us with his fear of death yet he struck off the head of the young knight. Now he saves his own head.' And nowhere could Lancelot see the ladies and damsels who cry out in their lamentations.

Then he came to the palace where he slew the knight and alighteth and tied his horse to a ring near the mounting stone. At this, a knight appeared with the same axe that Lancelot had used to strike off the head of the young knight. And the knight did sharpen the axe with a stone. Lancelot sayeth, 'Are you to slay me?'

The knight sayeth unto him, 'You have vowed to set your head in jeopardy as did the young knight who was my brother. Him you slew without defence and now you must stretch out your neck so that I may strike off your head. Let there be no contention in this matter for it was your deed and your vow that hath brought you here.'

Lancelot sayeth, 'May I see a priest that I may confess?'

But the knight sayeth, 'There are none here that will help you. You shall die as you are.'

And Lancelot knelt down and crossed himself saying, 'Have mercy on me Lord and accept my soul to your service. I surrender myself to you not as a good knight but as one who hath tried to do your service in this world.' At this, he remembered the Queen and sayeth, 'Dear kind, gentle, lady, never again shall I see you. Death does not trouble me but never to see you again is the worst death a man should ever know. My love for you has never failed nor shall the love of my soul if God should allow. Thus permitted, you should know well, dear lady, that you are loved in the next world as is no other in this world.'

And Lancelot did come upright and bare his neck that he might receive the axe and the knight raised the axe and brought it down right forcefully. As he did so an Angel spoke to Lancelot and sayeth that God was with him. At this, Lancelot bowed his head in worship and the axe came past his head. And the knight was sore angered and sayeth that Lancelot should keep his head still and he raised the axe again. But as he did so, two damsels of great beauty came to a window and one of them crieth out, 'Sire, if you would have my love for ever more throw down the axe!'

And the knight cast aside the axe and sayeth to Lancelot, 'Sire, I beg your mercy, pray forgive me!'

Lancelot sayeth, 'But, Sire, it is for me to cry mercy from you that you slay me not.'

The knight then sayeth, 'Though you have slain my brother, I will not do this. Rather, Sire, that I will defend you to the utmost of my power for by your valour you have saved this city and the people.'

And the two damsels came to Lancelot and sayeth, 'You, Sire, are the knight we loved most in the world for we are the sister damsels to whom you, Gawain and another knight did give the houses and treasures of the forest robbers that you slew. Many knights, Sire, have come by here as you did and vowed to return to face the axe but none have done so as you have done. Should you have failed us, never again would the city rise and be returned of its people.'

And they took Lancelot to the great hall and disarmed him and set him at ease whereon came a great noise of joyfulness. The damsels took him to the window and showed him the many people who came from the forest to return to the city. Ere long priests arrived in procession and went to their abandoned churches and praised God for the knight who hath rescued them by his knightly virtues. And Lancelot received much honour.

Part the XXIst

King Arthur and Gawain rode through the forest until they came upon a knight riding at great pace. And Gawain asked him from whence came he. And the knight sayeth, 'I, Sire, am from the land of the Queen of the Golden Circlet where the Queen hath sore troubles. Her land and castles have been taken by Nabigant of the Rock and he now demands the Golden Circlet that was won by the son of the Widow Lady when he slew the Knight of the Dragon.'

'How doth he make such a demand?'

'A damsel is to take the Golden Circlet to the Meadow of the Tent of the Two Damsels where Gawain did away with the evil custom. There an assembly of knights is to be held and Nabigant of the Rock intends to win it by combat on the field.'

'Will you, Sire, be attending the assembly?' sayeth Gawain.

'I shall, Sire, but first I must inform all the knights I can find to tell them of this event.' With this, the knight took his leave and departed.

And Gawain took the King to the Meadow of the Tent of the Two Damsels for he knew the path from the time he had vanquished the evil custom.

The tent was as before richly decorated within and without. And Gawain took the King in and sat him on a couch with a quilted cushion and they washed in water brought by squires who also disarmed them. At the head of the couch was a noble chest wherein where many rich clothes and Gawain dressed the King and he in white silk laced with gold.

Thereupon, the two Damsels of the Tent entered and Gawain sayeth, 'Welcome, damsels.'

But the damsels sayeth, 'Sires, you are welcome, but it seemeth to us that you take from us that which is ours. Yet you, Gawain, would not do as we requested when we last met.'

And the elder damsel sayeth, 'There is not a knight in the kingdom who would not be joyous at my desire to love him. I prayed for your love, Sire, but you would not grant it, but you come to our tent and take that which is not yours as if we were lovers.'

And Gawain sayeth, 'I act only in accordance with the custom of the land and in expectation of the courtesy you should show. For you hath told me that when the evil custom was overthrown, all knights may come here for lodging and find they are honoured as guest knights should be.'

'This is indeed true, Sire, but you gave us churlishness and must expect churlishness in return.'

The elder damsel then sayeth, 'The three-day assembly of knights begins tomorrow and the prize will be the Golden Circlet. If nought else, you and your comrade will be able to boast that you have the most noble lodging in the land.'

And the younger damsel looked at King Arthur and sayeth, 'Sire, will you be as a stranger to us?'

'No damsel need be a stranger to me, for any damsel will be safe in my presence. Happy I am to honour you and obey your commands.'

'I thank you, Sire, and have but one request of you. Will you, Sire, be my knight in the assembly?'

'Even should I wish so to do, I cannot refuse such a request for no true knight shall refuse a damsel.'

'What, Sire, is your name?'

'My name is Arthur, and I am from Castle Cardoil.'

'Have you ought to do with King Arthur?'

'Damsel, I have oft been at his court, and if he were not the king to whom I am most loyal, I should not be in the company of loyal Gawain.'

And the King smiled upon the damsel who knew not who he was. But his showing was not as his heart for he loved his Queen and would not countenance dishonour upon her.

That night they lay in great comfort and the damsels would not depart until they were asleep.

On the morrow, knights came from across the land and set up their booths and tents in rich array. And the elder damsel came to Gawain and sayeth, 'Sire, for my hospitality I request that you carry a shield of red at the assembly and that you shall be known as the Red Knight.' And Gawain agreed right willingly.

And the younger damsel came to King Arthur and sayeth, 'Sire, it is my wish that you bear a shield of gold. For it will be better on you than any other knight. And I ask that you thinketh of me as I shall think of you this day.'

'Thank you, damsel,' sayeth the King, 'the knight doth not live who would not think of your worth and courtesy.'

And they heard that the damsel hath brought the Golden Circlet and Nabigant of the Rock had issued the laws of the assembly. And the younger damsel sayeth to the King, 'Know, Sire, that there is no other knight here today more worthy than you nor hath arms so noble. Take care you honour them and show you to be a good knight for my love.'

King Arthur replieth, 'May God grant it so.' And the King with Gawain mounted their horses and went to the assembly.

The younger damsel sayeth to the elder, 'What think you of my knight? Doth he not please you?'

The elder damsel sayeth, 'He doth, sister. But I have no liking for Gawain for he doth not do as I ask of him. And for this he shall suffer dearly.'

And the King and Gawain charged upon the field as two lions unchained. Two knights did they knock from their horses and sent the horses to the two damsels who received them with much joy. Gawain then saw Nabigant of the Rock and caused him and his horse to tumble. King Arthur sent many a knight to the ground until it was time for evensong when they left the field. That night all the knights in assembly agreed that the Red Knight and the Knight of the Golden Shield were the best among them.

King Arthur dined with the younger damsel by his side and Gawain sat with the elder damsel. Much wine did they have until they went to the couches to sleep full weary of the buffets they had received that day.

On the morn, the younger damsel came to King Arthur and saluteth him saying, 'Sire, it is my request that this day you shall bear a shield of blue, and since you can do no better than you did yesterday, you should do no worse.'

The King replieth, 'May God so will it.'

The elder damsel came to Gawain and sayeth, 'Sire, have you remembrance of a time when you won the sword that struck off the head of Saint John the Baptist?'

'I do,' sayeth Gawain.

'Remember you also the covenant you made with the king who tried to take the sword from you? A covenant that you would obey the request of the damsel who first gives you his name?'

Again, Gawain sayeth, 'I do.'

'Then, Sire,' sayeth she, 'be aware that I am that damsel and I tell you in truth that the king was the King of Wales. And my request is that you bear your own shield of red with the golden eagle and that on this day you prove to be the worst knight on the field.'

And Gawain was sorely troubled for never hath he broken a covenant and sayeth, 'Damsel, you know I can do no other than grant your request.' At this, he departed from her and rode on to the field.

King Arthur rode as before and sent two knights to the ground. Gawain came in the midst of the combat and the knights all sayeth, 'See, here comes Gawain, a brave knight who is the nephew of good King Arthur.' And Nabigant of the Rock seeth Gawain and came at him at full gallop but Gawain cast down his shield and did flee from the field. There being no knightly virtue in defeating a fleeing knight Nabigant of the Rock did not pursue him. Gawain came against other knights and did flee from them also and they sayeth, 'Never have we seen such cowardice of a knight!'

As other knights came to engage him, Gawain fled to the protection of King Arthur who was sore put to the effort of defending him and was much confounded by the cowardice shown by Gawain. And the many knights sayeth, 'Now can I take vengeance on this knight for what he hath done to my family or my brother knights.' And the King did keep them away for the long day. Both knight and King were pleased that the end came with evensong and they could leave the field without much buffeting.

At the tent a dwarf appeared and sayeth to the damsels, 'Your knights are worse than may be imagined! He of the blue arms did fare well enough, but Gawain is of such cowardice that even I may send him to flight.'

To the King he sayeth, 'And you, Sire, why do you keep him company? Had he not been there you would have been the best today, but he skulked by you to avoid the buffets. No good knight should stand by a coward even though before he did slay two knights by this tent.' And the elder damsel did smile at these words.

The knights that left the field at evensong could not agree to whom belonged the Golden Circlet for the Red Knight and the Knight of the Golden Shield had not appeared on the field that day.

When the damsels and the dwarf had left the tent Gawain told the King of his covenant and his duty to observe it. And the King sayeth, 'Sire, you have had much blame this day and I have had great shame put upon me for my defence of you. Never did I believe that you could have pretended cowardice for your valour is renowned throughout the land. Pray God that on the morrow you are not required to do the same for your name shall be cast down as never before.'

And Gawain sayeth, 'Sire, I am still bound by my covenant. May God grant me ease of my suffering.'

In the morning the elder damsel came to Gawain and sayeth, 'Sire, it is my wish that today you bear the gold shield first borne by your brother knight on the first day of the assembly. And furthermore that you prove yourself to be the best knight on the field but you shall not say your name other than it be the Knight of the Gold Shield.'

And Gawain sayeth, 'As it pleaseth you, damsel.'

The younger damsel came to the King and sayeth, 'Sire, pray grant me that you will bear the shield of red this day and that you will do as well as the first day or better.'

And the King replieth that he was right pleased with such a request.

They galloped to the field and fell upon the knights so that many are knocked to the ground. The King did lay low many knights but did not seek out combat as willingly as he would, for it was his wish that Gawain should win the Golden Circlet. But the King did seek out Nabigant of the Rock and tumbled him most severely from his horse. As the procession to evensong was passing, the damsel bearing the Golden Circlet came on to the field and the knights were called upon to name the best among them. And they said that the best knights were the Red Knight and the Knight of the Golden Shield but of the two the best knight must be the Knight of the Golden Shield, for he hath done best on the first day and on the last. But had the Red Knight done as well as he had done on the first day it was he who would have won. And the Golden Circlet was awarded to Gawain but none there save King Arthur knew whom he was.

They returned to the tent where the damsels made great joy of them. And the dwarf came and sayeth, 'Damsels, it is better that you lodge these knights than the coward Gawain for had you lodged him great shame would you have brought upon yourselves.' And the damsels laughed at him and made him begone.

And the damsels say unto Gawain, 'Sire, what will you do with the Golden Circlet?'

'I shall return it to the knight that won it first and thus lift the burden from the Queen of the Golden Circlet.'

That night the King and Gawain lay asleep in the tent when the younger damsel came to the King and sayeth, 'Sire, much have you done as my knight. Now I come to reward you.'

But the King, whose heart was full of his Queen Guinevere, sayeth, 'Damsel, honour I love above all else and nought I put above your honour. May our Lord God help you to preserve that honour.'

The younger damsel then sayeth to the elder that such knights gave them neither comfort nor solace and may God preserve them from such guests. And the elder damsel sayeth that, but for the Golden Circlet, neither knight should leave the land but she hath loyalty to her Lady, the Queen of the Golden Circlet. And the damsels departed.

As the King and Gawain departed on the morrow, Meliot of England came upon the knights who had been to the assembly and sayeth to them that he is in search of Gawain whose man he was that the knight could aid him to take back his castle and land robbed of him by Nabigant of the Rock. And the Knights telleth him that Gawain had proved a coward and his aid would be of no avail and Meliot turned away in his sadness.

The King and Gawain rode until one night they came to the Waste Manor where Gawain had been led by the hound and where he found the body of the knight slain by Lancelot. They lodged the night there and were known by the knights therein. And the Lady of the Waste Manor sent for knights to come to her aid for she held King Arthur and his nephew Gawain that were both brother knights of Lancelot. Many knights came and she chose seven that were to lay in wait outside for when the King and Gawain did depart and find themselves on the points of their lances.

Meantime, Lancelot had left the Waste City where he was much honoured and came upon Meliot. And Meliot told Lancelot that Gawain who had once been full of much valour had now turned coward. But sayeth Meliot that he would still search for Gawain for he did not believe what he had heard of him. And Lancelot sayeth unto him that he would join him in his search.

Together they rode until they chanced upon the Waste Manor where the King and Gawain were lodged. And the King and Gawain sayeth to one another that they should face the knights that waited outside although there be seven of them. They came fully armed to the gate and rushed out to fall upon the knights, and the sound of swords upon steel fell upon the ears of Lancelot and Meliot. These knights then came to the gate and came upon the waiting knights as hawks among sparrows. The knights of the Lady were fallen or scattered with great swiftness and the King and Gawain gave great greetings to Lancelot and Meliot.

And the Lady of the Waste Manor did come to the gate holding the hand of a young squire and seeth Lancelot and sayeth to him, 'Sire, you did slay the brother of this squire and one day he or another shall come to slay you.' But Lancelot did not make reply.

The King and his knight departed and Meliot told them of Nabigant of the Rock who hath taken his land and will not return it except by combat with Gawain. And Gawain asked leave of the King to go with Meliot to gain return of his lands and the King doth grant it willingly. At this, the King and Lancelot rode on towards the Castle of the Holy Grail.

Gawain and Meliot repaired without delay to the castle robbed by Nabigant of the Rock and came before the gate. And Nabigant rode out with no other knights for he knew Gawain to be a coward and therefore aid needed he none. Nabigant sayeth no words to Gawain but came at him full furious with lance lowered. Gawain did hurtle at him and strike him through the breast even to the heart and he fell slain. The knights of the castle that serveth Nabigant then issued from the castle but were soon sent in flight from the field by Gawain and Meliot. More knights came from the castle but they brought the keys and paid homage to Meliot as their lord.

Now Gawain departed in pursuit of the King and Lancelot and came upon a damsel riding at a fast pace through the forest. And he sayeth, 'Damsel, God's greeting be upon you. Why do you ride so fast?'

The damsel sayeth, 'Sire, I am going to the great assembly of knights that is to be held at Palace Meadows where I shall search for the knight that won the Golden Circlet at the Meadow of the Tent.'

'Why so?' sayeth Gawain.

'I am sent by the Queen of the Golden Circlet to beseech the knight to come to her aid. For Nabigant of the Rock hath robbed her of her castle and there can be none better in the world to defend her than the knight who hath won the Golden Circlet.'

'Then, damsel,' sayeth Gawain, 'both you and the Queen may rest in ease for the knight who won the Golden Circlet hath already slain Nabigant.'

'Sire,' sayeth the damsel in joy, 'Can this be true?'

'Indeed, for I know the knight well and I saw him slay Nabigant. Furthermore, damsel, I have here the very Golden Circlet which I bear on behalf of the knight to the Castle of the Holy Grail.' And he showed the damsel the Golden Circlet in its ivory and jewelled box. He then sayeth, 'Thus it is that your Queen shall no longer bear the guardianship of the Golden Circlet and may be at ease.'

And so the damsel departed to tell her Queen of the joyous news. Gawain turned towards the assembly at Palace Meadows for he knew if the tidings of the event had reached the King and Lancelot there they would repair straightway. As he rode he came upon a squire full weary from a long journey and asked him from whence he came. And the squire answereth, 'Sire, I am from the land of King Arthur where there is a great war, for none know the whereabouts of the King. Many say that he is slain for none have heard of him since he left Castle Cardoil with Gawain and Lancelot. Now the Knights Briant of the Isles and Kay burn all the land and carry plunder from the houses. The knights of the Round Table number no more than five and thirty and of them ten are sore wounded and they are all that remain to defend Castle Cardoil.'

And Gawain took the squire and rode hard to the assembly where he found the King and Lancelot already in combat. They had heard that the prize of the assembly was to be the golden crown of a queen and her white horse and whosoever was the victor would have the duty of defending her country for she was now dead. And Gawain rode hard in to the fight and like Lancelot sent many knights to the ground. But none fought as did King Arthur who seemed like a lion against stags and scattered all before him. With the end of the contest, the knights sayeth that none fought as well as the Knight of the Red Shield, for so King Arthur had armed himself.

And a knight brought forth the golden crown and the white horse and put them before the King who sayeth, 'To whom doth the crown and horse belong?'

The knight sayeth, 'Sire, they belonged to Queen Guinevere, the wife of King Arthur whom many believe slain. As her knights may not leave Castle Cardoil, where they defend the land of the Queen, I was sent to attend assemblies that I may hear of tidings of the King or of Gawain and Lancelot and much sorrowed am I that nothing can I find of them for the land is in great despair.'

Of the sorrow of the King no words can be known for he loved his Queen beyond all measure, and his knights took him to one side where he fell to his knees and wept. At his side knelt Lancelot that loved the Queen but in his heart alone and he wept also for that all his deeds of knighthood were now as nought, for no longer had he a bright soul to be championed. By them knelt Gawain in full sorrow for the loss of his Sovereign Lady and the good wife of his King.

And Lancelot sayeth to the King, 'Sire, allow me to return to Castle Cardoil that I might defend your land. Thus may you and Gawain continue to the Holy Grail and obtain the help of God to give you strength in your loss and victory over those that despoil your realm.'

Gawain sayeth, 'Truly, Sire, it should be as Lancelot has asked. No better knight could you send and no better cause can you now have than finding the help of the Holy Grail.'

And the King sayeth to Lancelot, 'Go, Sire, and be the guardian of my land. Look to its proper rule and hold it for me until God allows me to return. For now I have no heart to return and see the ground where she walked and live in halls that no longer hear her laughter.'

And Lancelot did leave for Castle Cardoil full of sorrow and sadness.

Part the XXIInd

King Arthur and Gawain rode to the Castle of the Holy Grail. And the King took with him the white horse of the Queen and held her gold crown close to him. Percival greeteth them with great joy but fell to weeping when he heard of the death of the Queen. He took them to the Chapel of the Holy Grail and they saw the sepulchre of the good Fisher King where the rich covering was changed anew every day by the hands of angels only. They saw also the sword that had struck off the head of Saint John the Baptist, which had been brought thither by Gawain. Now Gawain gave to the Chapel the Golden Circlet that was the Crown of Thorns worn by Our Saviour and the King gave the golden crown of the Queen.

And the King saw that the castle was of great strength and beauty and was known by names other than the Castle of the Holy Grail, these being the Castle of Eden, the Castle of Joy, and the Castle of Souls. By the castle ran a river which was said to rise in Eden. It encircled the castle and flowed to the hermitage of a holy hermit and there did go beneath the ground and was not seen again. It was said that all good men that stayed there had souls that went straight to Paradise when their life in this world.

And the King was looking from the castle windows with Gawain when he espied a long procession led by a man dressed in white. This man carried a large Cross and all the others carried smaller Crosses and candles, save for the man at the rear who bore around his neck a golden ornament the like of which had not before been seen. And they asked Percival who these folk were and he sayeth that they were hermits that gathered three times a week to pray at the Chapel of the Holy Grail, but the man behind with the golden ornament he knew not.

The King did meet the hermits and the knights bowed their heads in reverence at the Crosses and saw the words in stone above the chapel door which sayeth:

All who entereth herein
Shalt be as silent as the rose
For God is herewithin
And any tumult shall be his
And those who carry out his works
And them alone.
Thou shalt speak only if God looketh
Upon thee.

As they came together in the Chapel the golden ornament was taken from the last man and placed upon the altar where it was raised and issued forth a sound that the King knew full well for it was the same sound he had heard every hour. And the hermits then prayed full reverently and sang sweet psalms and the King and the knights knelt before the altar. Then the golden ornament was raised again and the sound came forth three times whereupon there did appear the Holy Grail in five manners, the first four of which it is not permitted to say, but in the last appeared as a chalice the like of which there were none in England. And the chalice was borne by an angel bathed in pure light and the angel looked upon Percival. And the knight raised himself from his kneeling and, knowing full well that God looketh down upon him, placed his hand on his heart and sayeth, 'Whom doth the Grail serve?'

At his question, the nine orders of Angels filled the height of the chapel singing 'Holy, holy, holy is the Lord God of Hosts: the whole earth is full of His glory!', the sound of their voices echoing from the farthest hills. Then cometh the sound of beating wings, and a silver dove spoke the words, 'It serveth Him whose eye looketh down upon you and seeth naught but the virtues of Man and Angels. Of such shall the Seraphim be made.'

And the light fadeth as the words sang across the forests, meadows, rivers and seas.

And all in the chapel knew that only the most virtuous knight could have asked the question and received the answer. Now all throughout the world should know that evil shall ever fall before the virtuous for they wear the armour of God and carry the shield of Our Saviour and bear the sword of the Holy Ghost. And the Holy Trinity shall reign triumphant throughout all the ages.

At this, King Arthur did set in mind the law that henceforth throughout England all wine at the sacred Eucharist shall be taken from such a chalice in remembrance of that day.

At the end of the Mass, the King asked the man who bore the golden ornament by what name it was known. And the man sayeth that he was the King for whom Gawain had slain the giant, thus winning for him the sword that had struck off the head of Saint John the Baptist and now lay on the altar of the chapel. That King had been baptised in the presence of Gawain and his people had also become Christian. Thereupon, he had become a hermit and had lived by the sea where he saw a ship come ashore that held three priests all named Gregory who had come from the Holy Land. And they sayeth to him that in ancient times King Solomon had three bells to be cast. One bell was for the Saviour of the World, the second was for His Holy Mother, and the third was for all the saints. And God had commanded that the priests bring the third bell to England for no bells were there in that country. And the Hermit King was commanded to show the bell at this castle that others may be cast both great and small. For this all his sins would be forgiven. And King Arthur ordained that all the chapels in England should have bells in memorial of this day.

And Gawain sayeth to the Hermit King, 'Truly, Sire, you are a worthy King, for thy held to your covenant with me.' With this, the Hermit King and all the hermits did depart for their hermitages there to do the work of God.

The King was at meat with Percival and Gawain when the second damsel who was in the company of the Damsel of the Carriage came in to the great hall. On her right arm she bore a great wound as if by a sword or lance. She sayeth to Percival, 'Sire, have mercy upon your poor mother and your sister and on us. Aristor of Moraine, who is cousin to the Lord of the Moors that you did slay, wars upon your mother and hath carried off your sister. He sayeth he will take her to wife but he is of great cruelty and hath the custom of cutting off the head of his wife after the night of the wedding. This he hath done many times before. Sire, I was with your sister when he took her and he wounded me thus. Pray, Sire, that you heed the cry of your mother and go to her aid for great shame will fall upon you should you fail her.'

And Percival sayeth, 'Damsel, there shall be no failing. This very hour shall see my departure.'

And the King sayeth, 'Sire, Gawain and I would count it an honour to be by your side in this endeavour.'

But Percival sayeth, 'Thank you, Sire, but no. Better, Sire, that you repair to Camelot, there to guard the castle and the land for my mother that when she returns she shall find it safe under your protection.'

And to this the King assented.

Part the XXIIIrd

King Arthur and Gawain departed from the Castle of the Holy Grail and rode until they came upon a much ruined castle that once was of great richness. And they lodged therein that night and went to hear Mass in the chapel with the priest that lived alone in the castle. And the priest told them that the castle was named the Castle of Hope, for he prayed in hope for the return of the lord of the castle. They saw that the chapel walls were decorated with fine paintings in bright colours of red, gold, blue and green. And the King sayeth to the priest, 'What know you of these paintings?'

The priest sayeth, 'Sire, the paintings were done by a true and loyal knight who dearly loved the lady and the boy therein. They show the true happenings of that time.'

And Gawain sayeth, 'And what, Sire, is the story they tell?'

The priest then sayeth, 'The good knight Gawain was born in this castle and was given his name in honour of the knight that lived herein. His mother was the wife of King Lot but she did not want it known and she sayeth to the lord of the castle that he should take the child and leave it in the forest to perish or have some other do so. This other Gawain was loathe to do, and had letters that sayeth the child was of royal blood put in his cradle with gold and silver. He then travelled to a far part of the forest and found a humble dwelling wherein lived a worthy man and his wife and he asked them to care for the child. This Gawain then did return to the Castle of Hope and on his death asketh me to remain here until the boy returned. I now hear that the young Gawain is among the best knights in the world and pray God daily that he will return to this castle.'

And Gawain was sore ashamed that he learned of his birth in this manner and that his mother should have sought his death as a child. But King Arthur sayeth, 'Fair nephew, let not your heart be troubled by such tidings. I also have but recently learned of my own coming into this world. None of us can choose how we come or how we depart. You are honoured far and wide for your knightly virtues and none but you hath brought such high esteem.'

The priest, now that he knew to whom he spoke, sayeth to Gawain, 'Sire, you are confirmed in the laws of God and were born of the lawful marriage of King Lot and your mother. Let God be praised that you have come thither.'

Part the XXIVth

It was a hound that led Gawain to the Waste Manor where he found the body of a knight that had been slain by Lancelot. And the knight had a son named Meliant who determined to avenge his father. This Meliant heard that Briant of the Isles had a great and mighty army and he did war upon the land of King Arthur, and many of the King's knights were slain. He journeyed to find Briant and found him in the Castle of the High Rock and there told him of his father's slaying and his desire to find vengeance, and in this told he would help Briant in his war on King Arthur. And Briant received him with joy and made him a knight. Thus raised he wished to find Lancelot and challenge him. But no one knew the whereabouts of Lancelot and some sayeth that he is slain. But he was whole and sound in body yet in great despair at the death of the Queen and deep sorrow did lay heavy in his heart.

Lancelot rode through the forest and came upon a knight and a damsel who did play and laugh with each other. And Lancelot sayeth 'Sire, do you know of any lodging hereabouts?'

And the damsel sayeth, 'You shall not find lodging so good as we have, Sire, for already it is eventide.'

Lancelot sayeth, 'This, damsel, is good tidings indeed for I am greatly wearied.'

'So are all they who come from the land of the Fisher King, Sire, for none may journey from there without suffering as all good knights must.'

And Lancelot sayeth 'Damsel, where is this lodging of which you speak?'

The knight sayeth to Lancelot that he must follow the path before him and he will find it. The knight and the damsel sayeth, however, that they will go another way and meet Lancelot at the lodging.

As Lancelot departed the damsel sayeth, 'That is Lancelot but he knoweth me not. Much do I dislike him for he made a knight that loveth me marry another. And that damsel he loveth not and maketh her sit to eat with the squires and command that none aid nor obey her. But the knight will not abandon her for fear of Lancelot and for his honour.'

Lancelot rode along the path and seeth a large castle strongly walled and at its gate were hung the heads of fifteen knights. And he seeth a knight close by the castle and sayeth to him, 'Sire, what is the name of this castle?' The knight answereth that it is the Castle of the Griffon.

'Why, Sire, do the heads of knights hang there?'

'The daughter of the lord of the castle is the most fair damsel in the land but she will give herself only to the knight that draws a sword from a stone column in the great hall. All knights that lodge there must enter the contest for her hand and try to take the sword from the column. Those that fail must lose their heads. As you may see, Sire, none have succeeded. Now it is said abroad that none but a Grail Knight may draw the sword. But, Sire, take heed of what I say and seek lodging elsewhere for it is an ill adventure that needs place life at risk. No blame will fall on you for leaving, for there also lives in a cavern below the castle a lion and a griffon that have devoured half a hundred knights.'

And Lancelot sayeth, 'Thank you, Sire, but it is evening and I know not the forest. Better I chance the Lord within than the devils without.'

The knight sayeth, 'As you will, Sire, and may God go with you and grant that you depart in safety.'

Lancelot came to the castle gate and entered in to the courtyard where he dismounted and climbed the steps to the hall. Therein he found many knights and damsels but none saluted him or greeted his coming except the lord of the castle who sayeth that he should disarm himself. Lancelot sayeth that it was his wish to be allowed to wear his arms. But the lord of the castle sayeth that none shall sit at meat until he be disarmed and had two squires aid Lancelot in disarming. They dressed him in rich apparel and sat him at the table. Then the damsel of the castle came forth from her chamber and seeth Lancelot and thinketh him most comely. But she also thinketh it would be sore pity for him to have his head struck off.

When they had taken meat the damsel Lancelot had met in the forest came in to the hall and sayeth to the lord of the castle, 'Sire, you have lodging tonight your most deadly enemy, he who slew your brother at the Waste Manor.'

And the lord of the castle sayeth, 'This cannot be! Nor shall it be until it is proven.' He sayeth to Lancelot, 'Sire, ask the question.'

Lancelot sayeth 'Which question, Sire?'

'That you may have my daughter. For if you are worthy you shall have her.'

But the mind of Lancelot is full of the memory of the dead Queen and he hath no desire for neither damsel nor lady. But the custom of the castle was before him and he must follow it if only in courtesy. And he sayeth, 'Sire, any knight would feel himself adorned by such a damsel for his wife should she be willing. Had I thought you would let me take her for a wife I would have asked most willingly.'

And they took him to the column and showed him the sword therein. The lord of the castle sayeth, 'Go, Sire, follow the custom as have other knights.'

Lancelot stepped forward and grasped the hilt of the sword and pulled mightily, and the sword came free of the stone which did shiver at the deed. And the damsel of the castle was much pleased but the damsel from the forest sayeth to the lord of the castle, 'Sire, I tell you plainly that this is the foul knight that did slay your brother. He hath slain many knights and many more will he slay if you allow him to leave the castle alive.'

And the lord of the castle sayeth to Lancelot, 'Sire, I will not be bound by my covenant for you are a mortal enemy who did slay my brother. My daughter will not seek your company lest she be a fool.' But his daughter thinketh she would like to be deep in the forest with Lancelot. The lord of the manor then sayeth to his knights that they should bar the gates to the castle that Lancelot may not depart and they should meet the next dawn full armed for it was intent that Lancelot should have his head struck off and placed above the gate. But the daughter knew of her father's commands and bid haste to send a messenger to Lancelot.

The bearer of the damsel's message came to Lancelot bringing a hound and sayeth, 'Sire, my mistress bids me say to you that her father intends for you to have your head struck off. Twelve knights shall be within the gate and twelve without all armed, and though you be a good knight, this shall be over many for you to contend. There is beneath this castle a cavern which leads to the forest but it is guarded by a most fierce lion and a griffon that hath the beak of an eagle, from which it breaths fire, the eyes of a hawk, the teeth of a wolf, the ears of an owl, the feet of leopard, and the tail of a serpent. There is, Sire, no more hideous beast in the world. My mistress sayeth that you should go this way and she shall meet you with your horse where the cavern reaches the forest.'

'By all that is Holy,' sayeth Lancelot, 'It would be better for me to face the knights than this ill-formed creature.'

And the messenger sayeth, 'Sire, my mistress sayeth that she can aid you no more if you do not do as she directs. She doth it in love for you and sendeth you this hound that you should put before the griffon, for the beast doth love this hound greatly and will not harm it. But for the lion, Sire, you must depend upon God and your own valour.'

'This I shall do,' sayeth Lancelot, 'but the damsel should know by you that it is not cowardice that taketh me from the knights, but her wish.'

And the messenger telleth the damsel and she hath much happiness.

Lancelot armed himself and entered the cavern followed by the hound. And thereon did the cavern grow bright from the fire of the griffon as it came at Lancelot, but the light showed the hound and the griffon lay down and playeth with the hound as the knight went past. Then Lancelot seeth the lion which was of great fierceness. It ran at him but Lancelot moveth not, and the lion opened its jaws wide and in its last leap the knight put aside his shield and ran at the lion and thrust his sword down its throat. And the lion fell slain.

When he came to the forest there he found the damsel with his horse and she asketh him if he is hurt, and he sayeth that he is not. And she looked at him and sayeth, 'Sire, you seemeth not over joyous.'

And Lancelot replieth, 'No, damsel, I am burdened with much sorrow for I have lost that which I love most.'

The damsel sayeth, 'But, Sire, you have won me. It is said that I am the fairest damsel in the kingdom and I have brought you safely from the castle. You, Sire, have my love and much would I have it that you loveth me also.'

Lancelot sayeth, 'Damsel, much would I make of your love and your beauty but my heart owes its loyalty to another who cannot know it. For your service to me, damsel, I can do no more than offer you my protection when I am able so to give it.'

But the damsel was sore at heart and sayeth, 'This, Sire, is betrayal. Better that you were slain in the castle that I may be able to worship your head above the gate.'

And Lancelot commended the damsel to God and rode in to the forest.

The lord of the castle waited for Lancelot that morn and sent his knights to find him, but they found him not. He commanded two knights to enter the cavern where they were devoured by the griffon. The lord of the castle then went to the chamber of his daughter and found her weeping and without consolation. And no knights had the courage to go forth in pursuit of Lancelot.

That day Lancelot came upon a great valley that had forests on both sides and he saw a new and rich chapel upon a hill with a roof adorned with gold Crosses. Nearby were three new houses each facing the chapel. A stream ran by the chapel and fell in to the valley with many waterfalls and a pleasing sound. The knight then heard chanting from the chapel and, alighting, led his horse up the hill. And three hermits came from the chapel and he sayeth, 'Sires, what is this place called?'

And the hermits sayeth, 'It is Avalon, Sire.'

Leaving his sword, lance and shield outside, Lancelot entered the chapel and saw that it was like unto no other chapel that he hath seen. The walls were hung with silk cloths fringed with gold and the ceiling painted with images, and many other images of Our Saviour and His Mother were stood about. In the centre of the chapel were two tombs covered by rich cloths and with candles in gold candlestick at each corner. At each side of the tombs priests knelt and sang psalms. And Lancelot sayeth, 'For whom are these tombs made?'

And the hermits replieth, 'They, Sire, are for King Arthur and Queen Guinevere.'

And he sayeth, 'But King Arthur lives.'

'In truth he doth. But the Queen is herein buried with the head of her son for whom she died in great sorrow. It was the command of the Queen that she be placed by the tomb of her beloved King that he may join her at the side of Our Saviour.'

And the heart of Lancelot was as if torn asunder, but he may not show it at the tomb of the Queen. He goeth to an image of Our Saviour's Mother and knelt down weeping saying, 'It is my greatest desire that I never depart from this place but my honour and the memory of this sweet Lady doth forbid it. I pray therefore that when I die my body may be returned to this place and I might be shrouded and buried close by her. May death come soon for I know no longer the light nor joy of this world.'

And the hermits did come to him and ask him to join them at meat and then to rest. But Lancelot sayeth that he wished to keep a vigil that night by the image of the Saviour's Mother.

As the morning light dimmed the candles Lancelot rose from his prayers and took Mass with the hermits. Before he departed he placed his hands most tenderly upon the tomb of the Queen and commended her soul to the hosts of Heaven, and as he rode from the chapel he turned many times until he could see no more the golden Crosses.

And Lancelot came that night to Castle Cardoil where he seeth the land and manors were spoiled and wasted which angered him greatly. He then saw a knight that had been grievously wounded riding on the path and asketh him, 'Sire, whence have you come?'

And the knight sayeth that he had come from near Castle Cardoil where he had seen Kay and two knights taking as prisoner Yvain le Aoutres, the father of Chaus the squire who had brought the golden candlestick to King Arthur and died so doing.

'Are they far?' sayeth Lancelot.

'No, Sire.' sayeth the knight. 'I will lead you and help you as my wound may allow.'

And they came up to Kay and the knights and Lancelot sayeth loudly, 'Hold, Kay! Be it not enough that you hath slain the son of King Arthur that you now must war upon him?'

Kay replieth not but ran at Lancelot with his lance lowered. But Lancelot was ready to meet him and knocked him hard from his horse. And the knight that led him to the place also tumbled one of the knights of Kay. Lancelot gave the horse of Kay to Yvain as the traitor knight mounted the horse of his fallen knight and rode off to the Castle of the High Rock wherein was Briant of the Isles. Kay telleth Briant of what had happened and Briant sayeth, 'Was the King there?'

But Kay sayeth that he had no time to enquire of such. But Briant and Meliant of the Waste Manor believe that Lancelot is come to Castle Cardoil for the King is slain, and they much rejoiced.

And when Lancelot cometh to Castle Cardoil he telleth the knights there that the King is alive and they have much joy. But many of the knights are sore wounded.

On the morrow Lancelot looked from the castle walls and saw sixty knights on the field below. Among their number was Briant and Meliant but not Kay who was wounded from the buffeting of the day before. And Lancelot did muster seven knights amongst whom was Lucan and sayeth unto them, 'Knights! Nothing can we achieve by skulking behind these walls. Yonder is our foe and with God's will we shall scatter them. Pick your enemy and run at him most mightily, for we do this in the name of our sovereign lord Arthur and the memory of his dear Queen.' And they issued from the gate like arrows newly barbed with steel.

Meliant seeth Lancelot and ran at him so they hurtled with a mighty clash, but Meliant and his horse go to the ground and

Lancelot is minded to alight and run at him with his sword but Briant seeth this and ran at Lancelot. They struck each other so that sparks flew from their armour and their helmets were much buckled. Like lions they fought, and Meliant came to the aid of Briant but Lucan did knock him over again. The knights fought until they were separated by night and Briant returned to the Castle of the High Rock with many knights slain and wounded.

When the knights thereabouts heard that Lancelot had returned to Castle Cardoil and had dealt hard knocks to Briant they began to return. Ere long, Lancelot could muster five and thirty knights and others were mending of their wounds.

Part the XXVth

King Arthur and Gawain had gathered about them five knights within the Castle of Hope when they saw a multitude of knights come to the castle gates. But these knights were loyal to Ahuret the Bastard who had brought them to take vengeance on Gawain for the death of his brother Nabigant of the Rock, whom Gawain had slain on behalf of Meliot of England. For many days the castle was locked from without by these knights, and King Arthur became much angered for it became not a King to avoid combat. Gawain also did think it to be wrong to stay within the castle when the foe was camped outside. And they sayeth one to the other that better to face the foe and die with honour than stay inside to live with shame. And so they gathered their few knights and armoured them all and led them on to the field against the many knights of Ahuret.

The King and Gawain led the charge and they overthrew the knights that came against them, but Ahuret ran at the other knights and they were all slain. Now the King and Gawain commended each other to God, for both knew they were to be slain this day. And Ahuret ran full hard at Gawain and hit his breastplate so forcefully that Gawain lost his stirrups. But Gawain struck back and bent Ahuret back from his saddle. At this, Ahuret saw the King and ran at him but the King did hack at him with his sword and cause him to have a great wound. And the knights of Ahuret were much angered and gathered round to fall upon the King and Gawain. But there was an outcry from the rearmost of the knights for they hath seen more knights come on to the field.

Meliot of England had been given tidings that the King and Gawain were besieged in the Castle of Hope and gathered about him many good knights. Now he fell upon the knights of Ahuret and scattered them until many were slain and the others fled.

And Gawain taketh Meliot by the hand and sayeth, 'Thank you, dear Meliot, for the King and I were sore pressed and may have been very busy this day.'

Meliot replieth, 'Think little of it, Sire, for there was nought else I had in mind to do this day.'

And the King sayeth, 'Then thanks be to God, Sire, that He ordaineth you should rest in quiet this day.'

Then sayeth Gawain to Meliot, 'Meliot, I have need of a good knight to live in this castle and guard it well. Will you undertake so to do?'

And Meliot sayeth that he would right gladly. He sayeth also that as Gawain's man he will come to Gawain's aid without delay for it was proper for a knight to defend his lord without measure.

Gawain thanketh him. And the knight and the King departed as Meliot did build the castle back up.

Part the XXVIth

King Arthur and Gawain rode until they came to a deep forested valley beneath a hill. And the King seeth a rose bush and alighteth from his horse. There he took many roses to the wonder of Gawain, who knoweth not why and why the King is silent thereof. They then rode to the Chapel of Avalon and, after disarming themselves, entered. And the King in great sorrow placed the roses upon the tomb of his Queen. Then Gawain knoweth why the King hath picked the roses, for the knight had not known of the chapel nor of the riches tombs therein. They lodged that night with the hermits and rode to Castle Cardoil after Mass.

At Castle Cardoil the King was greeted with great joy for many thought him to be slain. And the news came to the Castle of the High Rock and Kay is much afeared and taketh him across the sea to Lesser Britain and hideth him in the Castle Chinon. Briant and Meliant stayed at the Castle of the High Rock and doeth much to spoil the land and take plunder where they may. But the knights at Castle Cardoil that came to Lancelot are mended of their wounds and many other knights came there also that the King may soon take vengeance on his foe.

One day the King was sat at meat. With him were sat also Lancelot, Gawain, Yvain the son of King Urien, Sagramors le Desirous and Yvain le Aoutres and other knights. And Lucan brought the King a gold cup that maketh the King think of his Queen. At this, a knight well armed came in to the great hall and bringeth himself before the King and sayeth, 'Sire, I bring you message from my sovereign, King Madeglant of Oriande. He demandeth that you yield up the Round Table for he is close kin and inheritor of the Queen and since she is dead you have no right to hold it. He is also your enemy for you hold to the new laws of God which he sayeth is an abomination. But he sayeth that if you abandon the new laws of God and marry his sister, Queen Jandree, you may hold the Round Table. If you do not do this, such misfortune that comes about will be upon your head.' With this, the knight left the hall and departed the land.

And Gawain sayeth to the King that his knights would follow him to smite his enemy. And he continueth, 'Sire, all Greater Britain is yours and no castles have been taken by your enemies. Only land and houses have been harmed and such shame is lightly mended. King Madeglant is mighty in words only and not in deeds and might easily be vanquished. Indeed, Sire, you need but send one of your best knights against him.'

The King doth order his knights to prepare themselves for conflict and prayeth the Lord God that He should defend that which is right in His eyes. The King also seeth that his ordinance is obeyed, that chalices of the manner of the Holy Grail be used throughout the land for the Eucharist wherein the blood of Our Saviour is taken by the people. And he doeth the same with the bells and seeth that all chapels hath one or more bells according to their means. And the people rejoiced much at the sound of the bells.

One day tidings came to the King that Briant and Meliant were intent on taking Castle Pannenoisance and did take a great army of knights there. At this, the King departed from Castle Cardoil, taking many knights with him, and he came upon Briant upon a field of red clover. And the knights ranged against each other and ran one upon the other with much hurtling. Great was the shock of their meeting and the ground shook with the fury of their combat. Meliant of the Waste Manor sought Lancelot and ran at him so that he pierceth the knight's shield. But Lancelot thrust his lance through Meliant's shoulder. Meliant then turneth and brought his sword down upon the helmet of Lancelot. Then Lancelot brought his sword down upon the shoulder of Meliant and the knight fell from his horse greatly wounded. And many knights fell upon Lancelot but Gawain doth aid him and they drove the knights away. King Arthur hath challenged Briant and they give great blows one to the other and Briant doth stumble, and his knights come to his aid and circle the King. Thereon Yvain and Lucan ride in and bring aid to the King. Sagramors le Desirous met with Briant and knocked him from his horse. He then took his sword and would have slain the knight but the King cried unto him to desist.

With Briant fallen to King Arthur the knights ceased their combat and tended the slain and wounded. Meliant was borne on his shield to the Castle of the High Rock where he died. Briant was taken prisoner to Castle Cardoil and gave his loyalty to King Arthur. Thereon he was made Steward of all the King's lands, and some of the King's knights did think this to be wrong and were downcast, but Briant seemeth to serve the King well. But the King did command that any who did take vengeance on Kay would do so in his name.

One day the King was at Castle Cardoil when a damsel came in to the Great Hall and sayeth to the King, 'Sire, I bear a message from my Lady Queen Jandree. She commandeth me to say to you that she wishes to be Queen of your land, mistress of your household, and your wife. She sayeth that you must give up your obedience to the new laws of God and follow those of the god whom she worships. If you do this not, King Madeglant is ready to fall upon your country. He hath taken oath that he will not end his war upon you until he hath the Round Table which you hold in defiance of him. My Lady would not bring you this message for she cannot look upon any that hold to the new laws of God and hath bound her eyes that she might not see such by mischance. Thus all day and all night she is blind to the world around her.'

And the King sayeth to the damsel, 'Pray say to your Lady that none shall sit here as Queen lest they be as worshipful as Queen Guinevere and the Lord God maketh not her like nor shall He so do. Tell your Lady also that the law given to us by the death of

God upon the Cross shall I never renounce. Further say to her that even though she unbind her eyes she shall not see truth unless she believeth in Our Saviour.'

'Then, Sire,' sayeth the damsel, 'you should prepare yourself for such evil tidings as never before have you known.'

And the damsel goeth to Queen Jandree and telleth to her the King's message. And the Queen sayeth that she would love this king but, as he hath no regard for her and refuses her will and command, he would fall. She sayeth to her brother, King Madeglant, that he should not take his knights to Greater Britain for she would seek her own vengeance on the King.

Part the XXVIIth

Despite the wish of his sister that she might take vengeance on King Arthur, King Madeglant gathered himself a mighty host and came to the shores of England with ten ships. The people defended themselves but cried to King Arthur for aid in their troubles. And his knights sayeth that he must send Lancelot for he was the best among them. Arthur sent for Lancelot and sayeth unto him, 'Sire, there are none that are your measure in knightly virtue and many are they who will follow you. King Madeglant wages war on my kingdom and I have need of a good knight to protect my land. I therefore earnestly pray you will take up my cause and rid England of King Madeglant.'

And Lancelot sayeth, 'Sire, there are many good knights in your court whom you could send. I am but one among many who would willingly serve you thus.'

King Arthur sayeth, 'Sire, modesty is becoming in a knight, but honour is more so. And your honour, Sire, is brighter even than my crown. Such honour have you I know that by it England can be saved.'

That day, Lancelot rode forth with forty knights in search of King Madeglant and discovered him by the coast where he warreth upon the people. And the people were of great joy when they saw Lancelot and joined his company of knights.

And King Madeglant issued forth from his ship and took his knights to do battle with Lancelot. Many of the King's knights were slain and many did run back to the ships but Lancelot had the ships burnt excepting two. King Madeglant took one ship and did flee right willingly and the other ship did follow with conquered knights. And the people sayeth that if King Arthur was willing they would much desire that Lancelot stay to be their king for he was a knight of much goodness and valour.

At Castle Cardoil the King sat to meat when a knight entered the great hall and come before the King without salute and sayeth, 'Sire, where is Lancelot?'

And the King sayeth that Lancelot is elsewhere in the land. The knight then sayeth, 'Sire, wherever he is, he is the mortal enemy of my sovereign King Claudas. And so, Sire, are you if you give this knight aid.'

'Why so? sayeth the King.

'For he hath slain Meliant of the Waste Manor, the son of the sister of King Claudas, as he also slew the father of Meliant. King Claudas grieves much for his nephew and is determined on vengeance against Lancelot.'

And the King sayeth, 'Sire, you should know that I hold not in great honour the name of King Claudas for he hath taken castles from his father and not by conquest. You should further know that I shall stand firm at the side of Lancelot against all the world may send against him. If Lancelot sayeth this demand you make against him is false then the knights of this court and the knights throughout the land shall stand firm by him, for his name in honour is without equal. Should he admit as you accuse him, then his cause for these deaths will be weighed to his advantage for nought would he do in meanness of spirit.'

'That may be, Sire,' sayeth the knight, 'but Lancelot is the enemy of King Claudas and should you aid this knight the consequences will be on your head.' And the knight departeth to return to his king.

The King sent for his knights and held them in council to ask what he should do. And Yvain sayeth that Lancelot had slain Meliant in the service of the King and should not be held to account thereof.'

But Briant of the Isles sayeth, 'Yvain, it is known well that Lancelot did slay the father of Meliant. It is right that he should have sought peace and accord with Meliant. Instead, he did slay him also.

And Gawain sayeth, 'No, Briant, I will not have it. Lancelot is not here to take up his cause for he is on the King's business. It was you who knighted Meliant and loosed him upon his warring against the King. And this whilst the King was far away in pilgrimage of the Holy Grail. It was the King that sent Lancelot to guard his lands that you had under conflict. On the return of the King Meliant knew of it well but did not come to the King nor did he send a messenger to put forth his grievance. Meliant did war against the King who hath never done him a wrong nor rejected a plea. The blame, Sire, doth go to Meliant and to no other. In this matter I will willingly take on the cause of Lancelot and defend his name.'

Briant sayeth, 'In that, Sire, there is no one who will take up your challenge, nor should any of us make enemies of friends but stay our hand for the defence against those kings that make war upon this land. My mind sayeth the King should keep Lancelot far from these lands for a year that King Claudas may see that the King doth not associate with Lancelot. Then will King Claudas seek accord with this court.'

But Sagramors le Desirous then sayeth loudly, 'What? Would you have Lancelot created a coward who hideth from his accusers? Shall we so treat a knight who hath served his King with much honour? No, Sire, we should run upon King Claudas and his knights and send them bruised and limping from this land as would Lancelot were he here.'

Briant sayeth, 'Far better it would be for the King to send Lancelot away for a year than to fight his enemies for the next ten years.'

At this, the good knight Orguelleux entered the hall and heareth what Briant sayeth and himself sayeth, 'Briant, no knight should wish another harm who hath done good service with the King. None are better than Lancelot in this and he is not here to make answer. And so you should not speak ill of him. Much renown hath this court from the works of Lancelot and no braver knight exists in this realm than he. Few enough are the knights in this court who are beyond replace such as he. If King Claudas wars upon this land in the name of hatred of Lancelot, then so be it. For the King and his knights shall suffer warfare on behalf of a good knight in the sight of God. And He shall be pleased.'

And Briant was much angered at this but sayeth nothing for Orguelleux was a hardy knight.

Part the XXVIIIth

When King Arthur learned that King Madeglant had been defeated and the land was quiet he sent to Lancelot and asketh him to return to Castle Cardoil. Though the people in the land where Lancelot had conquered King Madeglant sorrowed that he had returned, the people of Castle Cardoil made great joy. Lancelot was told of the tidings of King Claudas and of Briant but sayeth nothing for in his own mind he thinketh what to do. Briant much disliked Lancelot and wished him away from the place as he had asked the King. Unknown by all, Briant it was that had counselled King Claudas to send his knight.

King Madeglant did hear that Lancelot had returned to Castle Cardoil and he came back and wasted the land and did much plunder. The people asketh the King for the return of Lancelot but the King sendeth Briant and forty knights. And Briant did not protect the land and was defeated by King Madeglant who burned many towns and castles and struck of the heads of those who would not abandon God.

Briant returned to Castle Cardoil as war against the King spread on all sides. He had no liking for the King but pretended to be his loyal servant. Nor had he any liking for Lancelot and the fellowship of knights that gave him company.

On Whitsuntide, the King and the knights were at meat in the great hall when, to their wonderment, an arrow came within and penetrated a stone column. The iron-tipped arrow was made of gold and carried many precious stones. At this, a damsel of great beauty entered the hall on a horse with a squire behind. The horse was attired with gilded harness and the damsel was clothed in the finest silk. And she saluted the King most worthily and sayeth, 'Sire, a favour must I ask of you, nor can I alight from my horse until you grant it.'

'Then alight, damsel,' sayeth the King, 'for no one could refuse to help such a fair one as you.'

And Yvain did lift her from the horse and place her lightly on the ground and take her to sit by him whereon he looked upon her often for she was fair and gentle and of good countenance. And the King sayeth to her, 'Damsel, what is that you wish of me?'

And she sayeth that she hath much need of the knight that could draw the arrow from the column. And the King asketh what the knight should do when he hath drawn the arrow but she sayeth that the arrow must be drawn first.

At this, the King sayeth to Gawain. 'Fair nephew, pull forth the arrow for the damsel.'

But Gawain sayeth, 'Sire, I pray you that you ask the other knights before me. You have here Lancelot who is a great knight than I. No, Sire, I could not take the shame of trying first.'

And the King sayeth, 'Yvain, you try the arrow for you cannot think yourself too humble.'

But Yvain sayeth, 'Sire, nothing in this world would I not do for you, but in this I pray that you excuse me.'

Again the King sayeth, 'Sagramors, or you, Orguelleux, will you do it?'

But they sayeth, 'Sire, we pray you ask us only after Lancelot has tried.'

Now the King sayeth, 'Damsel, pray ask Lancelot that he attempt to remove the arrow that if he fails the others may follow.'

And the damsel sayeth to Lancelot, 'Sire, pray render not my request in vain. In the memory of that you hold most dear, try the arrow that others may follow should you fail.'

But Lancelot sayeth, 'Damsel, there are many knights within this hall and much as I would willingly give you aid I cannot be seen a fool and a braggart by taking first try.'

And the King sayeth, 'No, Sire, you would be seen as a true and courteous knight that giveth aid to a damsel. Pray, sire, do as she asketh.'

Lancelot remembereth the damsel had asked him in the memory of that he held most dear. He held the memory of the Queen most dear and would not bring dishonour upon that memory. At this, he stood up and went to the column wherein was the arrow and pulled it clear with a grasp that caused the column to tremble. And the damsel sayeth to the King, 'Sire, none other could have obtained the arrow but this knight. Now I ask that you honour your covenant and let him give me his aid.'

And the King sayeth, 'Damsel, as Lancelot wishes.'

Lancelot thinketh of the Queen and sayeth, 'Truly shall I do as the damsel requires.'

The damsel sayeth, 'Sire, you must go to the Chapel Perilous wherein you will find the body of a knight shrouded. You shall take the shroud and the sword thereby and take them to the Castle Perilous. Then, Sire, you are to go to the Castle of the Griffon whence you escaped by slaying the lion and return to me at Castle Perilous bringing the head of the griffon. For at that castle lies a knight who cannot be healed but by the shroud, the sword, and the head.'

'It seemeth to me, damsel,' sayeth Lancelot, 'that you care little for my life, but only for the success of your wish.'

'No, Sire,' sayeth the damsel, 'I know full well the dangers you face. But your life you must not lose for the knight who needs to be healed cannot endure without you fulfilling your trial. Also you shall see the damsel most desirous in the world to see you and she is fair beyond all others. Pray go now, Sire, for to tarry will increase the hazard.'

And the damsel departed from the court and sayeth to herself, 'Lancelot, you go to the two most evil and fearful places in the world yet I do not wish for your death. But you I ought to hate above all others for you took away my lover and made him marry another. This I shall never forget.'

Lancelot taketh his leave of the King and his brother knights and issued forth all armed into the forest and commendeth himself to God.

Part the XXIXth

The people who suffered under the slaying and plunders of King Madeglant sent a message to the King and sayeth that they are in sore want of Lancelot to defend them. For Briant did return to the court with but fifteen knights whereof he had taken forty. And the King was troubled for now he hath lost many brother knights and sayeth to Briant, 'How, Sire, did you have so many knights slain?'

And Briant sayeth, 'Sire, King Madeglant hath a mighty force whom none may endure against. No people war so savage as do they. Sire, this land that they war on is far from you and is of little worth. I counsel you to let King Madeglant take it and let it cause you no more trouble.'

'Briant,' sayeth the King, 'both blame and shame would be upon me should I act as you counsel. No man of honour would let another take what is his. A worthy man counts not the value but the honour of what is his. I will not have men say that I have not the heart to defend that which is mine. Already I am at great shame for they bring their ungodly law to my land. If Lancelot were here he would take forty knights and drive King Madeglant and his evil knights back to their own land; Pray God that he returneth soon.'

And Briant sayeth, 'Sire, you should know that the people of that land think nought of you but seek to have Lancelot as their King.'

The King sayeth, 'Sire, they may seek as you say, but Lancelot is my loyal knight and would do nought against my will.'

'Then, Sire,' sayeth Briant, 'I shall say no more on the matter since you choose not to believe me. But I am certain, Sire, that this knight will do great harm to you should you not guard yourself against him.'

Part the XXXth

Lancelot rode through the forest towards the Chapel Perilous and came upon a knight who did bear a grievous wound. And Lancelot sayeth, 'Sire, from whence come you?'

The knight sayeth that he came from Chapel Perilous and Lancelot asketh him of his wound. The knight sayeth, 'Sire, I could not defend myself from the evil people that were there. But for a damsel who came there I would not have escaped alive. She asketh me that, should I come upon a knight they call Lancelot, or another named Percival, or a knight named Gawain, I should ask of them that they go to her straightway for none but such good knights could enter the Chapel Perilous. Indeed, Sire, I marvel much that the damsel there entereth but she oftimes entereth alone. There is inside the chapel the body of a knight that hath of late been slain. He was a strong knight but foul and cruel.'

'What was his name?' sayeth Lancelot.

'He was named Ahuret the Bastard,' sayeth the knight. 'He received a great wound from King Arthur before the walls of Castle Hope and did die thereafter. And his knights did lay siege to Castle Hope and Meliot of England defeated them but was sore wounded by a knight with the sword of Ahuret, which now layeth with him in the Chapel Perilous. Meliot must have the sword and the shroud to save him from death of the wound. May God grant that I meet one of the knights that I might give him the message.'

'Knight' sayeth Lancelot, 'you have found one of the knights for my name is Lancelot. I tell you this that you may leave to restore your wound.'

'Thank you, Sire,' sayeth the knight, 'and may God grant you his protection for you go in great peril. But the damsel hath great desire to see you and will give you what aid she can.'

'Knight, God hath brought me through many a peril and if He so desires He shall bring me through this also.'

With this, Lancelot departed from the knight and came upon the Chapel Perilous at evensong. The chapel standeth in a great forest which pressed hard upon the graveyard walls. At the entrance stood a great Cross and Lancelot did cross himself when he entered the many-tombed graveyard. There also did he see many tall men clothed in black who stand near one to the other and say nothing to him. When he cometh to the chapel he alighteth from his horse and leave his lance and shield outside. He entered the chapel and saw it to be dark but for a small lamp which giveth a poor light. But he seeth therein the coffin in which lay the knight. After kneeling and praying before an image of Our Lady, Lancelot went to the coffin and opened the lid. Therein lay the body of the knight in a shroud all bloody. And Lancelot lifted up the head of the knight to loose the shroud and a great noise issued from the coffin but whence it came he knew not. He teareth away part of the shroud and taketh the sword that lay beside the knight and closed the coffin. And he came to the chapel door and saw that the gate from the graveyard was full barred by many tall knights clothed in black and mounted as if for combat. At this a damsel came running with skirt lifted to aid her haste. And she sayeth to the black garbed knights, 'Do not move until we know who the knight is.'

And she sayeth to Lancelot, 'Sire, lay down the sword and the piece of shroud you have taken from the coffin.'

And he sayeth, 'Damsel, how doth this concern you?'

The damsel sayeth, 'You have taken them without my leave for I have the body of the knight and the chapel in my charge. Tell me, Sire, what is your name?'

And he sayeth, 'My name, damsel, is for the friends that love me, or for the foes that fear me. Tell me, damsel, how would you gain if I give you my name?'

And the damsel sayeth, 'I know not, Sire, whether I would gain or not, for oft I have been deceived.'

He sayeth, 'My name, damsel, is Lancelot of the Lake.'

'Then, Sire,' sayeth she, 'you have right to the sword and the cloth. But, before you depart, come with me to my castle and see the rich tombs I have made for Percival, Gawain, and for you.'

And sayeth Lancelot, 'Damsel, no desire have I to see my sepulchre so early in my life.'

The damsel sayeth, 'If you do not come to my castle, you shall not issue forth from this graveyard, for the knights you see before you are fiends of Hell that guard this graveyard and are at my command.'

But Lancelot sayeth, 'Damsel, no fiend from Hell or from this world can harm a true Christian.'

Then sayeth the damsel, 'Sire, I beg you to come with me to my castle and I shall save your life from these fiends. If you do not come with me, I demand you yield the sword and you may leave in safety.'

And Lancelot sayeth, 'Damsel, I have neither desire nor leisure to enter you castle. Nor shall you have the sword, for it is needed to heal a brother knight and great pity it would be if he were to die at my yielding to you.'

'You, are both vile and cruel to me, for had I the sword you would not escape this graveyard, but with it in your keeping the knights here cannot bar your path. Had I but the sword you would have been taken to my castle there to remain and I would no longer have guardianship of this chapel and graveyard. Now I must come here for ever more.'

But Lancelot is not sorry on her behalf for she was a damsel that caused her own troubles. He took up his lance and shield and mounted his horse and rode slowly to the gate. The knights there, now hideous on being close, moved apart and let him pass and he thanketh God for his deliverance.

Lancelot rode through the forest until the sun rose and came upon a hermit with whom he heard Mass and took a little food.

He rode that day until the sun set and no house nor lodging could he find.

Then he came upon some high walls which surrounded an orchard and gained entrance therein by an unlocked gate. He unbridled his horse and lay down his shield for a pillow and went to sleep. He did not know that the orchard was hard by a castle hidden by the walls and the tall trees. It was the Castle of the Griffon where he had slain the lion and where he was to seek the head of the griffon.

From the castle issued a damsel leading a hound to guard against the griffon. She was come to lock the orchard gate but instead she seeth Lancelot asleep inside. The damsel did run most fast to her mistress and sayeth, 'Rise, Damsel! Lancelot is asleep in the orchard!'

And the damsel ran from her chamber at great pace and came to the orchard and seeth Lancelot but knoweth not what to do. She sat near him and looked at him and sighed and then came more close to the knight. She then sayeth to herself, 'Dear God, what shall I do? Desperately I wish to kiss him, but if I wake him he may not grant me a kiss. If I kiss him whilst he sleeps, he will wake up and perhaps fend me away. Better perhaps that I kiss him now and know that I have done so albeit without his blessing. Such blessed memory will I have of such a kiss.'

And the damsel kneeled by his side and kissed him three times most tenderly on the lips. And Lancelot did leap up and cross himself and say, 'Holy God! Where am I?' And he seeth the damsel.

She sayeth, 'Sweet Sire, you are at the side of her that loveth you. A damsel whose heart is yours for ever.'

But Lancelot sayeth, 'Damsel, truly no one should hate those that love him, but my heart is given to a Lady whose love is beyond this world. This love is deep rooted in my heart and may not be quenched by another although it be the most pure and fine.'

And she sayeth, 'Dearest Sire, come with me to the castle where you may know my thoughts towards you. And where your thoughts of love may turn toward me.'

'Damsel, I seek the healing of a knight that may not be healed but by the head of the griffon.'

'This well I know,' she sayeth, 'for it was my plea that the damsel did send you here that I may see you once more.'

'Then,' sayeth Lancelot, 'I have come in answer to your deception. Now I shall depart, for the head of the griffon is not needed.'

She sayeth then, 'Lancelot, they say you are a good knight, but I say great are your faults. No other knight in the world would have refused my love, but your base heart hath done so. I kept the griffon at bay that he might not harm you. Better I think that it had slain you, or my father came whilst you sleep and put you to death. Better also that I could love you more dead than alive and that your head was put over the gate where I might gaze upon it for ever more. You, Sire, won me by taking the sword from the stone column. I am your prize yet you will not take me.'

And he sayeth, 'Damsel, much have you done for me, but your kisses betray you, for they who doth kiss in like manner may not cause ill against those they kiss.'

And the damsel sayeth, 'Sire, I took only that which never may I have again.'

Lancelot mounted his horse and, after commending the damsel to God, rode from the orchard into the forest. And she looked after him as long as she may, her heart heavy with pain. She then returned to her chamber and wept amongst the silence.

Lancelot rode until noon when he came upon Castle Perilous wherein lay Meliot of England. As he alighted at the mounting stage he met the damsel who had been at the court of King Arthur and she sayeth, 'Welcome, Sire. All here have much joy at your coming.'

And he sayeth, 'Thank you, damsel. May God see your kindness.'

She taketh him to the hall and had him disarm. And he sayeth, 'Damsel, I have here some of the shroud with which the knight was wrapped, and the sword from his side. But you, damsel, did make a fool of me by sending me for the head of the griffon.'

'I did that, Sire,' sayeth the damsel. 'for the sake of the damsel that loved you greatly. Now that she hath seen you, no more shall she place me under her plea.'

The damsel then led him to the place where Meliot lay and sayeth, 'Here, Sire, is Lancelot.'

And Meliot sayeth, 'Much welcome have you Lancelot. How fares Gawain? Is he well?'

'He was most hearty when I departed from him. But had he and King Arthur known of your wounds they would have been most sorrowful.'

And Meliot sayeth, 'The knight that wounded me so is now dead of the wounds I gave him. But the wounds I have rage within me and nothing can I do for them but they are touched by his sword and bound with his shroud all bloody. And only the best knight in the land can find them.'

At this, the damsel sayeth with great joy, 'See, Sire, they are here, brought by Lancelot.'

'By God's mercy!' crieth Meliot. 'Truly they speak of you as the best knight for no other would the coffin open. You would not have had the sword or the cloth and the foul knights that waited in the graveyard would have had you slain. But your goodness and virtue have triumphed and now I may turn away from death's shade.'

They uncovered his wounds and the damsel touched them with the sword and Lancelot bound them with the shroud, and Meliot was comforted and need wait only mending. And Lancelot was with great joy for he knew Meliot to be a good and loyal knight.

And the damsel sayeth unto Lancelot, 'Sire, for long I have hated you for you did take from me the one I loved and gave him to another. Many are the times I have sought to bring you harm for my loss and often I have prayed to God to bring you low. But now, Sire, the time of your offence against me is long gone and the pain has gone from my heart to my fading memory. For that you have done this thing for Meliot you may know that never again shall I seek vengeance upon you, and my grievance against you has withered away.'

Lancelot sayeth, 'Thank you, damsel. May you walk in grace beneath the favour of God.'

That night Lancelot lodged at the castle and departed after Mass the following morning. He returned to Castle Cardoil where he found the King much dismayed, for King Madeglant was despoiling much of his land and the people were turning from God. And Gawain and Yvain had departed from the court for the King trusteth Briant more than he should. And Lancelot thinketh the same and would have departed, for he liketh Briant but little and hath no trust in him. But the King sayeth to him, 'Sire, let your loyalty guide your heart and go on my part and put King

Madeglant to flight for there are none here that might do as you may. Bring the land back to the realm and the people back to God for no better adventure is available to you in this world.'

Lancelot sayeth to the King, 'Sire, I shall not fail you as you would not fail me.'

And the King sayeth, 'Sire, in truth I will not, for to fail you would be to fail myself.'

The King giveth Lancelot forty knights but Lancelot goeth not to find King Madeglant. He goeth instead to the ships which saileth from Oriande bearing King Madeglant's men. And Lancelot doth burn the ships until they be destroyed. He then cometh against King Madeglant and did slay him and his knights. He then rode through the land destroying the copper idols and false images until all the people are brought back to the law of God. And the people sayeth that they need a king and they look to Lancelot to be their ruler, but he sayeth he will not be king for he was a knight of King Arthur and that he would not be against his sovereign.

King Claudas, who still warred against King Arthur, heard that Lancelot had slain King Madeglant and taken King Arthur's land back. And King Claudas sent a secret message to Briant that he should tell the King to keep Lancelot out of his court that King Claudas might take vengeance on King Arthur. And Briant replieth that Gawain and Yvain had gone from the court and that he would put Lancelot at enmity with King Arthur.

Tidings had come to King Arthur that King Madeglant was slain and that the people were back in God's law. He heareth also that the people are want to have Lancelot for their king. At this, Briant sayeth to the King, 'Sire, the lands taken back from King Madeglant have banded together and made treaty that they will attack you under the kingship of Lancelot. This I tell you from my loyalty due to your many kindnesses to me.'

But the King sayeth, 'This cannot be, for Lancelot is my most loyal knight. Such evil would he not do to me.'

And Briant sayeth, 'Sire, long has it been known among many in this court that Lancelot is a traitor to you but none dare to say this to you. I say this from the loyalty of my heart and that I am the most powerful knight in your service and you may depend upon me.'

The King then sayeth, 'For the faith you have shown me I shall send for Lancelot and ask him of this matter. For no worthy king should have disloyal knights about him or in his service.'

The King's messenger found Lancelot in the kingdom of Oriande and, when he had read the letters, he set forth to Castle Cardoil straightway.

And Briant sayeth to the King that he should have forty knights armed beneath their mantles come to the great hall and be ready to take Lancelot and make him prisoner at the King's command. And the King agreed.

These tidings came to Lancelot but only that forty knights were to attend upon the King with arms beneath their cloaks and he came to the hall likewise armed. Briant seeth this and sayeth to the King, 'Look, Sire. Lancelot comes to the hall full armed without your leave so to do. Demand of him why he wishes to do you harm.'

And the King sayeth to Lancelot, 'Sire, why are you full armed within the hall?'

'For I had heard, Sire, that there would be knights within the hall full armed and I feared that they might do you harm.'

'And, Sire,' sayeth the King, 'I have heard right differently for it seemeth that it was you that was intent on harming me.' And the King commanded that Lancelot be taken prisoner.

Briant and his knights fell upon Lancelot who drew his sword and ran at them such that they are all much disconcerted. But there were many of them and the King sayeth that they may not harm him, but they brought him to the ground at cost of seven slain and many others wounded, amongst whom was Briant with a grievous wound. And Lancelot was cast into prison saying to the King, 'This is an evil reward, Sire, for the service I have done you.'

And all they of the court save for Briant and his knights sayeth this must be the end of King Arthur, for Gawain and Yvain have departed and Lancelot is taken prisoner though he hath always done well in the eyes of God. And they knew that this was Briant's doing and they wished him an evil reward and the protection of God upon Lancelot.

Part the XXXIst

Percival rode from the Castle of the Grail with heart full sore at the tidings of his sister brought by the damsel with the wounded arm. The Damsel Dindrane had been taken by Aristor of Moraine to be his wife, whereafter he would strike off her head as was his cruel custom. Percival decided to ask his uncle the King Hermit for guidance in the matter. As he came upon the hermitage he saw three hermits come forth and they sayeth unto him, 'Do not enter, Sire, for a damsel is preparing a body in there.'

'Whose body is it?' sayeth Percival.

'It is the body of the good King Hermit who hath been slain by Aristor of Moraine on account of Percival whom Aristor doth hate with much vigour.'

And Percival is full of sorrow at these tidings for the King Hermit was his uncle and a good and holy man. He staith at the hermitage for the burial of his uncle and intendeth to depart after Mass to find Aristor and take vengeance for his uncle and save his sister. But the damsel who prepared the body of his uncle came to him and sayeth, 'Sire, a full long time I have been seeking you. In a rich box of ivory that hangs at my saddle I carry the head of a knight who ought to be avenged by none other than you. Please help me, Sire, in this matter for I have carried the head for a long time as witnessed by King Arthur and Gawain at court where I asked for you but none knew where you are. My castle is forbidden to me until the knight is avenged.'

'Who is the knight?' sayeth Percival.

'He, Sire, was the son of your uncle Bruns Brandalis. Had he lived, he would have been one of the best knights in the world.'

'And who slew him, damsel?'

'The Red Knight of the Deep Forest that taketh a lion on a lead. He came upon your cousin all unarmed and slew him in cowardly manner.'

'Damsel,' sayeth Percival, 'it greiveth me to know of his slaying as I grieve for my uncle the King Hermit. Him I would avenge more than any in the world for he was slain in my name. This Aristor hath slain a holy man who wished no ill on him, and may God grant that I find him for my vengeance.'

'Sire, he so hateth you that he would come to find you had he tidings of your whereabouts.'

'Then,' sayeth Percival, 'may God grant him the knowledge of my coming, for soon I wish to meet him.'

And the damsel sayeth, 'Sire, pray do not forget your cousin or the foul knight that slew him. To reach the castle of Aristor you must pass through the Deep Forest wherein lives the Red Knight who leads the lion. May God grant that you find him also.'

And Percival departed in haste.

Part the XXXIInd

As Percival rode through the forest he came upon two squires carrying venison and sayeth to them, 'Sires, whence carry you this venison?'

And they sayeth to him, 'To the Castle of Ariste where Aristor is lord.'

Sayeth he, 'Are there many knights at the castle?'

'Not one, Sire, but in four days the castle will throng with thousands for our lord is to marry. He is to take the daughter of the Widow Lady who he hath carried off by force from the Castle Camelot. She is placed in the house of one of our lord's knights until she be married. But we are right sorrowful at this for she is a noble damsel of great beauty, but he shall strike off her head thereafter as is his custom.'

'Might a good knight carry her off to save her from this fate?'

'Yes, if it pleases God for our lord hath such great cruelty. Already he hath slain a good hermit and is greatly desirous of meeting the brother of the damsel, for he sayeth that he is one of the best knights in the world. He sayeth that much pleasure would he have to slay the brother of the damsel.'

'Do you know where he now is?'

'Truly, Sire, we have just left him in combat with a knight.'

'Know you the name of this knight?'

'He is named the Knight Hardy, Sire. He came upon Aristor and telleth him that he is a knight that oweth much to Percival and our lord did run at him with great hurtle. We left them in full fight and could hear the blows of sword upon armour for many a long time. Aristor will surely slay him as he doth all knights he meets in the forest.'

Percival departed at great pace and goeth to the place said by the squires. There he heard the sound of sword and shield and came upon the two knights engaged in combat. Aristor had been wounded in two places but the Knight Hardy hath a lance through his body and blood ran from his armour. At this, Percival gave spur to his horse and cried to God as he lowered his lance and ran at Aristor. Percival hit him hard on the breastplate and bowed him back along his horse. And Percival sayeth in a loud voice, 'Behold, Sire, I am come to my sister's wedding!'

But Aristor came up again and dealt Percival a hard blow on the helmet. With this, Percival drew his horse back and lowered again his lance and hurtled once more at Aristor and tumbled both knight and horse to the ground. Percival alighted and took his sword and removed the helmet of his foe.

And Aristor sayeth, 'what do you intend, Percival?'

'I intend, Sire, to cut off your head which I shall give to my sister whom you have treated in most foul manner.'

'Stay your hand, Sire, I pray you, sayeth Aristor. 'If you let me live, I will forgo my hatred of you.'

'Your hatred, Sire, I can abide, but you are of such foul and cruel manner that neither God nor I will have you in this world!' With that, Percival struck off his head and tied it to his saddle.

He then goeth to the Knight Hardy and sayeth, 'How is it with you, brave Knight?'

And the Knight Hardy sayeth, 'Death comes before me, Sire, but I surrender my life in the good knowledge that I stood and faced fear as you taught me.'

Percival taketh the reins of the Knight Hardy's horse and leadeth him to a hermit where the Knight Hardy did confess his sins before his soul departed his body. And Percival gave the hermit the Knight Hardy's horse and armour that he might have a good and honourable burial. He also giveth him the horse of Aristor.

After Mass there came to the hermitage the damsel who carried the knight's head at her saddle, and she sayeth to Percival, 'Sire, still you have much to do. You have rid this country of the foul Aristor, but you needs must find the Red Knight that slew the son of your uncle. No doubt have I that he you shall conquer, but I have great fear that the lion may be beyond defeat for it is a cruel and savage beast that fights with right hardiness for its lord.'

Percival rode into the forest with the damsel at his side. They had not travelled far when they came upon a knight sore wounded as was his horse. And the knight sayeth, 'Hold, Sire! Do not enter the forest for I have just escaped from a Red Knight who is guarded by a foul lion. And I have to pass by the land of Aristor who wouldst attack any knight that passes that way.'

'Have no fear of that,' sayeth the damsel, 'for his head hangs at the saddle of this knight.'

'Praise God for that,' sayeth the knight.

Percival sayeth unto him, 'Go, Sire, to the hermit that is a little beyond and sayeth to him that he should give you one of the horses I left with him for he hath no use for them.'

And the knight thanked Percival and rode on to the hermitage where he chose the horse of Aristor. This dealing, however, was much to his misfortune for he came upon a knight of Aristor's household who did slay him to retake his master's horse.

Percival and the damsel were deep in the forest when they came upon a glade wherein lay the lion guarding the path of its master and waiting for passing knights. The damsel withdrew in much fear and Percival lowered his lance as the lion came at him with eyes of fire and with jaws wideagape. The knight thinketh to thrust his lance down the throat of the lion but the beast did swerve and jump on the hindquarters of the horse, wounding it much. At this, the horse did kick backwards and break the lion's frontmost teeth whereon it gave a great roar that sounded through the forest. Percival then thrust at the lion with his lance and pierced it through the body and it was slain.

The Red Knight had heard the roar of the lion and came full pace to the place and saw the beast slain upon the ground. And he sayeth to Percival, 'You did falsely slay this lion when it was wounded by your horse.'

And Percival sayeth, 'And you brought about your own death when you slew my uncle's son whose head is borne on the saddle of this damsel.' Without more ado he ran at the knight who came at him with his lance and broke it on the white shield with the red cross. Percival thrust his lance through the breast of the Red Knight and bore him dead to the ground.

Percival then mounted the horse of the Red Knight, for his own was sore wounded by the lion. The damsel sayeth to him, 'Sire, the castle which the Red Knight did steal from me is within this forest and I pray that you accompany me thither that I may take it without conflict from any within.' And Percival sayeth that he will.

When they came to the castle, Percival could see that it was a most fair castle, well walled with battlements and with a many windowed hall. When those inside heard of the death of the Red Knight they yielded the castle most eagerly and accepted the damsel as their mistress. She had the head of the knight buried with great honour and commanded that Mass be said every day for the soul of the dead knight. Percival rested therein until he was ready and departed with the prayers of the damsel for his restoring of the castle to her inheritance.

Percival then returned to the house wherein was held his sister, the Damsel Dindrane. The knight who guarded her for Aristor was of a most kindly nature and had comforted her often when she wept at her fate. Percival came to the gate of the house full armed and the knight came and welcomed him, for he took him to be a knight of Aristor. But he saw the head of Aristor when Percival held it by the hair and marvelled much at the sight. And Percival walked in to the house and seeth his sister that wept in great sorrow. 'Damsel,' he sayeth, 'weep no more for there shall be no wedding. Proof you will have of this token.' And he threw the head of Aristor to her feet.

The damsel looketh at the knight and seeth that it was her brother Percival. Great joy she made of him and thanked Our Saviour that he was alive and had come to her aid. And the knight of the house gave them both much honour for he was joyous at the slaying of Aristor. The Damsel Dindrane took the head of Aristor to the river and threw it in and sayeth, 'Thus may all foul and cruel men be done by, God willing.'

Brother and sister then rode back to Camelot where the Widow Lady was in great sorrow. As she wept in her chamber Percival took the hand of his sister and entered therein saying, 'Dear Lady, look upon what God hath preserved for you.' And she fell to her knees in joy. She then kissed them and sayeth, 'Blessed son and daughter, now my great joy hath returned to me. Thus my life is ended in joy, for I have lived long enough and I am ready to meet Our Saviour.'

'Lady,' sayeth Percival, 'in your life you have harmed no one and deserve tranquillity at your end. You shall live at the Castle of the Holy Grail, and thus when God calls for you, you shall be in the presence of many hallowed and sacred objects.'

And the Widow Lady sayeth, 'It is as you say, fair son, the castle of my good brother hath seen much that is holy.'

Sayeth Percival, 'And I shall see that should my sister wish to marry she shall be honoured as your daughter.'

But sayeth the damsel, 'Thank you brother, but only God will I marry.'

And the Widow Lady sayeth to Percival, 'The Damsel of the Carriage seeks you and will not end her search until she finds you.'

'Narrowly have our paths crossed. She will hear of my whereabouts.'

The Widow Lady then sayeth, 'We have here with us the damsel who was wounded in the arm by the foul knight. She it was that brought news of your sister and now she is healed.'

And Percival sayeth, 'Through her I am well avenged.'

Percival stayed with his mother until the land thereabout was put at peace. The Widow Lady and her daughter led a holy life and placed a chaplain in the chapel between the forest and Camelot that Mass be said therein. In later times the chapel grew to be an abbey which remains to this day.

Percival took leave of his mother and departed from the castle and rode in the forest until he came to a small house wherein he lodged for the night. The house belonged to a knight of simple means who gave Percival great honour but often did he sigh most sorrowfully. And Percival sayeth to him, 'Why, Sire, do you have this downcast countenance?'

And the knight sayeth, 'Sire, my brother was killed but recently by a knight in the service of Aristor, for my brother had been given

255

the horse that had belonged to Aristor. It had been given to him
by a hermit for his own horse had been maimed by the lion of the
Red Knight. And my brother was a good and worthy knight who
harmed no one.'

These tiding were not good for Percival for it was he that had
slain Aristor and had given the hermit the horse. He sayeth to the
knight, 'Sire, your bother did not deserve his death for he did not
slay the knight.'

'I know, Sire, for it was the same knight that slew the Red
Knight.'

On the morrow, Percival came upon a hermitage where he heard
Mass. The hermit sayeth to him, 'Sire, I counsel great care in this
forest for there are knights full armed that waiteth for the knight
that slew Aristor and the Red Knight and his lion. Any knight they
meet they will slay for the deaths of the two knights.

'Then, Sire,' sayeth Percival, 'may God keep me from such evil
knights.'

But he hath not left the hermitage long when he saw two knights,
one of whom rode the horse that had belonged to Aristor. And
the knights seeth Percival and one sayeth to the other, 'Look, this
knight beareth the same shield as he who slew Aristor.'

They came at great pace at Percival who spurred his horse to
meet them. Both knights broke their lances upon his shield and
Percival pierced the knight that rideth the horse of Aristor and bore
him dead to the ground. The other knight returned to the combat
but Percival did slay him by the sword. Percival then took the two
horses of the slain knights to the hermit and telleth him to give the
horses to deserving travellers, 'For it is great courtesy to aid a man
when you may.'

And the hermit sayeth to him, 'Sire, I knew of your deed in
the forest against the two knights, for three knights came to this
hermitage. They did flee from the chance of meeting you and
I praised their flight and sayeth unto them that death in combat
brings them closer to Hell than to Paradise.'

On the morrow, Percival chanced upon a knight who came fast
upon him for the knight knew Percival by his shield. And the knight
sayeth, 'Sire, I am come from the Castle of the Black Hermit. There
you will find the Damsel of the Carriage who asks you to attend

upon her with great pace. Also, Sire, I ask your aid of a most pitiful thing I saw in the forest. There I saw a knight leading a damsel against her will and beating her with a cruel rod. The damsel crieth out for the son of the Widow Lady who hath given her back her castle, and the knight doth hate the son of the Widow Lady and for this intends to put the damsel into a pit of serpents. They were followed by an old knight and a priest who prayed the knight to cease his torment of the damsel but he doth threaten them with death for their pleas.

Percival followed the pointing of the knight and heard the cries of the damsel as he approached the valley, wherein was the pit of serpents. And he heard her cry for mercy whereon the knight did beat her more cruelly. As he rode upon the scene the damsel seeth him and cried out, 'Sweet Sire, please give me your aid for this knight would steal my castle!'

And the knight sayeth to Percival, 'That horse I know. It belonged to the Red Knight of the Deep Forest. I know therefore that it was you who doth slay him!'

'And it was well that I did slay him, for he hath cut off the head of the son of an uncle of mine, and the head was carried by this damsel for many a long time.'

'Then,' sayeth the knight, 'you are my mortal enemy.'

At this, they ran at each other as fast as their horses could carry them and Percival knocked the knight from his horse to the ground. He then alighted and came to stand over the knight who cried him for mercy. And Percival sayeth, 'Have no fear, I shall not slay you, but I shall do to you as you would have done to the damsel.' With this, he commanded the old knight and the priest to carry the knight to the pit of serpents and cast him therein. Thus he died of the serpents biting unmercifully.

And the damsel gave great joy for his mercy. And she returned to her castle never again to be troubled by foul knights for fear of what Percival hath done.

The good knight Percival knew that his Godly labours would be at an end on his visit to the Castle of the Black Hermit and thinketh that he should do more before it endeth. These endeavours would he dedicate to God. He came thus upon a land where he met many strong knights and where the laws of God were not followed but they worshipped false idols and devils. There he met a knight who sayeth to him, 'Turn back, Sire! This land is full of non-believers and I pass through by truce only. The Queen of this land is the sister of King Madeglant of Oriande who was slain by Lancelot, who then turned the land thereabouts back to the true worship. And the Queen hateth God's laws and hath blindfolded herself that she might not gaze upon the true believers. Now her eyes have gone blind of their own accord and she thinketh that the false gods have done such in punishment for the coming of the true faith. Now she prays for the return of the false gods that she may see again. I tell you this, Sire, that you may not face the enemies of God herein.'

But Percival sayeth to the knight, 'Thank you, Sire, but there is no knightly virtue more fair than that which stands by God. This is the greatest knightly endeavour that may be done. As Our Saviour set His body at pain for us, so we should do likewise for Him.' And he departed joyous in the knowledge that Lancelot hath done God's work but he knoweth not that King Arthur hath cast Lancelot in prison.

That nightfall Percival came upon a great castle with many battlements and ancient towers. The castle was guarded by a drawbridge, and at the gate stood a squire with a metal collar around his neck from whence a chain was fastened to a large heavy piece of iron. And the chain length allowed the squire to come to the edge of the drawbridge from whence he sayeth to Percival, 'Sire, do you believe in God and His Son, Our Saviour?'

'Young friend,' sayeth Percival, 'I most certainly believe in God and I do so with all my heart.'

'Then, Sire, for the sake of Our Saviour, do not enter this castle.'

'Why do you thus say?'

And the squire sayeth, 'Sire, I am a Christian and have been enslaved to guard this castle. It is the most cruel place I know and is known as the Raging Castle for within are three young knights who on sight of a Christian knight become raging mad and would slay him. Their hands may be delayed however by a most fair damsel whom they dare not disobey. Full many knights hath she saved thus but many have not escaped this place alive. I live only that I guard the gate.'

'Young friend,' sayeth Percival, 'as a Christian you should know that the power of God is much beyond that of the Devil.' With that he rode across the bridge and entered the courtyard and alighteth from his horse. And a damsel of passing great beauty did see him from a window and came down to the courtyard. There she seeth from his shield that he is a Christian and sayeth, 'Sire, do not go to the great hall for there at table sit three knights that are my brothers. Should they see you they will lose their senses and go mad as they do at the sight of all things from God.'

'Damsel,' sayeth Percival, 'I pray that you are wrong, but it is known that the sight of any Godly matter doth send the non-believers mad.'

With this, Percival doth enter the hall full armed whereupon the three knights saw him and leapt up all maddened. And they took up swords and axes and run upon him but he standeth like a rock before them and they saw that God was in him. At this they fell upon each other and slayeth each other despite the damsel crying for them to cease. And she wept for the loss of her brothers. But Percival sayeth, 'Weep not, damsel, but repent of your false belief for all those with no belief in God die in their madness.'

Then Percival set the squire free of his chain and brought him to the great hall and clothed him in rich robes. At this, the damsel seeth the squire and thinketh that he is of a comely figure and made great honour of him. But still she sorrows for her brothers. And Percival sayeth unto her, 'Damsel, do not sorrow for that which cannot be amended. Comfort yourself instead as you may.'

At this, the damsel thinketh to herself that she may turn Percival from God to her false gods and sayeth, 'Sire, will you renounce your God? For should you so do I would be at your entire commanding.'

And he sayeth, 'Remember, damsel, had you been a man you would have been slain as a non-believer. I hope the lesson will turn you away from such falsehoods.'

The damsel sayeth, 'Sire, then will you promise me that should I accept your God, you will love me as a knight should love a damsel?'

And Percival sayeth, 'Damsel, should you receive baptism you have my word of honour as a Christian that I will love you as a knight who firmly believeth in God should love a damsel.'

'Then no more will I ask of you.'

And they sent for a hermit who came and baptised her with the name Celestre. And those who denied Our Lord were slain that they may soon see their errors. And those remaining in the castle were also baptised, and the hermit did stay with them to teach them the ways of God and the service of the Lord. The damsel became of a good life and did many good works.

Percival departed the Raging Castle praising God that he was able to turn the castle from its cruel ways to those of God's law. He rode a long distance and came to a land that was without cheer and the people said that he was come to destroy their worship for he had already won the strong Raging Castle. And he came upon a great and ancient castle whereat the gate was a great throng of people. From them came a squire, and Percival asked to whom the castle belonged. And the squire sayeth, 'Sire, it is the castle of Queen Jandree, who hath commanded the people to come to her that she may hear of the fall of the Raging Castle and the slaying of the knights therein and the baptising of the damsel. Now that her brother King Madeglant of Oriande is dead she hath no one to defend her and she hath heard that the knight who conquered the castle is the best knight in the world and none may endure against him. She is preparing to go to a stronger castle for her safety.'

And Percival rode to the castle and the people at the gate seeth him come and say to the blind Queen, 'Lady, a Christian knight is come to the castle!'

The Queen sayeth, 'Is it he who is about to overthrow our gods?'

Percival entereth the castle and alighteth and came before the Queen full armed. And the Queen asketh him what he sought. Percival sayeth that he sought nought but what was good for the Queen. She sayeth to him, 'But, Sire, you come from the Raging Castle where there has been much sore loss from the three slain brothers.'

And Percival sayeth, 'True, Lady, I was at the castle, and now it is at the command of Our Lord Jesus Christ as I wish was this castle.'

'And has your God so great a power as it is said?'

'Lady, God hath much greater power than ever it was said.'

'Then,' sayeth the Queen, 'will you stay with me until the power of your God hath been proven?'

'That, Lady, I surely will.'

And Percival taketh her hand and led her in to the great hall of the castle. And the people marvel at this for the Queen would not before allow any Christian knight to be near her. But now she wisheth that she could see, for Percival seemed to her to be a comely and a good knight. And Percival wished that she would turn to God for then the people throughout the land would follow in like manner.

Percival lay the night at the castle. On the morn the Queen sent for all the powerful people of the land to come unto her. She then walked in to the hall where was Percival and all marvelled that she could now see.

When the powerful people had assembled the Queen sayeth to them, 'Well you know of my loyalty and faith to the gods. Last night yet again I prayeth to them to restore my sight but they answereth me that they could not and full sorrowful am I. Then I remembered the God of whom Percival hath spoken and I prayed to Him as sweetly as I may. I asked Him that if He was as powerful and had such virtue of which it was oft said, He would restore my sight for now hath I belief in Him. I then fell asleep and it seemed to me that I saw the fairest Lady in the world who hath with Her a Child that had about Him a light as if from the sun. About the Lady and the Child were a host of angels who were in great joy of Her and Her Son. And an ancient man telleth me that although She was the most worshipful mother ever in the world She was a virgin, for none could surpass Her purity. Then I saw a man bound to a stake and He was beaten right cruelly with rods and scourges and I wept in pity of Him. I then saw the man nailed upon a Cross by evil men and they did thrust a spear in His side until the blood ran therefrom and I wept even more for Him. At the foot of the Cross I saw the Holy Lady and we wept together and she was comforted by a man who had no joy in him. There also was a man who held a vessel to the wound of the man on the Cross and collected the blood therefrom and he bore a shield of white and with the blood he maketh a red cross upon it. This same man then taketh down the body of the man from the Cross and placed it in a simple sepulchre, and such pity did I have that I thought that I would weep forever. And my tears did wash my eyes and made me see again. Such a Lord one ought to believe in for He suffered death when He could have lightly avoided it had He so wished. And this He did for His people. It is now my command that you shall all believe in this Lord and renounce all false gods as devils. And if any do not believe this way they shall be slain or put to a shameful death.'

The Queen was baptised with the name Salubre and she had all non-believers slain or banished. She was a good Lady and believed well in God and led a life so holy that she died in a hermitage. And Percival departed from the castle with joyous heart that the Lady and her people did now believe in the one true God.

Part the XXXIIIrd

Meliot of England had departed from the Castle Perilous with his wounds well healed by virtue of the sword and shroud that Lancelot had brought him. But he was in great sorrow when he heard tidings that Gawain had been cast into prison by two knights who were kin of those who killed each other at the Raging Castle. They had taken Gawain on account of him being a brother knight of Percival who had taken the castle for Our Saviour. And Meliot set his heart on finding Gawain and rode into a dark and gloomy forest. Finding neither house nor hermitage Meliot rode on in the darkness until he saw a damsel sitting alone and much forlorn beneath a tree. He sayeth to her. 'Damsel, why are you here at this hour?'

And she sayeth, 'Sire, I may not depart from here. You may see the reason above me.'

Meliot looked above her and seeth two knights hanging from the branch of the tree. He sayeth, 'Damsel, who hath done so foully of these knights?'

She sayeth, 'Sire, it was the Knight of the Galley that saileth upon the sea.'

'And why?'

'Because they believeth in God and His Holy Mother. I am placed here by command of the knight for forty days to prevent their being cut down for if they are he will lose his castle and would cut off my head.'

And Meliot sayeth, 'Such a watch is shameful for a damsel. Rise, damsel, for you shall not stay here.'

'Then,' sayeth she, 'I am a dead woman for none may face this knight most fearsome.'

'Damsel,' sayeth Meliot, 'I will not take the reproach of good knights for leaving them hanging here. Nor will I take the shame upon myself.'

Thereupon he cut them down and made their graves with his sword.

And the damsel sayeth, 'Sire, the Knight of the Galley will look for me and strike off my head for you have no thought for me.'

But Meliot lifteth up the damsel to his horse and rideth to a hermitage where the Knight of the Galley hath slain the hermit. The damsel and he entered therein and seeth in a great brightness of light a damsel that sitteth by a dead knight. And he sayeth, 'Damsel, when was this knight slain?'

And she sayeth, 'Sire, he was slain by the Knight of the Galley on the sea shore whereof I am commanded to keep watch over him until the Knight of the Galley doth return tomorrow before he attends to the death of Gawain.'

'He hath schemed that Gawain shall die tomorrow?'

'Yes, Sire.'

'But first he will come here?'

'With certainty, Sire.'

'What more do you know of Gawain?'

'He is to face a lion all unarmed, and when he is slain by the beast, the Lady who is mistress of both of us shall be brought to the lion and slain likewise, for she will not renounce the law of God that she accepteth from the knight who took the Raging Castle and through whom her brothers did slay each other. Then the damsel that accompanieth you and I shall be slain by the lion also for you have taken down the hanging knights. Sire, you may save this damsel if you take her away for the knight may not wait for the lion to do its ill, but will cut off her head straightway. For you also have I great fear.'

'Damsel,' sayeth Meliot, 'this Knight of the Galley is a man like any other.'

'No, Sire,' sayeth she, 'He is more strong and cruel than you.'

But Meliot was not afraid and stayed the night at the chapel. In the morning he heard the knight coming from far off for he bringeth the Lady from the Raging Castle and doth loudly and foully revile her. Meliot accordingly was full armed and waiting.

A dwarf that ran behind the Knight of the Galley seeth Meliot and crieth out to his master, 'Look, Sire, it is the knight who hath cost you your castle for he cut down the hanging knights. Haste! and avenge yourself that we may go and attend the death of Gawain!'

And the knight cometh before Meliot and sayeth as a braggart, 'Is it you that hath trespassed on my land and taken down my knights?'

And Meliot replieth, 'They, Sire, were not your knights for they were knights of God. And you have committed an outrage by their shameful death.'

Without more words, Meliot hurtled hard at the knight and pierced his breastplate and wounded him. The knight replieth with a thrust that pierced the shield of Meliot and the dwarf crieth out, 'Go to him, Sire; let him not endure more than the many knights you have slain!'

And the knight ran at Meliot and broke his lance upon his shield in such strong manner that both knight and horse staggered. But Gawain thrust his lance through the knight and he fell dead to the ground. The dwarf thought to escape but Meliot cut off his head and the damsels were both of much joy.

Meliot buried the knight that lay slain in the chapel and sayeth farewell to the damsels. He rode in search of Gawain and came upon a knight full armed and riding at a great pace. And the knight sayeth to Meliot, 'Sire, have you tidings of the Knight of the Galley?'

'Why do you ask?'

The knight sayeth, 'For Gawain is brought to the forest and is to face a lion all unarmed. And they wait for the Knight of the Galley who is to bring two damsels who shall likewise face the lion after Gawain.'

'When will this take place?'

'Soon, Sire, for Gawain is already bound to a stake until such times as the lion comes. He is guarded by two knights meantime. Tell me, Sire, have you tidings of the Knight of the Galley?'

And Meliot sayeth, 'Go on your passage, Sire, and you will hear of him soon enough.'

At a great gallop Meliot came to the part of the forest wherein was Gawain bound to the stake.

There he seeth Gawain and the two knights that guarded him and great pity hath Meliot. He rode hard at the two knights and thrust his lance through one of them. On seeing this, the other knight tried to flee but Meliot did slay him with his sword. Then he went to Gawain and cut his cords and set him free whereof Gawain had great joy.

The tidings came to the land that Queen Jandree was baptised, that a knight had come that was of such might that none may endure against him, that the Knight of the Galley was slain, and that Gawain was set free. And the people of the land that had thought to see Gawain devoured by the lion fled across the sea.

And Gawain and Meliot did depart at great pace and marvelled that none came after them. But their foes had gone away in fear. The knights rode until they came to the sea and seeth a great clashing of arms. And they saw a knight in battle against those who would come on his ship and he keepeth them off with much valour. And they came close and saw that the knight hath a shield of white with a red cross and they knew it to be Percival. But as they went to his aid the ship was blown by the wind from the shore and was set to drift to parts unknown. And they knew great sorrow for they could not aid him nor did they know of the land whence the ship goeth. They watched Percival fending off his foes until they could see him no more and they turned away in sorrow and rode on.

Thereupon they saw a knight who sayeth he was from the court of King Arthur. And they asketh for tidings of the King and the knight sayeth, 'Sires, I have nought but bad tidings for the King neglects his knights for the words of Briant of the Isles, and he hath put one of his best knights in prison.'

And they sayeth, 'Which knight hath he put in prison.'

The knight sayeth, 'Lancelot of the Lake. He had taken back all the lands lost to King Arthur and hath slain King Madeglant and conquered the land of Oriande which he made turn to the Lord God in worship. But the King sent for him and put him in prison on the advice of Briant. Now King Claudas hath assembled a great army to take back Oriande and to fall upon the King on the advice of Briant.'

And Gawain sayeth, 'Surely a king who setteth aside the counsel of good knights for the advice of a traitor must bring his crown to great risk. But to put the good knight Lancelot in prison is to risk all.'

Part the XXXIVth

And King Claudas hath conquered the land of Oriande and now cometh nigh to the lands of King Arthur that was saved from King Madeglant by Lancelot. And the people desired much the return of Lancelot but the King sendeth Briant and nought was gained thereby. Thus the people sayeth that if the King doth not send them aid they will yield up the land and turn away from God. But Lancelot was in prison and Gawain and Yvain and the other good knights did not resort to the court for shame of King Arthur's trust in Briant.

And the King was heavy hearted at this and sat alone in the great hall. At this, Lucan did come to him and sayeth, 'Sire, you seem to be without joy.'

King Arthur sayeth, 'Truly, Sire, I have been without joy since the death of the Queen. Those who may have heartened me come here no longer and I know not their aid yet King Claudas wars upon me and would conquer my lands.'

'Sire,' sayeth Lucan, 'to the blame of no one can you put this save your own. You have done evil to him that hath served you best, and you have honoured the traitor. None will come to your aid whilst you hold Lancelot in prison. He hath served you most honourably and hath faced death many times in your name but your treatment of him keepeth away Gawain and Yvain and the other good knights.'

And the King sayeth, 'You speak truly for I have done a great discourtesy to him. Think you, Sire, that he would ever trust in me again? Lancelot hath a great heart and knows the lesson of forgiveness taught by Our Saviour, yet he would not pause at gaining vengeance where he took his right to be offended.'

'Sire, Lancelot knoweth that you have been ill-advised and loyalty to his King runs through his bones. He pines in prison for service to you. I well believe that you should release him, Sire, that he may take up your cause. The good knights will return and you lands shall be saved. Do otherwise, Sire, and all shall be lost.'

The King thanketh Lucan and had Lancelot brought before him from the prison. And the King sayeth, 'Are you well, Lancelot?'

And the knight sayeth, 'Prison hath made me weak, Sire, but I shall recover soon.'

'Lancelot,' sayeth the King, 'listen to my words for they are the words of a King though no King should have to speak them. I put you in prison for fear of losing my people and my lands. I was ill-advised in this matter and I repent that I did this to you. If your honour has been stained by my deeds I shall do all I can to amend the matter for no better knight could any King have in his court.'

The King would have spoken more but Lancelot sayeth quickly, 'Hold, Sire! I am your loyal knight. All that I do, I do for you. It matters to me none whether your command takes me to the field of battle or to your prison. I know full well that I was not in prison for treason for I have no room in my heart for such evil. I see it not as shame or dishonour to obey my King whatever he commandeth. No, Sire, all I ask is to serve you again that my honour be tested in your cause.'

And the King cometh to Lancelot and taketh his hand saying, 'Sire, my court is rich beyond measure with knights such as you. Get you well with haste for these times doth place us all at hazard.'

But nought made Lancelot well until he encountered Briant in the forest. And Briant tried to flee but Lancelot came upon him with his sword and left the body of the traitor knight for the wild beasts.

Part the XXXVth

Percival hath slain those who would board his ship and only his horse and the pilot remaineth. The pilot, seeing the valour of Percival, did enter in a covenant with him to become a Christian. And for many days the ship was blown by the wind of God until no land could be seen and the pilot knoweth not the stars. Then they came upon an island whereon was a rich castle. At each corner of the castle was a tower which hath a bell within which did make a most pleasing sound across the water.

And the ship came to the castle and took the ground beneath its walls. And Percival did take his horse and the pilot and they go to the castle gate. They entered and saw within the most fair halls and chambers they have ever known. Beneath a tree in the courtyard they seeth a fountain surrounded by tall pillars and thereby a pavement of precious stones. By the fountain sat two Masters with white beards all dressed in white robes whereon the breast thereof was a red cross. When they saw Percival they came to him and knelt in greeting before kissing the shield of white with the red cross. And they sayeth, 'Sire, do not marvel that we do this for we knew full well the good knight who bore this shield before you. Many times did we see him since Our Lord's crucifixion.'

But Lancelot did marvel for they talked of a time long past. And he sayeth, 'Know you the name of this knight?'

'Sire,' sayeth they, 'he was Joseph of Arimathea, but the shield was all white at first. Only upon the death of Christ was the red cross put on with His blood.'

And Percival layeth the shield down and one of the two men placed upon it a wreath of flowers and herbs. Beyond the fountain Percival could see a large ivory vessel wherein stood a knight full armed and he spoke to the knight but reply received him not. And he asketh the two Masters who was the knight and they say he may not yet know. They took him to the great hall and bore his shield before him and all that were in the hall made great joy of his coming. He saw that the great hall was rich indeed and hung with costly cloths of silk. In the centre of the hall was an image of Our Savour in Majesty with His apostles around Him. And in the galleries were many people who all seemed to be of much holiness.

And the two Masters sayeth to Percival, 'This, Sire, is the Royal Hall.'

And he sayeth, 'Such a hall could be nought else but that of a King.'

Percival saw that the hall was full of rich tables of gold and ivory. One of the Masters clapped his hands three times and three and thirty knights entered the hall all of a company. They were clad in white garments and all had a red cross upon his breast. They went to the tables and prayeth to God whereon they put down their cups and washed their hands in a large golden bowl. Then they sat down. The Masters put Percival among them on the Master's table. Thereon they were served with meat and other foods in full worshipful manner.

As they sat at meat Percival seeth a golden crown descend on a golden chain as if from Heaven. At this, the Masters opened a great pit in the floor from whence issued the sound of much sorrowing and all there assembled stretched forth their hands to God in prayer. The crown, the chain, and the sound of sorrow stayed until the meal is finished whereon the Master closed the pit and the crown and chain ascended and could be seen no more. The good knights then gave thanks to God and left the hall.

Percival sayeth to the Master, 'Pray tell me, Sire, of the golden crown and chain.'

But the Master sayeth, 'Sire, until you swear by your honour that you will return to this island when you are called by a ship carrying a white sail which bears a red cross, you can neither leave the island nor be told of the golden crown and chain.'

And Percival sayeth, 'Sire, I promise you faithfully in the name of God that as soon as I have attended to the needs of my mother and my sister I shall return on the ship you send thither.'

'Then, Sire,' sayeth the Master, 'on your return you shall wear upon your head the crown of gold which you saw come down on the chain. And so you shall be seated on a throne and be king of the Isle of Plenty that lacks nought for the good of man. Your uncle, King Hermit, was king of this island and, by his good works, the island is well furnished with all manner of good things. Now he is king in another realm and the people have asked for another worshipful man to be their king. You must continue in a worshipful manner and govern as a true and loyal king as did your uncle. Should you fail in this, the crown will be taken from you and you will be sent to the Isle of Poverty whence you heard the sound of great sorrowing when you sat at the table for meat. They also were kings of the Isle of Plenty but they broke their covenant with the people and were cast out. Also on the Isle of Poverty are many that were not kings but did forget their duties to God and are punished accordingly. And we know not if they should be ever released. One thing more should you know, Sire. Before you return on the ship with the white sail and the red cross, you must obtain the head of a king and queen sealed in gold.'

And Percival sayeth, 'Thank you, Sire. Pray tell me also of the knight full armed that stands in the ivory vessel and also of the name of this castle.'

But the Master sayeth, 'These you may not know until you return. But, tell me, Sire, of the most Holy Grail with which you spoke. Is it still at the chapel of the castle of the good Fisher King?'

'It is, Sire,' sayeth Percival, 'with the sword which struck of the head of Saint John the Baptist, and with many other holy relics also.'

And the Master sayeth, 'I saw the Holy Grail in the hands of Joseph of Arimathea who had used it to collect the precious blood of Our Lord. All your family I know, but you should know that it was your valour and cleanliness of mind that caused God to bring you hither. It is God also that shall choose where the place shall be, and when the time shall come, that you shall see the ship with the red cross.'

Percival sayeth, 'Be assured, Sire, that there is no other place under Heaven where I would rather be than this isle. Were it not for my duty to my mother and sister, I would never depart willingly.'

After a night lodged at the castle where they did him great honour, Percival went to hear Mass in the rich chapel of the castle. The service finished, a Master came to him with a shield of purest white and sayeth unto him, 'Sire, you will leave your shield here as a token of your coming. Instead you will take this shield.'

And Percival sayeth, 'As you wish.'

He goeth on board the ship with the pilot and it sailed from beneath the castle walls with the bells sounding over the water as before. Fast goeth the ship under the guidance of God for within He knew was a good knight.

After many days the ship came to an isle whereon was a castle that once had known greatness but now was in poor condition. They came to the wharf below and Percival entered the castle full armed. On the steps of the castle hall he seeth a lady that hath the bearing of a gentlewoman and two young damsels with her. All were dressed raggedly. And the lady sayeth to Percival, 'Welcome, Sire, for long it hath been since we have seen a knight enter this castle.'

'May God grant you joy and honour, lady,' sayeth Percival.

'We have need of both,' sayeth the lady, 'for none have we seen this many a year.' Then sayeth she, 'Sire, will you lodge in this castle this night?'

Percival sayeth that he would lodge that night. The damsels disarmed him and brought him a robe to wear saying, 'Sire, none better do we have for you than this plain mantle.' And he sayeth that it will do right well.

And Percival seeth that the damsels have by nature been formed well and they have all the sweetness and simplicity of manner that maketh a good woman. And he hath pity on their condition.

'Lady,' sayeth Percival, 'doth this castle belong to you?'

And she sayeth, 'Sire, I am the widow of Calobrutus, a good knight who hath been dead these many years. He is the father of my daughters that you see here. I have also a son who is known as a good knight but hath been taken and put in to prison by the evil knight who hath robbed me of all my land save this castle. My husband was the brother of Alain le Gros but he is dead also and we have no kin nearby to aid us. I have heard that Alain hath a son who is the best knight in the world but he knoweth not of us or I should have my son returned to me. I have also an uncle called King Ban of Benoic. He also is dead, but he hath a son that is also one of the best knights in the world. If either of these knights should come this way, they would return our joy to us.'

The pity Percival hath for the two damsels now grows as they are the daughters of his uncle. And he sayeth, 'Lady, what is the name of your son, and wherein is he prisoned?'

Sayeth she, 'He is named Galobruns, and he is held by Gohaz in the Castle of the Whales.'

Sayeth Percival, 'Is this castle, lady, nearby?'

'It is on the next island, Sire. But none dare to challenge him for he is a mighty knight who hath fear of no one. And he hath come to me and sayeth that I must send him one of my daughters or he hath sworn that he shall rob me of my castle.'

At this Percival sayeth, 'Lady, not all oaths are kept, nor shall this one be. For I am Percival, son of Alain le Gros, and the damsels are daughters of my uncle that is called Calobrutus. And you, Lady, are kin to my brother knight, Lancelot of the Lake, the son of King Ban of Benoic. Neither he nor I will live with this evil that is upon you.'

And the lady and the damsels were overcome with joy and they kisseth his hands and prayeth unto God that he shall find Galobruns and take them from their poverty. Percival sayeth unto them that he shall do all within his powers to help them.

He took his ship until he came to an island whereon he saw a cave above the shore. In the cave he saw a man and took a path from the shore to the cave where he found a most comely knight. And the knight was chained by the neck and foot to the rock from whence he could not depart. Percival sayeth unto him, 'Sire, it seems you are made well fast to this rock.'

And the knight sayeth, 'Truly said, Sire, but I wish it were not so.'

Sayeth Percival, 'Have you food and drink?'

'I have, Sire, for the daughter of the Sick Knight that lives on an island close by brings me meat and drink every day. He that hath prisoned me here hath stolen her castle as he hath those of my mother.'

'Can none free you?'

'Only he that hath prisoned me here for only he hath the key to the lock and he sayeth that I shall never be freed from this place.'

'Does he, Sire? Then he should know that you are the son of my uncle Calobrutus and I am the son of your uncle Alain le Gros. Never would I endure the reproach of leaving you here. Be assured, Sire, that I shall return with the key and you shall be returned to your mother and sisters.'

Percival went to his ship and departed and came upon an island most fair. Near to the shore he saw a small island whereon was a tree. At the top of the tree a knight could be seen and below him on the tree was a damsel who cried out to Percival, 'Sire! Come to the aid of this knight and of me, a damsel.'

And Percival replieth, 'What is it you fear, damsel?'

And she sayeth, 'A great dragon, Sire. It hath driven us up this tree and, in truth, I ought not to be sorry for this knight hath carried me from the house of my father and would have done me shame of my body had it not been for this dragon.'

'What is the name of the knight?'

'It is Gohaz of the Castle of the Whales. This land is his and he hath taken the lands of my father and of others also.'

All this time the knight sayeth nothing for great shame of his deeds and his flight from the dragon. Percival now knoweth that it is he that hath put Galobruns in chains and came ashore with his sword and shield. The dragon came upon him and breathed strong fire but Percival raised his shield and the flame could neither penetrate nor sully the whiteness of the shield. Again the dragon did take breath to send forth more fire but Percival stepped forward and thrust his sword down the throat of the dragon and it fell slain at his feet.

And he sayeth to them in the tree, 'Now, Sire, you may come down and you also damsel.'

The knight sayeth from his place in the tree, 'Sire, one thing more may you do for me. A key hath fallen from me and the dragon did swallow it. Much honour would I give to him that found it for me.'

Percival goeth to the dragon and opened its throat. There lay the key and he taketh it and sayeth, 'I have the key, Sire, now you may come down.'

The knight came down and goeth to Percival with intent to give him good thanks for what he hath done. But Percival doth put him at the point of his sword. And the knight sayeth, 'Have a care, Sire, for I rule all that you see about you.'

'That, Sire, is good for it is with just such a ruler that I would have business. You will come with me.'

And the damsel sayeth, 'Sire, pray do not leave me here but help me return to the castle of my father, the Sick Knight who grieves for me.'

Percival now knoweth that the damsel is she of whom Galobruns gave great praise for her sweet kindness in his troubles. He taketh the knight and the damsel to his ship and goeth to the cave wherein is Galobruns. And much glad is the knight to see him. And Percival put forth Gohaz and sayeth, 'Here, Sire, is your mortal enemy. Do with him as you wish.' Percival taketh the key he had found in the throat of the dragon and unlocked the chains that bind Galobruns and the young knight put them on Gohaz and sayeth to him, 'Look upon this key for the last time, Sire, for you shall not see it again.' At this, he threw the key in to the sea.

Percival took Galobruns and the damsel to the castle of Gohaz and called there all the powerful people and sayeth unto them, 'See here before you your new ruler Galobruns. Before God and before him shall you bow or you heads shall be flung in to the sea.'

And the people of the land made much honour of Galobruns and Percival commended the care of the damsel to Galobruns whereon the young knight looked with much tenderness upon the damsel and calleth her to sit by his side.

Percival then departed and sailed until he came to a shore whereon was a great castle from which issued much flame and smoke. And he went on the shore and came to a hermit and sayeth to him, 'Sire, what is this castle and why doth it burn?'

And the hermit sayeth, 'It is the castle where Joseus, the son of King Pelles, did slay his mother. And it hath been ordained by God that it shall burn for ever and from these flames shall come those that shall cause the world to burn.'

Percival now knoweth that it is the castle of his uncle the King Hermit and he departed at great pace and sailed for many a long time until he saw twelve hermits on the shore. And he goeth to them and asketh them from whence they come and they sayeth. 'Sire, we come from nearby where there are twelve chapels and twelve houses and a graveyard wherein are the graves of twelve knights who are all brothers. We keep watch over them. None of the knights lived for more than twelve years as a knight save one. They all took much land and kingdoms from the misbelievers and they all died under arms. The name of the eldest brother was Alain le Gross who came to this land to avenge the death of his brother Alibans of the Waste City. He had been slain by the Giant King and Alain came from the Valleys of Camelot and avenged him but died of his own wounds after.'

And another hermit sayeth, 'Sire, I was at the death of Alain and to me did he confess his sins. But nought mattered to him more than to see his son, Percival.'

With this, Percival asketh the hermits to take him to the graveyard and they did gladly. Therein did he see the tombs both rich and fair with bright adornments. Then sayeth he, 'Which is the tomb of Alain le Gros?'

And they sayeth, 'The highest, for he was the eldest and the greatest.'

And there goeth Percival who prayed and gave great worship in honour of his father. And when the hermits heard that he was the son of Alain they made great joy. He lodged with the hermits that night and heard Mass in the morning at his father's chapel. Then he departed and came to the shores of Greater Britain where he mounted his horse and sent the pilot and ship away commending him to God.

Percival rode long through the forest until he came upon a house where at the gate he saw a knight lying on a bed where at the top sat a lady of great beauty who hath the head of the knight in her lap and sayeth sweet things to him. But the knight doth revile her and say that he would cut off her head and that he was sick and not well. And the knight seeth Percival and asketh him if he was to lodge the night.

And Percival sayeth, 'If it pleases you, Sire, I would gladly lodge in your house.'

'We should be honoured by your staying,' sayeth the knight, 'but I ask you not to think ill of me for what I may say to my wife.'

'Sire,' sayeth Percival, 'the lady is your wife and you may do as you must, but I would counsel you that courtesy cometh at no cost.'

And the knight commandeth his wife to honour Percival and commanded also that squires take him to his bed in to the house for it is near evensong. And the lady disarmed Percival and gave him a scarlet robe to wear and took him in to the hall of the house. And the knight sayeth to her, 'Be sure you sit with the squires for you shall not sit and eat with me or those that lodge herein.'

Percival asked the lady why her husband reviled and rebuked her in such manner. And she sayeth, 'It is because, Sire, the good knight Lancelot made him marry me. Since that time he hath ever shown me great dishonour. Now he hath become ill on account that his brother is also sick and that Gohaz of the Castle of the Whales hath robbed him of his castle and lands. My husband is of the sort that rages at small things and is overjoyed at small things and always there is something that they desire. For him it is a golden cup he hath heard tell of that is borne by a damsel. It is a golden cup of much richness and the damsel is guarded by a knight and it is said that the cup will go only to the best knight in the world. My husband sayeth that he will treat me lowly until such times he hath the golden cup. But he rages over his brother's lost lands and I have to pay the forfeit for, although I do all that he wills, he giveth me no fair treatment. But, Sire, no churlishness may he bring against me, no ill-manner, and no harsh reviling will set me against him, for he is my husband through the eyes of God and the command of the blessed Lancelot. I have loved my husband in health and I will love him in sickness yet I pray to God to bring him to a better mind towards me.'

'Lady,' sayeth Percival, 'you may set his mind at part ease for I tell you truly that his brother hath both his lands and his daughter back in safety. I was at the reconquering thereof and know this to be true. But of the golden cup I know nothing.'

The lady made Percival sit at the table and when the meat was provided she went to sit with the squires. Percival was ashamed of this but sayeth nothing for he would not provoke the knight.

Percival lodged the night in the castle and departed the next morn after Mass. He thinketh that it would be a good thing to gain the golden cup for the lady but also he thinketh of the ship with the white sail bearing the red cross for at the island castle did he most wish to be. He rode until he came to the forest of the Black Hermit that was a loathly place where grew no green leaves and no birds did sing. There he came upon the Damsel of the Carriage who was changed mightily. 'Sire,' sayeth she to Percival, 'Bald have I been since we first met, but look now upon me.'

And she threw back the hood of her cloak and showeth much hair as golden as the dawn. And Percival sayeth, 'Damsel, before you were indeed comely, now you have beauty surpassing even the whitest lily.'

'Thank you, Sire,' sayeth she, 'also my arm I no longer carry from a cloth of gold about my neck. And the damsel that once walked behind me now rides as she should. And this, Sire, for that you brought about the Holy Grail by the goodness of your heart.'

'No, damsel,' sayeth Percival, 'the Holy Grail was revealed only at the command of God.'

And the damsel sayeth, 'Sire, we come nigh the Castle of the Black Hermit and further I dare not go for there are bowmen at the walls that loose arrows at all who come near them. Only if you live to reach the gate will they stop and then only for they mean to slay you within the walls. You, Sire, need have no fear of those within for they will do you no evil save for the Black Hermit who will gladly slay you.'

And Percival bid the damsel to stay and spurred his horse on to a great gallop. As he came to the castle the bowmen loosed their arrows and he raised his shield and many arrows were lodged therein but he flinched not and rode to the drawbridge which was lowered on his coming and whereon the arrows ceased. The gate was opened, for the knights within thought to slay him but when they saw him they knew him to be Percival and they fell back with great dread.

Percival rode up the steps to the great hall and entered on horse and full armed. And the hall was full of many knights all foul featured. At the far end of the hall was the Black Hermit of great height and seated on his horse full armed also. And the knights cryeth to the Black Hermit saying, 'We have often guarded and defended you, now you defend us from this knight!'

And Percival lowered his lance and raised his shield and ran full hard at the Black Hermit who cometh at him in like manner. And the hall resounded to the clash of steel as the Black Hermit broke his lance on the shield of Percival and was sent to the ground horse and all by the lance of the good knight. When they seeth him fall, the knights of the castle ran upon him and opened a pit from whence came a foul smell and did throw him in. Then all of a company they yielded the castle to Percival and put themselves at his mercy.

With this, the Damsel of the Carriage entered the hall and the knights of the castle gave her the head of a king in a silver box with a golden crown and the head of a queen in a box of lead with a copper crown, which have been robbed of her when she came nigh with Gawain. And she departed joyfully for the Valleys of Camelot.

And Percival put the knights in covenant that they would turn to God and the Holy Mother that they would be saved from the torments of Hell and that they would give courteous lodging to any passing knight that so required. And he departed in full joy that he hath brought the knights to God and for ever after faithful masses were sung in the castle for ever after.

Percival rode until he came upon a damsel and a knight riding through the forest. The damsel carried a golden cup and Percival saluted the knight saying, 'May God be with you this day, Sire.'

And the knight replieth, 'And with you also, Sire.'

Sayeth Percival, 'Is this damsel one of your household?'

And the knight sayeth, 'No, Sire, rather I am one of hers. We go, Sire, to the assembly of knights where they shall contest for this golden cup.'

Percival sayeth, 'That will be a fair sight to see. For now damsel, Sire, I shall depart but mean to meet you again before this day is out.'

With that, Percival rode to the ground of the assembly and seeth there many knights begun in combat and he hurled himself in to the clashing of arms. The assembly continued until evensong when it was time to choose the best knight. All agreed that the Knight of the White Shield did overcome them all in valour and chivalry and the damsel cometh to give Percival the golden cup. She sayeth to him, 'Sire, I present to you this cup of gold for your knightly virtues. You should know, however, from whence it came, for it carries with it a duty which you must discharge.

This cup was given to Gawain by the elder Damsel of the Tent whereat he had defeated the evil custom. But the joy of Gawain was destroyed when that most courteous of knights, Meliot of England, was treacherously slain by Brundans, the son of the sister of Briant of the Isles. Gawain now prays that whosoever should win the golden cup would undertake to avenge the death of Meliot. Brundans carrieth a shield of green and silver.'

Sayeth Percival, 'Damsel, were there no cup of gold, I would willingly do as Gawain requests for both he and Meliot are well deserving of the aid of good knights. Be assured, damsel, that from this moment Brundans lives only with me waiting in his shadow and he shall know soon that treachery brings its own vengeance.'

He then sayeth to the knight with the damsel, 'Sire, I request and charge you that you take this golden cup to the house of the Sick Knight and tell his lady that it was sent thither by the Knight of the White Shield.' And the knight sayeth that he will gladly do as Percival requests.

Percival then rode to Castle Perilous where Lancelot had brought the sword and piece of shroud to cure the wounded Meliot. Therein he found a damsel who was full sorrowful and sayeth that Brundans hath slain the most courteous knight by treachery. As she speaketh another damsel came fast on horse and sayeth to Percival, 'Sire, you must come quickly and give us your aid. You are the only knight in this forest I can find.'

And Percival sayeth, 'How may I aid you?'

Sayeth she, 'A knight is carrying off my lady by force. He hath taken her when she was on her way to the court of King Arthur.'

'Who is your lady?'

'She is the younger Damsel of the Tent where Gawain overthrew the evil custom. For the sake of God, Sire, hasten for he treats her cruelly for her love of Gawain and King Arthur.'

Percival rode as fast as he may with the damsel by his side and come to the forest where they heard the damsel crying for mercy. They heareth also the knight saying that mercy would she have none as he beat her with the flat of his sword. And Percival seeth the damsel and the knight and he seeth also that the knight beareth a shield of green and silver.

Percival cometh up to him and sayeth, 'Hold, Sire! This is too harsh a manner to treat a damsel.'

And Brundans sayeth, 'Hold back. Sire! For this is my affair and I shall treat her as I am content so to do.'

Sayeth Percival, 'No, Sire, you shall not. No knight should treat a damsel thus.'

But Brundans sayeth, 'I have not yet begun to show my treatment of her, ere long she shall be the most sorrowful damsel in the world.' And with this he struck the damsel on the head with the flat of his sword and blood came from her mouth and nose and she fell to the ground.

And Percival sayeth, 'Doubly you hath earned vengeance of me. You hath slain the good Meliot and now you shame this damsel. Mount your horse and prepare to meet me!'

Brundans goeth to his horse and mounteth as Percival goes back apace. They came at each other with a mighty hurtle but Percival thrust his lance through the green and silver shield in to the breast of Brundans and knocked him hard to the ground. And Percival dismounted and went to Brundans and took off his helmet and then struck off his head. He gave the head to the younger Damsel of the Tent and sayeth, 'Damsel, take this with you to the court of King Arthur and salute them for me. Sayeth also to them that this head is the last gift I send them for I shall never see them again in this world. But tell them also they shall remain in my thoughts and never shall I bring to end the love I have for my brother knights. For ever they shall remain the example of knightly virtue to those who would follow.'

And the damsel departed thanking Percival for his aid and he commended her to God. He then rode to the Castle Perilous where the damsel made much joy on hearing of the slaying of Brundans. Percival lodged in the castle that night and heard Mass before parting on the morrow. He then came upon the knight who hath carried the golden cup to the Sick Knight and Percival asketh him how it goeth with the gift. And the knight sayeth, 'Sire, never was a gift received with such goodwill. The knight no longer grudges his wife and she sits at table with him and the household obey her commands.'

Sayeth Percival, 'I am well pleased with this and I thank you, Sire, for doing this on my behalf.'

And the knight sayeth, 'There is nothing I would not do for you, Sire, for you made my brother Knight Hardy that was once Knight Coward.'

And Percival sayeth, 'He was a good and true knight that met a good end, but I think had he been still Knight Coward he would have been alive.'

But the knight sayeth, 'No, Sire, he met death with honour and no more could he ask for otherwise he would have lived with shame. Yet I was not glad of his death for he proved a Knight Hardy and would have done more good had he lived the longer.'

Percival departed from the knight commending him to God and rode to the Castle of the Holy Grail. In his castle he found his mother and his sister brought there by the Damsel of the Carriage. They had brought the coffin from the chapel of Castle Camelot and had laid it in the chapel of the Castle of the Holy Grail also with the coffin from the chapel outside the Castle of the Holy Grail. Never more would they need to open in the presence of the best knight in the world. His sister, Dindrane, hath also brought the piece of shroud that she hath taken from the Chapel Perilous and placed it with the other holy relics.

Percival then stayed in the castle for a long time without any questing for adventure for he gave his loyalty entirely to God and worshiped Him most worthily. He and his mother and his sister did continually pray to Our Saviour and His Sweet Mother that the world should be rid of evil and that the light of God should be seen in every corner of the land. First his mother and then his sister were summoned to God. They were buried by the hermits who sang masses over their tombs. One day Percival was alone in the chapel praying when an angel voice sayeth, 'Percival, you shall not abide here for long. It is the command of God that you spread the relics herein among the hermits. No more shall the Holy Grail appear in this chapel but you shall know soon of the place where it shall be.'

When the voice ceased its speaking all the coffins and tombs within the chapel clattered with sound as the bodies within saluted the speaker.

In obedience to the command of God, Percival called forth the hermits and spread among them the holy relics. The hermits departed and went abroad throughout the land and built churches and abbeys wherein they housed the relics. And those sacred places remain here with us today. Only Joseus, the son of King Hermit, remained with Percival for he knew his time had come.

One day, Percival heard the sound of a bell ringing across the waters. He went to the chapel window and saw a rich ship which bore a white sail whereon was a red cross. In the ship were many good knights dressed in garments of white and with a red cross on their breast. And they came unto the chapel bearing gold and silver vessel which they placed in full reverence on the tombs therein. Percival took his leave of Joseus and the household and went on board the ship. And they watched as the ship departed, the knights standing on the deck with Percival as if to give him great honour. And the ship sailed to a sky red as if of fire and Percival was never seen again in this world.

When Joseus was summoned by God, the castle fell in to decay but the chapel remained as if untouched. No one dare enter the castle for dread of the mighty and virtuous knights that had walked its halls and chambers. But many years on, two young and brave knights came in to the ruined castle. No one knows what they had seen within but they became hermits and lived a hard and good life in the forest. When asked what they had seen therein, they sayeth only, 'We may not tell you, for the knowledge is only for them that hath entered.' They later became Saints.

About the Editor

E. C. Coleman served in the Royal Navy for 36 years, which included time on an aircraft carrier, a submarine, and Nelson's flagship, HMS *Victory*. During that time he mounted four Arctic expeditions in search of evidence from the 1845 John Franklin Expedition. He has written many books on naval, polar, medieval and Victorian subjects and contributed the foreword to two volumes of Captain Scott's diaries. His interest in the Grail legend is longstanding and he is currently researching a new work on the Knights Templar. He lives in Lincolnshire.